THE TRA
DIN(

REFLECTIONS ON
HANGING

Arthur Koestler was born in Budapest in 1905. He attended the University of Vienna before working as a foreign correspondent in the Middle East, Berlin and Paris. For six years (1932–38) he was an active member of the Communist Party, and was captured by Franco's troops in the Spanish Civil war and imprisoned under sentence of death. In 1940 he came to England, adopting the language with his first book written in English, *Scum of the Earth*. His publications manifest a wide range of political, scientific and literary interests, and include *Darkness at Noon*, *Arrival and Departure*, and *Thieves in the Night*, novels concerned with the ethics of revolution and survival. Arthur Koestler died in 1983 by suicide, having frequently expressed a belief in the right to euthanasia.

BY ARTHUR KOESTLER

NOVELS

The Gladiators
Darkness at Noon
Arrival and Departure
Thieves in the Night
The Age of Longing
The Call-Girls

AUTOBIOGRAHY

Dialogue with Death
Scum of the Earth
Arrow in the Blue
The Invisible Writing
The God that Failed (with others)

ESSAYS

The Yogi and the Commissar
Insight and Outlook
Promise and Fulfilment
The Trail of the Dinosaur
Reflections on Hanging
The Sleepwalkers
The Lotus and the Robot
The Act of Creation
The Ghost in the Machine
Drinkers of Infinity
The Case of the Midwife Toad
The Roots of Coincidence
The Challenge of Chance
(with Sir Alistair Hardy and Robert Harvie)
The Heel of Achilles
Suicide of a Nation? (editor)
Beyond Reductionism: The Alpbach Symposium
(editor with J. R. Smythies)
The Thirteenth Tribe
Life After Death
(with Arnold Toynbee and others)
Janus – A Summing Up

THEATRE
Twilight Bar

READER
Bricks to Babel

Arthur Koestler

THE TRAIL OF THE DINOSAUR

REFLECTIONS ON HANGING

VINTAGE

Published by Vintage 1994

2 4 6 8 10 9 7 5 3 1

Copyright © Arthur Koestler 1955, 1956, 1970

THE TRAIL OF THE DINOSAUR
First published in Great Britain by Collins 1955
Published by Hutchinson 1970

REFLECTIONS ON HANGING
First published in Great Britain by Gollancz 1956
Published by Hutchinson 1970

Vintage
Random House, 20 Vauxhall Bridge Road,
London SW1V 2SA

Random House Australia (Pty) Limited
20 Alfred Street, Milsons Point, Sydney
New South Wales 2061, Australia

Random House New Zealand Limited
18 Poland Road, Glenfield, Auckland 10,
New Zealand

Random House South Africa (Pty) Limited
PO Box 337, Bergvlei, South Africa

Random House UK Limited Reg. No. 954009

A CIP catalogue record for this book
is available from the British Library

ISBN 0 09 942501 7

Printed and bound in Great Britain by
Cox & Wyman, Reading, Berkshire

Contents

———

REFLECTIONS ON HANGING

Preface to the Danube Edition

The preface to the first edition of *The Trail of the Dinosaur* is dated February, 1955, the preface to *Reflections on Hanging*, October 3 of the same year. That year marks a turning point in my curriculum as a writer: a farewell to politics and a return to my earlier interests, as a student, in psychology and the sciences of life. The end of the first preface mentioned reads: 'The bitter passion has burnt itself out; Cassandra has gone hoarse and is due for a vocational change.' The 'bitter passion' refers to the disillusioned ex-Communist's attitude towards the Stalinite regime of totalitarian terror, the sufferings it inflicted on the people under its rule, and the threat it represented to the rest of the world. To refer to oneself as a hoarse Cassandra may sound like self-dramatisation, but so many hostile critics had called me that name so insistently that I felt justified in adopting it for once.

The essays in *The Trail of the Dinosaur* cover the decade 1946–55—the early or classical period of the Cold War. In that confrontation the West was on the defensive, and the majority of its progressive intellectuals was still turning a benevolently blind eye on Soviet foreign policy and the facts of life behind the Iron Curtain (see 'The Seven Deadly Fallacies'). In the dramatic contest between Whitaker Chambers and Alger Hiss, which has been called the Dreyfus Affair of our century, progressive opinion stood firmly behind Hiss. And when, in the *New York Times*, I took Chambers' part, I became, if possible, even more unpopular among self-styled progressives than I had been before. The intellectual climate of that period was even worse in France, and provided the background for *The Age of Longing*—the novel which is published in the Danube Edition simultaneously with the present volume.

The Trail of the Dinosaur was meant to be the end of this involvement, and its preface amounted to a kind of public vow to that effect. I have actually managed to keep to it, with a very few occasional lapses. The 'vocational change' announced in the passage quoted above resulted in a trilogy (*The Sleepwalkers—The Act of Creation—The Ghost in the Machine*) which attempted a scientific analysis of the creativity and pathology of man. Those three books took over ten years to write; but nobody who has led a politically active life can sit for ten years at his desk in scholarly quietude. Thus from time to time there were bursts of hectic activity, and the first of these was devoted to the National Campaign for the Abolition of Capital Punishment, which was launched by the late Victor Gollancz, Canon John Collins and myself on a Sunday afternoon in the summer of 1955, when I paid a visit to Gollancz' country house. It took fifteen years to achieve its aim, and even at the time of writing these lines there are forces at work, backed by the majority of the public, which advocate a return of the hangman. This, however, is not the main reason for including a substantial part of *Reflections on Hanging* in this collection. It was originally intended as a pamphlet, but grew into a full-sized book as I became more and more fascinated— and horrified—by the historical, psychological and philosophical background and implications of the death penalty in general, and its theory and practice in England. Thus *Reflections on Hanging* became, for better or worse, an essay on a lurid, but significant, aspect of English cultural history.

A.K.

London
  March, 1970

The Trail of the Dinosaur
and Other Essays

Preface to the First Edition

I

The essays, lectures and broadcast talks in this book date from 1946 to 1955 and are a sequel to a previous collection, *The Yogi and the Commissar*, completed in 1944. At that time the Western world lived in the euphoria of approaching victory, and the pessimistic forecasts in that volume were almost unanimously rejected as fantasies of a morbid imagination. In the ten years that have passed since *The Yogi and the Commissar* was published, all its pessimistic and seemingly absurd predictions have come true, but none of its optimistic and seemingly plausible ones—few and cautious though the latter were.

2

'The typical career of the French politician', I wrote some years ago, 'reads like a book, from left to right.' Though I am not a French politician, the evolution reflected in these essays could be regarded as a confirmation of that rule—if the words 'left' and 'right' still possessed any concrete political meaning. One of the submissions of the present volume is that they have lost that meaning, and that man, if he is to survive, must shift the focus of his eyes to more vital questions.

This book, then, is a farewell to arms. The last essays and speeches in it that deal directly with political questions date from 1950, and are now five years old. Since then I felt that I have said all I had to say on these questions which had obsessed me, in various ways, for the best part of a quarter-

century. Now the errors are atoned for, the bitter passion has
burnt itself out; Cassandra has gone hoarse, and is due for a
vocational change.

London
February, 1955

I. THE CHALLENGE

The Challenge of our Time*

I WOULD like to start with a story which you all know, but it will lead us straight to the heart of our problem.

On the 18th of January, 1912, Captain Scott and his four companions reached the South Pole, after a march of sixty-nine days. On the return journey Petty Officer Evans fell ill, and became a burden to the party. Captain Scott had to make a decision. Either he carried the sick man along, slowed down the march and risked perdition for all; or he let Evans die alone in the wilderness and tried to save the rest. Scott took the first course; they dragged Evans along until he died. The delay proved fatal. The blizzards overtook them; Oates, too, fell ill and sacrificed himself; their rations were exhausted; and the frozen bodies of the four men were found six months later only ten miles, or one day's march, from the next depot which they had been unable to reach. Had they sacrificed Evans, they would probably have been saved.

This dilemma, which faced Scott under eighty degrees of latitude, symbolises the eternal predicament of man, the tragic conflict inherent in his nature. It is the conflict between expediency and morality. I shall try to show that this conflict is at the root of our political and social crisis, that it contains in a nutshell the challenge of our time.

Scott had the choice between two roads. Let us follow each of them into their logical extensions. First, the road of expediency, where the traveller is guided by the principle that the End justifies the Means. He starts with throwing Evans to the wolves, as the sacrifice of one comrade is justified by the hope of saving four. As the road extends into the field of politics, the

* Opening talk of a BBC broadcast series, Spring, 1947.

dilemma of Captain Scott becomes the dilemma of Mr. Chamberlain. Evans is Czechoslovakia; the sacrifice of this small nation will buy the safety of bigger ones—or so it is hoped. We continue on the straight, logical metal road which now leads us from Munich No. 1 to Munich No. 2: the Ribbentrop-Molotov Pact of 1939, where the Poles go the way the Czechs have gone. By that time the number of individual Evanses is counted by the million: in the name of expediency the German Government decides to kill all incurables and mentally deficients. They are a drag on the nation's sledge and rations are running short. After the incurables come those with bad heredity—Gypsies and Jews: six millions of them. Finally, in the name of expediency, the Western democracies let loose the first atomic bombs on the crowded towns of Hiroshima and Nagasaki, and thus implicitly accept the principle of total and indiscriminate warfare which they hitherto condemned. We continue on our logical road, which has now become a steep slope, into the field of party politics. If you are convinced that a political opponent will lead your country into ruin and plunge the world into a new war—is it not preferable that you should forget your scruples and try to discredit him by revelations about his private life, frame him, blacken him, purge him, censor him, deport him, liquidate him? Unfortunately, your opponent will be equally convinced that you are harmful, and use the same methods against you. Thus, the logic of expediency leads to the atomic disintegration of morality, a kind of radio-active decay of all values.

And now let us turn to the second alternative before Scott. This road leads into the opposite direction; its guiding principles are: respect for the individual, the rejection of violence, and the belief that the Means determine the End. We have seen what happened to Scott's expedition because he did *not* sacrifice Evans. And we can imagine what would have happened to the people of India had Mr. Gandhi been allowed to have his saintly way of non-resistance to the Japanese invader; or what would have been the fate of this country had it embraced pacifism, and with it the Gestapo with headquarters in Whitehall.

The fact that both roads lead to disaster, creates a dilemma which is inseparable from man's condition; it is not an invention of the philosophers, but a conflict which we face at each step in our daily affairs. Each of us has sacrificed his Evans at one point or another of his past. And it is a fallacy to think that the conflict can always be healed by that admirable British household ointment called 'the reasonable compromise'. Compromise is a useful thing in minor dilemmas of daily routine; but each time we face major decisions, the remedy lets us down. Neither Captain Scott nor Mr. Chamberlain could fall back on a reasonable compromise. The more responsible the position you hold, the sharper you feel the horns of the dilemma. When a decision involves the fate of a great number of people, the conflict grows proportionately. The technical progress of our age has enormously increased the range and consequence of man's actions, and has thus amplified his inherent dilemma to gigantic proportions. This is the reason for our awareness of a crisis. We resemble the patient who hears for the first time, magnified by a loudspeaker, the erratic thundering of his heart.

The dilemma admits no final solution. But each period has to attempt a temporary solution adapted to its own condition. That attempt has to proceed in two steps. The first is to realise that a certain admixture of ruthlessness is inseparable from human progress. Without the rebellion of the Barons, there would be no Magna Carta; without the storming of the Bastille, no proclamation of the Rights of Man. The more we have moral values at heart, the more we should beware of crankiness. The trouble with some well-meaning ethical movements is that they have so many sectarians and quietists and cranks in their midst.

But the second and more important step is to realise that the End only justifies the Means within very narrow limits. A surgeon is justified in inflicting pain because the results of the operation are reasonably predictable; but drastic large-scale operations on the social body involve many unknown factors, lead to unpredictable results, and one never knows at what point the surgeon's lancet turns into the butcher's hatchet. Or, to change the metaphor: ruthlessness is like arsenic; injected in very small doses it is a stimulant to the social body, in large quantities it is deadly poison. And today we are all suffering from moral arsenic poisoning.

The symptoms of this disease are obvious in the political and social field; they are less obvious but no less dangerous in the field of science and philosophy. Let me quote as an example the opinions of one of our leading physicists, Professor J. D. Bernal. In an article called 'Belief and Action' recently published by the *Modern Quarterly*, he says that 'the new social relations' require 'a radical change in morality', and that the virtues 'based on excessive concern with individual rectitude' need readjustment by a 'change from individual to collective morality'. 'Because collective action is the only effective action, it is the only virtuous action', says Professor Bernal. Now let us see what this rather abstract statement really means. The only practical way for Tom, Dick or Harry to take 'effective collective action' is to become a member of an army, political party or movement. His choice will be determined (*a*) by his nationality, and (*b*) by his political opinions or prejudices. Once he has joined the collective of his choice, he has to subordinate his 'individual rectitude' to the interests of the group or party. This is precisely what, for instance, the accused in the Belsen Trial did. Their excuse was that they had to service the gas chamber and push the victims into it out of loyalty to their party, because their individual responsibility was subordinated to collective responsibility. Counsel for the Defence of Irma Grese could have quoted verbatim Professor Bernal's reflections on ethics—though politically Bernal is a staunch opponent of Nazism and supports, to quote his own words, 'the theories of Marx and the practice of Lenin and Stalin'. His article actually contains some reservations to the effect that there should be no question of 'blind and obedient carrying out of orders', which, he says, leads to the *Führerprinzip*. He does not seem to have noticed that blind obedience plus the *Führerprinzip* are nowhere more in evidence today than in the Party to which Professor Bernal's sympathies belong. In short, I believe that much confusion could be avoided if some scientists would stick to their electrons and realise that human beings do not fit into mathematical equations. And it should be realised that this is not an abstract philosophical quarrel, but a burning and very concrete issue on which it depends whether our civilisation shall live or die.

Let me return to my starting-point, the dilemma between expediency and morality. In the course of our discussion, the symbolic sledge of Scott's small party has grown into the express train of mankind's progress. On this train expediency is the engine, morality the brake. The action of the two is always antagonistic. We cannot make an abstract decision in favour of one or the other. But we can make temporary adjustments according to the train's progress. Two hundred years ago, during the train's laborious ascent from the stagnant marshes of feudal France towards the era of the Rights of Man, the decision would have been in favour of the engine and against the brake. Since about the second half of the nineteenth century our ethical brakes have been more and more neglected until totalitarian dynamism made the engine run amok. We must apply the brake or we shall crash.

I am not sure whether what the philosophers call ethical absolutes exist, but I am sure that we have to act as if they existed. Ethics must be freed from its utilitarian chains; words and deeds must again be judged on their own merits and not as mere makeshifts to serve distant and nebulous aims. These worm-eaten ladders lead to no paradise.

Land of Virtue and Gloom*

London, November, 1946

DEAR EDITORS,

If governments are to be remembered by epithets like 'the Hundred Days', or 'the Terror', this first government of the socialist era in Britain will pass into history as the Reign of Virtuous Gloom. Both, the virtue and the gloom, become strikingly evident if one compares our life here with conditions in France (whence I have just returned after a long visit). The contrast is truly remarkable.

France has emerged from five years of occupation in a state of almost complete economic sanity and moral insanity. She produces most of the food she needs, but the normal channels of circulation and distribution have broken down. This breakdown is due not to economic, but to political and moral causes. In other words, it is a functional, not a structural disease. There is plenty of wheat but little bread, because the farmers feed wheat to the cattle, distrusting the franc; there is plenty of milk, but not a drop in Paris, for similar reasons; there are plenty of consumer-goods, but prices soar because the goods are speculatively hoarded. During my six weeks' stay, there were six *scandales* or exposures of large-scale rackets in bread, wine, potatoes, pulse, petrol, and clothing coupons—each *scandale* implicating one of the political parties in the then tripartite government and being launched by one of the rival parties at the appropriate moment, as a routine move on the political chess-board. There is no longer a black market as it has practically swallowed the legal white one; the result is a general grey of various shades, expressing the degrees of

* Condensed version of three 'London Letters', published by *Partisan Review*, New York, in 1946–7.

illegality of the transactions to which the ordinary Frenchman is driven in order to obtain bread, fats, meat, apartments, clothes, cigarettes; and to obtain the money for obtaining them. The same routine of lawbreaking is forced upon shop-keepers, department stores, and business firms if they want to survive. Even the political parties were cashing in on the black market according to the production-branch they controlled through their ministries; the most notorious case was the sale of licences for the acquisition of private cars by the Com-munist Minister of Production, Marcel Paul, in return for contributions to the Party fund. Rationing had broken down so completely that nobody whom I asked even knew what the official rations were on which he was supposed to live. This inevitably led to the retort whether I knew what *our* rations were and whether *we* lived on them; and affirmative answers met with frank incredulity or a polite smile, implying that I was trying to sell British propaganda. But there was also a curious resentment, betraying some half-conscious national guilt complex, and expressed by sneers at the priggish virtues and lack of *débrouillardise* of the British. But, of course, not all Frenchmen have the knack of *débrouillardise*—so much the worse for them. As a public figure said: Two-thirds of France live in the jungle, the remaining third in the desert.

I repeat—and the fact is publicly admitted by the more sincere French politicians—that all this is due not to economic, but to political and moral causes. Medicine had to recognise that there are functional disorders without demonstrable struc-tural defects; social science will probably arrive at similar conclusions. Meanwhile I submit the matter for discussion in your symposium on 'the future of socialism'.

To return to this island of Virtue and Gloom: if you reverse the present condition of France, then you get roughly the idea of the present condition of England. From the economic point of view, England emerged from the war very nearly bankrupt. But at the first post-war elections it recorded the sanest vote in its history; and public morale, in accepting continued ration-ing and austerity, proved almost depressingly sound and firm. I say depressingly, because this patient acceptance is not so much based on foresight and voluntary sacrifice, as on resignation, puritan tradition, and lack of *joie de vivre*. The people in the suburbs and working-class districts accept the bad life because they have never tasted the good life; there is probably more rejoicing in heaven about one repentant French black marketeer than about ten British Ministry of Food Inspectors.

Still, one can't have it both ways, and the English chose the hard and sound one. In France, the contrast between rich and poor has become sharply accentuated since the war; here nobody starves and nobody gets a decent steak. This is meant literally: even in London's top luxury restaurants food is much poorer, both in quality and quantity, than in the average French *bistro*. The black market here is insignificant; though scarce goods are kept under the counter for old customers, they are sold at regulation price, and it is quite impossible, for instance, to buy a packet of cigarettes by offering more money for it—whereas in France any amount can be had by paying four times the official price.

In short, the socialist era in Britain started by a general levelling down of the living standard—precisely as the stupidest critics of socialist theory had predicted. Needless to say, this is not the Government's fault, but the aftermath of war and of decades of capitalist mismanagement (of the coal mines, for instance). Needless to say, too, this is cold comfort in an English winter marked by coal cuts, gas cuts, ration cuts, cigarette shortage, beer shortage, and by the dull, monotonous 'more austerity' warnings of the leaders, who seem to have retained nothing from the brilliant flow of Churchillian rhetoric except the sweat-and-toil motif. The irony of the situation is, that while the higher income classes (down to the skilled worker and small shopkeeper) suffer acutely from the levelling-down process, the lower income classes are not conscious of 'going up'. For their benefits are relative, not absolute: rationing does not give them more food, but merely prevents their getting even less; government-controlled building re-houses only a fraction of the bombed-out per year and merely prevents all building material from going to the rich; and so on. The objective impoverishment of the country makes it inevitable that the hardships caused by socialist policy are real, the benefits mainly theoretical. The consequence of all this is growing apathy and resignation. As a symbol of contemporary Britain the lion and the unicorn could be replaced by the varicose veins of the British housewife after six years of queueing. But as neither Tories nor Communists have any attractive alternative to offer, the keynote of the people's mood is resentment, not revolt; except for a few, so far isolated episodes—squatting, small mutinies against demobilisation delays overseas, and a series of unauthorised strikes—about which more below.

After eighteen months of Labour rule it is, of course, too early to draw conclusions. But it is not too early to point out two basic factors among the confusing multitude of threads. One is an objective, one a subjective factor, and both are relevant to socialist theory.

The first consideration is that socialist movements are apparently doomed always to ascend to power under the worst possible objective conditions. This, on the one hand, provides socialists with the ready excuse that the theory should not be judged by experiments carried out under such handicaps. The Paris Commune was handicapped by war, siege, and famine; the Soviet system was tried out first in the most backward country of Europe; the Weimar Republic carried the economic and psychological burden of Versailles, which broke its back. British Labour inherited the hostility of all coloured people, the bad international reputation of past colonial policies, and above all, a country economically on the verge of ruin; thus, once again, the experiment cannot provide conclusive evidence for or against the theory. It would only become conclusive, the theorist argues, if socialism could be tried out in a rich, modern industrial country, secure from external aggression— the U.S.A., for instance.

It seems to me that this argument puts the cart before the horse. You cannot expect any ruling class to hand in its resignation, nor the masses to listen to radical propaganda, while all goes well. Hence it is in the nature of things that socialist movements will always inherit a more or less bankrupt estate, that they will always ascend to power in the 'wrong' country or at the 'wrong' moment. As this factor is implicit in socialist theory it cannot at the same time be treated as an extraneous

accident and serve as an excuse. Socialism is meant to be a cure
for diseased society, and no doctor can get away with the
excuse that people only call him when they are ill.

This brings us to the second factor: every leadership has a
certain elbow-room of subjective freedom within the hard
limits set by objective conditions. Nobody can blame the
Government for being unable to provide more houses, food,
coal, dollars for imports, and so on. You cannot expect
socialism to do miracles—but you can and must expect it to
give the people a message and an inspiration, to bring home
to them the consciousness of the opening of a new era. This is
where the Labour Government has completely failed. Take, as
an example, the momentous event of Britain's coal mines
passing from private to national ownership after half a century
of socialist agitation, on 1st January, 1947. Coal is the hard
core of Britain's industrial life, and the coal miner is the pioneer
and symbol of the struggles of the working-class movement.
What a pageant Hitler or Mussolini would have staged to
impress upon the people's memory this historic event! What
a glorious ballyhoo, if it had happened in America! Well, I
have seen the great event on the newsreels. It took place in the
Ministry of Fuel's austere conference room, and was about as
inspiring as the annual visit of the welfare committee in a state
orphanage. Shinwell's speech and Lord Hyndley's reply were
in the greyest virtue-and-gloom key; and the only moment
when proceedings rose to the pathos of the historic occasion
came when Attlee referred to the future of the National Coal
Board with the inspired metaphor: 'It is going to bat on a
sticky wicket, but I think it will score a great many sixes.' You
can imagine how elated the miners must have felt at this flash
of Dantonesque oratory.

It is nonsense to pretend that people in this country don't
like noisy celebrations and public displays; each Derby Day
and Cup Final is proof to the contrary. It is equally stupid to
keep repeating that 'this is no time for celebrations'. No
people can live on bread-rationing alone. I am not arguing in
favour of circus games; I only want to say that socialism minus
emotional appeal, structural changes in economy without
functional changes in mass-consciousness, must always lead to

a dead end of one sort or another. The present Labour leaders do not seem to have even an inkling of this truth. While the Government passes its nationalisation bills, raises the school-leaving age, institutes its Public Health Services, votes old-age pensions and family allowances, pursues its legislative prog-ramme slowly, steadily, and on the whole with considerable success, it is doing nothing to change the atmosphere, the mental climate of the country. If a new Rip Van Winkle had gone to sleep under the Churchill Government two years ago and woke up now, he could spend weeks travelling all over England without discovering that anything has changed in people's lives. I happen to live on a sheep farm in North Wales, next to a slate-mining village called Blaenau Ffestiniog. As neither slate-mining nor sheep-farming are on the nationalisa-tion programme, the 'landslide', the 'new era' has changed literally nothing in the life of the village, in the thoughts and habits and emotions of the people. The advent of the Age of Socialism has affected their daily routine about as much as a change in government in Mexico. And the same goes for millions of the politically indifferent, all over the country.

'But what else did you expect?' the staunch Labour politi-cian will answer: 'you know that we are a reformist, gradualist movement; you can't expect Clem Attlee to dance the Carmagnole in Trafalgar Square, nor Lord Rothschild, a Labour peer, to swing aristocrats on lamp-posts. You are a romantic, my dear fellow, and your idea of socialism is half a century behind the times. "Business as usual" was our motto during the Blitz, and "business as usual" is the motto of our Socialist Revolution. For a revolution it is, though a slow and bloodless one; and even our ultra-radical Harold Laski brought a libel suit against a newspaper which had alleged that by preaching revolution he meant anything rash or violent.'

This is the typical kind of answer of the typical Labour politi-cian, based on the typical mistake of equating gradualism with dullness. With one half of the argument I fully agree: to wit, that the reformist way is the only possible one for this country; that a revolution on orthodox Marxist lines, apart from being unthinkable under present conditions, would lead to a catastrophe; and that, if all goes well and Labour remains in power, we shall see, within a generation or so, a quiet but profound transformation of the whole social and economic structure of the country. *But Labour will only remain in power if it succeeds in capturing the people's imagination.* They voted Labour because they were fed up with the Tories; after five years of Virtue and Gloom, they may turn Stalinite or back to the Tories, for the same negative reasons. Gradualism and long-term planning are no justification for the fact that the *Daily Herald* is the drabbest and dullest paper in this country. If it can't change its editorial traditions, why can't the victorious Labour Party find the means to start a new, truly popular paper and get the politically indifferent masses away from the influence of the Rothermeres and Beaverbrooks and Kemsleys? The best journalists in this country are on the Left; but they have to work for the *Mail* and *Express* because there is no scope for them on a socialist paper in socialist Britain. Why can't socialist Britain produce films on the lives of Marx, or Robert Owen, or Keir Hardy, or the Tolpuddle Martyrs—which would be just as exciting as films on Henry VIII or Lady Hamilton? Why has the British working-class family to spend its holidays at home, or on a miserable excursion which consists mainly of queueing—for the train, for a room, for tea, lunch, cigarettes, cinemas—whereas Mr. Butlin's private holiday-camps for the lower middle classes are a roaring success, with sport, dances, entertainments and no end of fun for very little money? Why can't the Government hire Mr. Butlin—or study the Nazis' 'Strength through Joy' organisation, which was in many respects a truly admirable thing? Why is the only place in any English village or town where a soldier can play billiards, read magazines, hear lectures and get cheap meals, the Y.M.C.A.—and why are Labour clubs the most cheerless places anywhere? Why is no serious attempt being made to show the people in this country what socialism is really about? We hear the news at nine o'clock; but where, to quote Eliot, where are the eagles and the trumpets?

The answer to these questions is, firstly, that each national branch of the working-class movement is bound to adapt itself to certain national characterstics. The ruthlessness of the Bolsheviks reflected the mentality of a semi-Asiatic country; the arduous theorists of the S.P.D. were steeped in German pedantry; the great tribunes of French socialism drew on the sources of latin eloquence; and the Labour Movement has inherited the Briton's proverbial main virtue and vice, his Lack of Imagination. (Lack of imagination has always been associated in this country with straightforwardness, reliability and tradition; its opposites, 'smartness' and 'cleverness', with dubious and mainly foreign practices.)

Furthermore, each political organism develops, as it advances in age, a kind of automatic filter system through the meshes of which only those are able to ascend to leadership who, in mentality and temperament, conform, by and large, to the required standard type; it is the equivalent of Natural Selection in the political field. Hence the prevalence in the British Labour Movement of the Transport House bureaucrat, and its contempt for 'intellectuals' like Laski and Strachey, for brilliant *enfants terribles* like Nye Bevan, for people who are considered too clever by half like Crossman or too passionately sincere like Michael Foot. I could continue the list; if the outsiders were insiders, Britain could have the most dynamic Government in its history.

Another paradoxical aspect of the situation is that the forerunners of the political Labour movement, the Trade Unions, have today become the heaviest drag on the Labour Government. While I am writing this, the London transport workers are out on an unauthorised strike, and the socialist Government has had to resort to the ominous measure of calling in the Army to maintain London's food supply. Although the troops are being used to get the goods to the people and not to break the strike, the workers are of course unimpressed by such subtle distinctions; so bitterness is mounting, and the Government's stock is falling. Now even Conservative papers admit that the men's demands are reasonable enough—the main point being the reduction of the lorry-drivers' working week from 48 to 44 hours. The Transport and General Workers' Union, to which the men belong, backs their claims. It is the most powerful Union in the country. If it cannot reach agreement with the employers through the national joint negotiating machinery, it can ask for a committee of inquiry, appeal to Parliament, and so on. But the Union leaders in charge have let the negotiations drag on *for nine months*—on points of dispute which could have been settled in nine days. They 'do not seem to have worried over the time wasted. They were unaware of the fact that the patience of the men was at an end. The leaders of this mammoth Union were clearly out of touch with the men they were supposed to represent. They seemed to know next to nothing of the mood of their members. So great is the gulf that has developed between the central executive and the rank and file, that both have come to obey different impulses . . .'

The above comment is from *Tribune*, the Labour weekly; I quote it to show you how generally it is realised among clear-sighted Labour politicians that the Trade Unions have become the most awkward problem of the socialist future. For it is almost mathematically predictable that as nationalisation and planning progress, and as the Unions become more and more absorbed into semi-governmental, managerial functions, the estrangement between their bureaucracy and the working masses will become even greater. The article ends with the pious hope that the Union leaders will regain the confidence of the rank and file. But it is an illogical hope. When the State becomes the biggest employer and the Unions part of the State bureaucracy, they cease to be an instrument of the working class and become an instrument for the coercion of the working class. That is what has happened in Russia, where the worker is once more as helpless as he was in pre-Tolpuddle days. *Who is going to protect the workers in the Workers' State?* The question is less paradoxical than it sounds, and I have found no answer to it in Labour's blueprints of the future. So that's another one for your symposium.

I have no space left to talk about foreign policy; that will have to wait until the next Letter. As for outstanding literary events, they don't have to wait—there haven't been any.

London, October, 1947

DEAR EDITORS,

Only an exceptional imaginative effort could enable the Labour Government to win the next election. The future

depends on its ability to stimulate the people's political consciousness and joy of life. Instead of which, they get 'Work or
Want' posters, unctuous sermons, and the death-sentence on
the motor-bike through the abolition of the basic petrol
ration.

> *The Cabinet takes Britain in its keeping*
> *In working partnership with sons of toil,*
> *But there's the rub—those partners now are sleeping,*
> *The revolution has gone off the boil,*
> *The plebs have lost that hectic* joie-de-vivre
> *That goes with revolutionary fever.**

Two more years of this, and Labour will have irretriev-
ably wasted its historic chance and will have gone the way
of the German, Austrian, and French social-democratic
parties.

The fatal pattern of the Continental precedents is equally
discernible in Labour's attitude towards the upper and the
middle classes. The Weimar Republic had sufficiently scared
the Junkers and the Ruhr industrialists to make them her
mortal enemies; it kept on provoking them with pinpricks, but
forgot to break the backbone of their power. Much the same
happened in Austria, and in the France of the 'Popular Front'
era. With local variations it is always the same distressing
spectacle. The young matador enters the arena, bows to the
enthusiastic crowds, flaunts his red cape before the bull until
the beast gets raving mad; then, in the decisive moment, it
appears that he has left his sword at home, and he is carried
out on a stretcher, past the booing spectators who throw
cushions and rotten eggs at him.

In other words, a Socialist government cannot escape the
fatal choice either of breaking the power of the old ruling
classes, or of coming to a *modus vivendi* with them. Every single
social-democratic movement in Europe since 1918 has tried to
evade this choice, and each has fallen a victim to its attempt at
evasion. In this respect, the predicament of British Labour is

* From Sagittarius' brilliant political satire: *Let Cowards Flinch*, London,
1947.

merely an example of the predicament of democratic socialism in general, and the muddled policy of the Government may be regarded partly as a consequence of the inadequacy and datedness of socialist doctrine itself. But no such excuse can be claimed for the treatment of the storekeeper, artisan, small businessman, white-collar worker. The requirements of socialist policy towards this amorphous, politically opportunist mass, with its decisive influence on the climate of public opinion, and its decisive 'floating vote', are clear and unambiguous: they must be won over to the side of the People, to which they belong. Experience both on the Continent and in this country has proved that the industrial working class alone, without middle-class support, can neither obtain a stable parliamentary majority, nor the necessary favourable *ambiance* of the street; it cannot govern.

To all this the staunch Labour supporter will answer that the Government has no choice, that all its actions are rigidly determined by Tory mismanagement in the past, by the dollar shortage and the export gap. It would be foolish to deny the extremely heavy economic odds against which the Government is battling; it is equally foolish and irresponsible to use facts, which were just as well known in 1945 when Labour fought its electoral campaign, to justify the ineptitude of, say, Shinwell's fuel policy last winter, or the symbolic lunacy of the abolition of motoring, or Bevin's running amok on Palestine. In my first letter to you I tried to show that this Government, like any other, had a wide elbow-room of subjective freedom for manœuvring within the hard limits set by objective conditions; and that goes for all fields of activity, from economics to public relations. At that time I said that after eighteen months of Labour rule it was too early to draw conclusions. Today, in the third year of the régime, it is becoming clear that it is squandering at a rapid pace the goodwill of the electorate, the benevolent neutrality of the Little Man, and the sympathy and hopes of the European Left. If, within the next year, the Labour movement still retains sufficient vitality to change its leadership, both in spirit and in body, the downhill trend may still be halted; if not, 1950 will see the Conservative Party, perhaps reinforced by a few neo-Macdonaldites, reinstated in power. The British Labour victory was the last chance of the social-democratic movement in our time; if it is lost, it means that a Tory England allied to a Gaullist France will, for better or worse, tackle the European problem which socialism has been unable to solve.

Land of Bread and Wine*

O N 1st JULY, 1947, *Sondage*, the excellent fortnightly bulletin of the French Institute of Public Opinion, published the results of a Gallup Poll on the question: 'Do you believe that at the present moment things are going well or badly with France?' The answers were: Going well: 0 per cent. Rather well: 4 per cent. Badly, or rather badly: 93 per cent. No opinion: 3 per cent.

The near-unanimity of the answers shows that the series of convulsions which constitute French post-war history are not a surface disturbance, but rather the results of what is called here a *lame de fond*, a ground-swell which affects all the basic values of life.

Now the paradox about this profound upheaval is that apparently it cannot be traced to objective causes. Unlike England, France has emerged from the war with a temporarily weakened, but structurally intact and essentially sound economy. Unlike Germany or Italy, whose tragedies follow the classic pattern of defeat, France is in the camp of the victors. Unlike Poland or Rumania, she has no expanding Power of superior strength leaning over her frontiers. To put it crudely, the French seem to have no excuse for the frightening mess into which they have got themselves.

Just as the storming of the Bastille was not a local French event, but the symbol of the collapse of the feudal system in Europe, so the present situation in France is like a dramatisation on the stage of all the relevant contradictions and conflicts of the post-liberal era, which in more conservative or politically less sensitive nations are still in a stage of latency. This has

* Condensed version of two articles first published in *The Observer*, February, 1948.

happened before—in 1789, in 1848 and in 1871; it is the glory and tragedy of French genius, to serve as a burning lens of Western civilisation.

A central feature of the French crisis is the world-wide problem how to integrate farming communities, whose mental climate, is, at the best, that of the nineteenth century, into the controlled economies of the twentieth. The Russian peasants in 1930 resisted the intrusion of the State by burning their crops and killing their cattle; the French farmer of today resists State control by turning his grain into pig-food instead of bread. The Russian State tried to break the resistance of the peasants by deporting five million to Siberia and terrorising the rest; the French, less single-minded, have to resort to the absurd expedient of importing foodstuffs which abound in the farms but never reach the market.

In all details the two processes are different; in their essence they represent developments parallel to each other and to developments in other parts of the world where peasant populations fight their stubborn rearguard actions against the planning and controls imposed by the industrial age. The French crisis, which began about two decades ago and was merely accelerated by the war, reflects the transformation of the last great bread-and-wine producing country of Western Europe.

The vicious spiral of wages and prices; the black, or rather grey market which, mainly based on direct barter between the urban population and their farming relatives, is to some extent a common-sense corrective to abstract planning; and a great number of other secondary factors of great complexity, are reducible either to this basic process or to factors other than economic. The present crisis was no more 'caused' by war-inflicted losses in capital substance than the crisis of 1789 was 'caused' by the salt-tax or the extravaganzas of the Court; it marks the end of an era in European economy in a typically French dramatised version.

If this diagnosis is correct, the crisis can be eased by foreign aid and other palliatives, but it cannot be solved within the framework of French economy alone. A plan of reconstruction as a self-contained economic unit is no more possible for France

than for Wales or California, at least for the basic trinity of
coal, steel, and cereals; blueprints for a French recovery can
only make sense within the framework of Western Europe, including Western Germany, as an economically integrated unit.

2

The French situation reflects yet another general European
trend over the past twenty-five years: the disgust with party-
politics, the crisis of the parliamentary system, a certain anti-
democratic nostalgia of the masses, and the division into two
extreme opposing 'blocks' which grind the softer mass between
like millstones.

The Communists today present the same dilemma to France
as the Nazis did to Germany in 1930. Should democratic
privileges be extended to a party which aims at the destruction
of democratic privileges? The dilemma is complicated by the
fact that, while Nazism frankly professed its intention to
abolish democracy, the Communists pose as its defenders.
Their disfranchisement could be justified only by circumstantial
evidence; once embarked on this course, democracy would
deny its own principles and become absurd. The farcical
proceedings in the French Chamber thus again merely reflect
the more profound European dilemma. A political system
which crystallised in the liberal era becomes increasingly in-
applicable in the epoch of quasi-mystical mass movements led
from abroad by remote-control switches, and liable at any
moment to scuttle the nation.

As the remote switchboard of the Cominform permits all
national extensions to display a certain amount of local colour,
the successive transformations of the French Communist Party
have been more picturesque than in any other country. A few
months ago it still posed as the party of the Little Man, of
bourgeois respectability and even sentimental jingoism. Its
posters in the provinces told the farmers: 'For the Defence of
Property—vote Communist.' Next came a brusque, ultra-
revolutionary turning to strike, sabotage, and terror.* As a

[1] The wave of strikes and riots during the winter of 1947–8 brought certain
areas of France to the verge of civil war.

result, the chances of civil war are discussed today in France in the same tone of voice as the possibilities of a new cut in the bacon ration in England.

In this respect again, what appears as a French internal crisis is in fact a function of the world crisis: for three centuries in succession, France has maintained its unenviable position as the centre in which the chronic stresses of Europe become acute. In retrospect, the country looks like a luminous canvas with fluid contours and coloured shadows, where all the major themes of our age are represented in the impressionist style, from the problems of the farming community to the collapse of ethical values. If France goes, Europe is gone, and this the French know; on the other hand France can only be saved as an integral part of Western Europe—and this they have so far refused to accept.

The Candles of Truth[*]

A FORMER comrade of my Communist days asked me recently with an ironic smile what would be done to members of the Communist Party if I had my say. I told him that I would condemn them all to one year of Forced Reading. The sentence would start with a course in Russian to enable the offender to read Russian newspapers and listen to the Soviet radio. He would have to read *Pravda*, *Izvestia*, and *Komsomolskaya Pravda*, one social-economic magazine and one literary magazine, day by day, column by column. Then the collected speeches of the leaders, both living and dead, and the confessions of the dead before they died; then the school books, a selection of average magazine short stories, and patriotic poetry. The course would be confined to reading matter authorised by the Soviet Government, and all counter-revolutionary literature would be banned, including, of course, all newspapers, periodicals and books published in the capitalist world. It is my conviction, based on experience at the *locus in quo*, that, before the year was over, this enforced exposure of and to Soviet reality would act as a complete cure. Evidence are the few thousand foreign workers—mainly Austrian *Schutzbund* people and German Communists—who were admitted into Soviet Russia. Unfortunately, their sentence did not come to an end after one year of forced reading of reality; theirs was a more drastic fate.

The facts of Soviet reality speak for themselves and constitute such an overwhelming indictment of the régime that, once they are known, comments can be dispensed with. The main difficulty is to get at the facts and to put them before the public.

[*] From the foreword to *Stalin's Russia*, by Suzanne Labin (London, 1949).

To get at them is difficult because of the double barrier of language and frontiers. To put them before the public is difficult because the facts are systematically drowned by floods of defamation and slander. The result is that the average Western European knows no more about the realities of every-day life in Soviet Russia than his forbears knew about China in Marco Polo's time.

Ignorance breeds illusions, and illusion, both of the positive and negative kind, is a mortal danger in politics. Soviet sym-pathisers contend that the existence of forced labour battalions, numbering approximately 10 per cent of the total Soviet population, is a counter-revolutionary illusion. What better service could be done to the Soviet case, what more crushing defeat inflicted upon the literary hirelings of the imperialistic war-mongers, than to invite a trade union delegation to tour the Arctic, Siberian and Central Asiatic territories in which the alleged forced labour camps are located? To forestall accusations of bias, the delegation should include Soviet sym-pathisers of such undoubted sincerity as Professors Haldane and Bernal, Mr. Zilliacus and the Dean of Canterbury. If these men were given unrestricted freedom of movement and inquiry to enable them to check their beliefs against reality, I for one would accept their evidence, and so would a con-siderable section of British public opinion.

Positive illusions are no less dangerous than negative ones. The French and Italian Communists' acceptance of a policy deliberately aimed at wrecking European recovery is only made psychologically possible by their illusions about the structure and aims of the Soviet régime. Moreover, the exis-tence of these strong Communist parties in various European and Asiatic countries, who in case of armed conflict are expected to side with the Red Army, is a potent inducement to the Soviets to continue their policy of expansion, and thereby to increase the risks of a third world war. Without the hope of support by civil wars, it would be suicidal for the Kremlin to challenge American military power; and the hope of civil war rests entirely on the masses of people whose addiction to the Soviet myth is based on their ignorance of reality.

It follows that if Soviet reality could be made accessible on a mass scale, the dangers of war would be considerably reduced. The myth-addict can only be cured by a shock-therapy of facts. What is needed is a Reader's Digest of the Soviet Press in English, French and Italian, featuring editorials, reports from the capitalist world, home news, literary criticism, all without comment; a monitored survey of Soviet home broadcasts, again without comment; popular editions in the Western European languages of the Soviet Labour Code, of Soviet electoral law and procedure, of Court procedure for dealing with political offences in public and in camera, of censorship regulations, of laws and administrative decrees regulating the Soviet citizen's rights to travel inside his country, to leave his place of residence, to apply for jobs and to leave jobs—all without comment; translations of Soviet first readers, extracts from Soviet textbooks of geography and history; a short booklet, exclusively based on translations from the Soviet Press and radio: 'Europe through Russian eyes.' What is needed above all is that our publishers and editors of the Left, who fed us for years on uncritical echoes of Soviet mythology, should awaken to their responsibilities. They have led the European public into a pink fog of half-truths. Their duty today is to help to dispel it before Europe suffocates, physically and morally; to dispel it, not by counter-propaganda and songs of hatred, but by the organised distribution of facts.

The world, tired of isms, its emotions burnt out, is thirsting for cold, clean facts. The torch of faith is extinct; let us fall back on the candles of truth.

The Seven Deadly Fallacies*

THE war hysteria from which a considerable number of people seem to suffer here in the United States is not a sign of mature awareness. Nor is the mentality of appeasement. Appeasement of an expanding power creates a fog in which neither of the opponents knows where he is; and so the world slides into war, without either of the opponents wanting it. Appeasement means playing poker; a firm, clearly outlined, principled policy means playing chess.

These are platitudes, the type of platitude which every reader of the *New Republic* or *The New Statesman and Nation* knew by heart in the 1930s. Today they have forgotten it, and arguing against them means regressing to the kindergarten level. I hope that in this meeting we shall remain at least on the level of the primary school. So I shall take it for granted henceforth that war hysteria and appeasement are our Scylla and Charybdis, and that the liberal's precarious task is to navigate like Ulysses between the two.

Allow me, as an aid to navigation, to point out some of the logical fallacies and emotional eddies in which young idealists frequently get shipwrecked. I have listed for myself seven of them—the seven deadly fallacies of what you may allow me to call Left Babbittism. Here they are:

First is the *confusion of Left and East*. Some sections of the reactionary Press are unable or unwilling to distinguish between liberals, New Dealers, Social Democrats and Communists; they are all damned Reds. Naturally we are indignant at such poisonous imbecility. But the Left itself is partly

*Compressed version of an extempore lecture in Carnegie Hall, New York, March, 1948.

responsible for this confusion. The Left Babbitt assumes that there is a continuous spectrum stretching from pale pink liberals to red socialists and so on to infra-red Communists. It is time that he got it into his head that Moscow is not to his left but to his east. The Soviet Union is not a socialist country, and Cominform policy is not socialist policy. So let us bear in mind that 'East is east and Left is left' and if the twain sometimes still meet, the meeting is purely coincidental.

The second fallacy is the *soul-searching fallacy*. The other day there was a press conference at which I mentioned that the frightened people in Italy and France look upon you Americans as their only hope of salvation, both from the economic point of view through E.R.P., and from the military point of view against open or disguised Russian aggression. Thereupon one of the reporters present said, 'Do you really believe that we can help Europe with our dirty hands?' I asked: 'What do you mean by "dirty hands"?' He said: 'Well, I mean our policy in Greece, and in Palestine, and backing up Franco, and the way we treat Negroes and Jews. We are dirty all over, and when we pose as defenders of democracy it is sheer hypocrisy.'

The answer to this fallacy is to project the argument back to 1938. Then it would have run as follows: 'We have no right to fight Hitler's plan of sending the Jews to the gas chambers so long as there are "restricted" hotels in America and so long as Negroes do not have absolute equality here. Once American democracy has become a perfect democracy, then and then only shall we have a right to defend what remains of Europe. And if Europe goes to the dogs before we have finished, that's just too bad and cannot be helped.'

Third, and closely related to the soul-searching fallacy, is *the fallacy of the false equation*. Its European version runs: 'Soviet totalitarianism is bad. American imperialism is equally bad. There is nothing to choose between them, so let us stay in No Man's land until fate catches up with us.' To prove that the American system is 'just as bad' as the Russian system, to make the two sides of the equation balance, your purist has recourse to half-conscious little subterfuges. He equates the Hollywood purges with the Moscow purges. He has never lived under a totalitarian régime, so when he draws comparisons he does not know what he is talking about. His conscience is in revolt against the appalling slums of Chicago, in which the Negro workers of the slaughter-house industry live like rats. I have spent a few days in Chicago, and I was appalled by what I saw and heard and smelled. Do not think I am a naïve tourist, a romantic admirer of your system. But now compare your treatment of racial minorities at its worst, with the Soviet treatment of the minorities of the Crimean Republic, the Chechen Republic, the Volga-German Republic, whose total populations were deported because they had, as the official Soviet communiqué said, 'proved themselves unreliable during the war'. Even the babes in their cradles were unreliable and had to go to Siberia. In Chicago I saw men on strike, and sympathised with them. In Russia strikes, or incitement to strike, are qualified as high treason and punished by the maximum penalty. In American elections political machines corrupt and distort the People's will. In Russian elections $99\frac{1}{2}$ per cent vote for the one official list—the remaining $\frac{1}{2}$ per cent presumably being in bed with influenza. Your enlightened Babbitt equates an imperfect democracy with a perfect totalitarian régime; his philosophy boils down to the maxim that there is nothing to choose between measles and leprosy.

Fallacy number four is the *anti-anti attitude*. It runs: 'I am not a Communist. In fact, I dislike Communist politics, but I don't want to be identified with anti-Communist witch-hunting. Hence I am neither a Communist nor an anti-Communist, but an anti-anti-Communist. If W. R. Hearst says that twice two is four, I shall automatically hold that twice two is five, or at least $4\frac{1}{2}$.' The $2 \times 2 = 4\frac{1}{2}$ mathematicians are usually Henry Wallace voters.

Don't laugh, for the roots of this fallacy are very deep in all of us, myself included. I remember how painful it was when a doddering elder in a London club walked up to me and said with a tap on my shoulder: 'Well, young man, I am glad that at last you have come round to see reason. I myself knew twenty-five years ago what Bolshevism means, and it's never too late to repent.'

You can't help this sort of thing; you can't help people being right for the wrong reasons. In the last war we fought in the name of democracy in an alliance with Dictator Metaxas of Greece, Dictator Chiang Kai-shek and Dictator Stalin. At that time Nazism was the main menace to the world, and politics is based on forming alliances. But there is a fundamental difference between a war-time alliance, and political identification with one's allies. Being allied to Chiang did not mean that we wished to imitate the Chinese régime. Being against our will in one camp with the Hearst press or Senator McCarthy does not mean that we identify ourselves with their ideas and methods. This fear of finding oneself in bad company is not an expression of political purity; it is an expression of a lack of self-confidence. If you are sure of yourself—politically and ideologically—you will no longer be frightened to say that twice two makes four, even if Colonel McCormick says the same.

Fallacy number five is *the sentimental fallacy*. For years we were allied to Communists in the struggle against Nazism, and now when we have to part company, the roots of past loyalty are difficult to tear out. Our bedfellows of yesterday do not share this sentimental squeamishness. Over the slightest disagreement they will denounce us as Fascists, traitors and cannibals. These emotional ties are one-way ties, and it is essential to bear in mind that they are entirely irrational and conservative in nature.

Fallacy number six is *the fallacy of the perfect cause*. It is related to number two, the soul-searching fallacy. Only absolutely clean hands have a right to reach out to protect and save what remains of Europe. Only an absolutely perfect cause is worth fighting for. And the search for the perfect cause becomes an excuse for quietism.

History knows no perfect causes, no situation of white against black. Eastern totalitarianism is black; its victory would mean the end of our civilisation. Western democracy is not white but grey. To live, even to die for a perfect cause is a luxury permitted to few. In 1942 or '43 I published an article which began with the words: 'In this war we are fighting a total lie in the name of a half-truth.' The total lie was Hitler's New Order. The half-truth was our democracy. Today we face a similar emergency and a similar predicament. Once more the choice before us is merely that between a grey twilight and total darkness. But ask the refugees who manage to escape, at the risk of their lives, from behind the iron curtain into our grey twilight world whether this choice is worth fighting for. They know. You don't.

The last fallacy, number seven, is the *confusion between short-term and long-term aims*. It is the most dangerous of all. By long-term aims I mean the age-old struggle for reform, for social justice, for a more equitable system of government. By short-term aims I mean the necessity of fighting an immediate emergency.

The danger of confusion is twofold. Your leftist Babbitt may refuse to fight against the short-term emergency until he has finished the job of creating a perfect government in his country, in a century or two. The opposite danger is to become so obsessed with the immediate emergency, that all principles of the long-term struggle are thrown overboard. Ex-Communists and disappointed radicals are in particular danger of toppling over to the other extreme. It is essential that we should keep in mind that there are two distinct levels involved in our struggle; that to defend our system against a deadly threat does not imply acceptance of everything in this system, does not imply giving up the long-term fight to improve it; and *vice versa*, that our criticism of the shortcomings of this system does not free us from the duty to defend it, despite its ambiguous greyness, against the total corruption of the human ideal.

This talk was mainly addressed to the progressive Left. I may have been harsh to the Left Babbitt; it was a brotherly harshness. To the Babbitt of the Right I have nothing to say; we have no language in common.

The power-vacuum which two world wars have created in Central and Western Europe, has inescapably linked your fate with that of the European continent. I feel the enormous burden which is falling on your shoulders. For there will either be a *Pax Americana* in the world, or there will be no pax. Never has such a burden and such a responsibility been borne by any single nation in history. It is the more unfair to you as yours is an adolescent civilisation, with adolescent enthusiasms and adolescent pimples. The task of the progressive intelligentsia of your country is to help the rest of the nation to face its enormous responsibilities. It is time for the American liberal to grow up.

Chambers, The Villain*

THE second trial of Alger Hiss happened to coincide with the publication of a book in which several former Communists and Soviet sympathisers, including myself, relate their experiences. This explains the letter from which the following extract is taken. The writer is unknown to me—she is a woman, obviously of German origin, who now lives in a Latin-American country.

DEAR MR. KOESTLER,

In the *Time* issue of January 9th, Latin American Edition, where the book *The God That Failed* and your account in it, is mentioned, there appears, once again, a piece on the Alger Hiss trial.

Many were the times when I wanted to write to you. Many were also the times when I wanted to write either to Alger Hiss or to *Time* when I read again and again of that ominous trial, to express my sympathy and/or to cry out: isn't there anybody who is interested to present the case of Hiss in the right light of psychology and human understanding? I didn't do that either, because I thought who cares if I write or not.

Still, today I write to you because it came to me in a flash that it is you who really should write that letter which would be nothing if it came from a nobody like me, but if it comes from you it will be a plea that will be heard.

Reading about Alger Hiss I always think: there but for the grace of God and the Communist Party, stand I. I

* First published in abridged form in *The New York Times*, February, 1950.

belong to your generation, in age and in spirit; I was one of those who, had the party only asked for it, would have spied on God Almighty without the least bit of a bad conscience. It is not my merit that they did never ask me things like that, because the only function I ever held was that of a dumb cashier of party dues, and later on I was fortunately only a no-account typist in one of their organisations in Berlin; still later, in Spain the same in a party office in Barcelona during the Civil War. It was around that time, summer 1937, when I changed my mind about our 'Religion' and no doubt, had Alger Hiss gone through this school he would have changed his mind also. But Americans were rather a few years later in finding out, you know the political reasons for that very well, I suppose. It seems one has to be a European with a left-wing past to understand the Hiss story . . .

That is where the call for you comes in. Defend Alger Hiss on ground of his motives. I only know of the Hiss case what I have read in *Time*. Still, the story seems in a way very clear to me and though I believe he did what he is accused of, I see it in the light of his then decent motives. The question would rather be: have the United States really been harmed through him? I cannot believe that. It must be his difficult position and regard for his family that makes him insist on his 'innocence' which, in a higher sense, is real. Come to think of it, for the American public the case is really a bit involved, but you could make it clear. Maybe, if you did, you would prevent a suicide. Could not this trial be brought around to the real issue: even if he did steal the documents, what were his motives? Probably, sometime between now and then, when Alger Hiss changed his mind as so many did who had been communists in good faith, he was in no position to announce that change. It must have been like this and Whittaker Chambers is the real villain because he didn't keep his mouth shut about things past and done with.

I have quoted this long extract because I believe that it expresses, in an admittedly exaggerated and overstrung manner, the vague feeling of uneasiness in a considerable section of the European and American public. The out-standing aspect of the trial was that it was not a case of the State calling a citizen to account for an alleged crime. It was a public and deathly duel between two individuals, one per-secutor, one persecuted. Thus, the abstract equation of justice between individual and society became transformed into a personal equation between two men, and the whole picture became distorted by the public's emotional reactions to these two so utterly different human types. As far as personal impressions and the testimonies of high-standing witnesses go, the persecuted Hiss appeared as the prototype of the decent, modest, hard-working, well-spoken, happily married, idealistic American liberal who, even if assumed to be guilty, could not be suspected of having acted for any base reason or for per-sonal gain. His persecutor, on the other hand, appeared as a man who unblushingly admitted having committed perjury, travelled with forged passports, lived with mistresses under false names, and was described by some academic gentlemen as a psychopath. To put the whole matter in a nutshell: from the spectator's point of view the casting of the parts was wrong—Chambers should have got the part of Hiss and Hiss the part of Chambers.

But the roles were only apparently miscast. For there is a tragic consistency and symbolism in both characters. There are many who, without doubting the verdict of the jury, agree that Hiss's innocence is 'in a higher sense real'. For my part I am convinced that Hiss did what he did out of misguided idealism, and that he kept passing the documents to the spy-ring happily like a boy scout performing his one good deed every day. He is the classic type who becomes addicted to the Communist drug, and never finds his way back from the lost weekend in Utopia. We always feel unhappy if it becomes necessary to send a man to prison for something he did in subjective good faith, based on a profound conviction—though if this necessity were neglected civilisation would disintegrate.

Hiss stubbornly persisted in his error; Chambers confessed and recanted his past. One would think that this decisive fact should have tilted the balance of sympathy towards Chambers.

Yet my correspondent excuses Hiss's impenitence by his 'difficult position' and calls Chambers the 'real villain' because 'he did not keep his mouth shut'. And here again she seems to lend a shrill voice to public sentiment. For though it is said that one repentant sinner causes more rejoicing in Heaven than ten righteous men, here on earth the public spectacle of the repentant sinner causes at best a feeling of embarrassment, at worst a feeling of revulsion. And there, I believe, is the core of the whole problem.

Some time ago at a New York cocktail party a lady journalist attacked me with some vehemence. She said that people who had once been Communists should shut up and retire to a monastery or a desert island, instead of going round 'teaching other people lessons'. She spoke with deep conviction, which expressed a widespread popular feeling: mankind's instinctive horror of the renegade.

This horror probably has its roots in the collective unconscious, in past loyalties to church, clan or tribe which, even if apparently buried, remain potent emotional forces. Even those who in principle agree that there are considerations which may force a man to override his loyalties, and who accept the ethical justification of a given act of renegation—even those feel aesthetically repelled by the spectacle of the act itself. People don't mind if you betray humanity in the name of some attractive cause; but if you betray your club or party, they will turn from you in contempt.

This leads us to the curious fact that in our society most people are in the habit of manipulating two mutually exclusive sets of ethical rules without being aware of the contradiction between them. The first is expressed by sayings like 'my country, right or wrong', or 'if the Party demands it I will spy on God Almighty Himself'. The second demands that a man should have the courage to become a traitor, renegade, or apostate if the interests of humanity demand it. Some of the War Trials of the last years were good examples of the confusion created by the simultaneous application of these contradictory rules of ethical conduct. Even more startling is the example of France, where people were shot, imprisoned or sentenced to 'national ignominy' for having obeyed the orders of their own legal government. If you feel contempt for the renegade Chamberses and Kravchenkos, then you should feel sympathy for the loyal Ribbentrops and Lavals; and *vice versa*, if you condemn people for having 'collaborated' with a totalitarian régime, then you must acquit those who have deserted such a régime.

But even if in theory you agree with this, the deserter remains an unwelcome sight, and like Coriolanus he may exclaim:

> *A goodly house: the feast smells well: but I*
> *Appear not like a guest.*

For of the two co-existent and contradictory rules of ethical conduct the first, which demands unquestioning loyalty to some flag, social body or institution, is much older and deeper embedded in our unconscious psyche. This may be illustrated by comparing the public's attitude to a Catholic convert on the one hand, to an unfrocked priest on the other. Everybody, including hardened atheists, respects the convert; but even atheists are embarrassed by an unfrocked priest taking a girl out to a dance. Now, in fact, both are renegades who have repudiated their former convictions. But the convert has only deserted the amorphous mass of unbelievers who do not represent a social institution and have no flags, emblems or party cards; whereas the priest has deserted a church with powerful binding symbols.

Chambers and Kravchenko and the rest of us who have once borne allegiance to the 'God that Failed', will always be looked upon as unfrocked priests. This would be without much interest if it merely concerned the few individuals in question. In this case the simplest solution for these would be to follow the lady journalist's advice and satisfy the demands of good taste by retiring to a desert island.

But if Chambers had followed this advice, his repentance would have become meaningless, for the public would never have learned certain facts which it was essential for it to learn. And the same is true of Kravchenko, and Barmine, and Silone, and Gide and the others. My correspondent asks why they can't 'keep their mouths shut about things past and done with';

and the public, repelled by this flood of renunciations, disclosures and ringing *mea culpa*'s, ask with a shudder the same question. The answer is, simply, that these things are neither 'past' nor 'done with'. The essential data for the ideological and strategical defence of our civilisation could never have been assembled if these men had had the discretion and good taste to keep their mouths shut. For only those who have worked inside the totalitarian machine know its true character and are in a position to convey a comprehensive picture of it; and in this sense at least it is true that one repentant sinner is a more valuable asset than ten righteous men who have never swerved from the path of democratic virtue.

The decisive fact about Chambers is that he has performed a service of great social utility. Not all acts of social utility curry favour with the public, or make the man who performs them appear in a favourable light. But it is essential that these two value-judgments, the first of an objective, the second of an emotive character, should remain neatly separated; and that the emotional factor should not obscure political judgment or interfere with the discharge of justice. It is not to be expected that the public should like the runaway priest—even if the church from which he has run away happens to be devoted to worshipping the devil. It is not even important that it should believe in the purity, or otherwise, of his motives to quit. The public is entitled to feel attracted or repelled by him, but it is not entitled to let its bias interfere with its judgment: to talk of betrayal where loyalty would mean persistence in crime, and to defend the agents of an evil régime on the grounds that those who denounce it are not saints.

II. DIVERSIONS

The Future of the Novel*

1

NOVELS date more than drama and poetry. The reason for this is the novel's pseudo-objectivity. The characters on the stage speak for themselves; the poet, whose method is direct and subjective, speaks for himself; but in the novel the author speaks for his characters, and pretends to give an objective account of their thoughts, feelings and actions. This alleged objectivity is, of course, pure swindle. For the narrative reflects not only the author's personal philosophy, idiosyncrasies and style (that in itself would be all right) but also smuggles in, still under the label of objectivity, the whole baggage of the prejudices and conventions of his time. As the narrator, *ex hypothesi*, is omniscient, ubiquitous and non-existent as a person, it is the period itself which speaks through him. The novel's period-character is implicit and mainly unconscious, therefore all the more revealing.

2

Elizabeth Bowen said somewhere that the object of the novel is the non-poetic statement of a poetic truth. As a recent convert to semantics, I began to doubt whether I knew what a poetic truth is, though I always thought I did. I imagined Professor Ogden taking the class:

'In current usage we call a scientific truth a statement of the type that the attraction of a heavy body decreases in inverse ratio to the square of the distance. Now, Bowen, will you give

* First published as a contribution to a symposium in *New Writing and Daylight*, September, 1946.

us an example of what you call a statement of "poetic" truth?'—'The wine-dark sea, I suppose.'—'Is that a *statement*, Bowen? And how, by expressing it in non-poetical form, is it supposed to become a novel?'

Still, I side with Miss Bowen, but her formula needs elucidation. As a next step I suggest this phrase of Gerhardt Hauptman's: 'Poetry is the distant echo of the primitive word behind the veil of words.' It seems to me that the action of the novel is always the distant echo of some primitive action behind the veil of the period's costumes and conventions. The word 'primitive' is used here in the sense of the archaic and perennial, the Jungian archetype. Archetypes are ever-repeated typical experiences rooted in the human condition; inherited patterns of instinct-conflicts; the psychic residue of the 'suffering and delight that has happened countless times in our ancestral history, and on the average follows ever the same course'.

The great significant works in the history of fiction are variations of such archetypal situations and conflicts, which first occur in mythology, and are re-stated in the specific language of the period. Prometheus, Job, Sisyphus, Samson, Oedipus, Tantalus, Narcissus, etc., are the eternal 'stories' of the inadequacy of the human condition. Their listing would be a gratifying task for a research thesis. Here is one example: the type of story based on the archetypal figure of the 'idiot', the inspired fool. Its heroes are ever-new incarnations of the ideas of charity and innocence. They appear to their environment as naïve, foolish, even mentally deficient—not because they lack intelligence, but because their system of values differs from the conventional values of their surroundings. Their simplicity moves on a higher plane than the craftiness of their time; so that their clever contemporaries, when they look down at them, have to lift their faces upward. Equally typical is the narrator's attitude to his hero: a tender ridicule, a sigh of regret for his own lack of courage to take the hero quite seriously, for alas one has to keep one's feet on the earth. Examples of this chain are: the *Perceval legend*; the *Lay of the Great Fool*; the Welsh and Germanic variations of it; *Don Quixote*; *Eulenspiegel*; numerous variations of the *enfant terrible* and the 'gentle-savage-goes-to-town' themes; Masereel's *The Sun*; Shaw's *Black Girl in Search of God*; Dostoevski's *The Idiot*; Thornton Wilder's *Heaven is my Destination*; Camus' *L'Étranger* (with a new twist); and so on. Other frequently recurring archetypes are: conflict between two loyalties (Penelope *v.* Trojan war, Katinka and the Five Year Plan); between instinct and convention (Bovary, Karenina); sensitive hero and callous world (all public-school novels and most auto-biographies); shock and conversion (a Russian speciality but also a favourite motif with E. M. Forster); the conquest of fear (from Hercules to Hemingway) and of the flesh (from Buddha to Huxley). There are perhaps a dozen or so more—but not many more. The themes of fiction are limited; only their variations are inexhaustible.

Novels which are not fed from archetypal sources are shallow or phoney. They are like a house with elaborate plumbing, bathrooms, cold- and hot-water taps, which the builder forgot to connect with the main.

3

We may thus distinguish in the novel a constant and a variable factor. The constants are the archetypes, the predicaments inherent in the human condition. The variable factor is the cultural pattern of the period, and its conscious and unconscious techniques of projection.

As far as the first factor is concerned, we need not worry about the novel's future. Novelists will not run out of themes as long as mankind has not reached a state of nirvanic perfection and diffused its emotions in social entropy. Moreover, their themes will always remain new, for archetypes enjoy eternal youth like their early incarnations, the Olympians.

As to the variable factor, my prediction is that the fiction of the period between the second and the third world war will be dominated by a trend towards three Rs: Realism, Relevance, Rhythm.

By *Realism*, I mean neither the naturalism of Zola, nor the philosophy of Babbitt, the diplomacy of M. Vishinski, or the portraits in the Royal Academy. Realism in fiction is the striving to approach the reality of the human condition with as open a mind and as much disregard for convention, prejudice and habit as one's capacities permit. It means discarding traditions which mask vital bands in the human spectrum, and taking in new extensions of the visible range offered by psychology, the social sciences, the evolution of language. The opposite of realism is smugness, and the ambition to be recommended by the Book Society. Realism requires courage and integrity. But alas, these manly virtues are not enough; the less spectacular and more difficult task of realism is to assimilate the new extensions of the spectrum—and to assimilate them so completely that no residue of learnedness, no label of the scientific department-store should remain.

Some critics deny the necessity for the artist to take in new extensions of the spectrum. They wallow in statements like 'Stendhal knew all that long before Freud' and 'Tolstoi wouldn't have gained much by reading Marx.' One might as well say that it makes no difference to the writer whether he knows that the earth is a small planet or believes that it is a disc supported by Atlas, and the centre of the world.

The approach to realism in the history of fiction is gradual. In the average Victorian novel, the whole range of sex was represented by a gap in the spectrum. Today, a number of its aspects are admitted; but it would be naïve to believe that these suffice to cover even the most recurrent unmentionable thoughts and emotions of real people. A writer may take his courage into both hands and allude to some of them; yet he won't be able to do it with grace and ease. The passage will hit the reader in the eye, and the author will feel that he is handling a hammer. The novel will not be able to digest the full implications of Freud for perhaps another half-century. Art is not yet ripe to represent the most fundamental act of reality, procreation; even a Hemingway fails when he tried it.

4

Relevance is a quality in fiction which connects it with the dynamic currents, the essential pattern, of the period. In our period, these currents have become tidal waves which spare no private island. It is no longer a question whether ivory towers are desirable; the point is that they have become physically impossible. One could easily ignore the Boer War and the Dreyfus affair; one cannot escape the implications of the atom bomb. As public concerns invade an ever-increasing sector of the space inside the individual's skull, his private interests become increasingly saturated with relevance. The fiction of the next few decades will be situated in a strong magnetic field which will impose its pattern on the raw material as on a heap of iron filings. This is true even of the deliberately escapist type of fiction. George Orwell has recently analysed the development of the crime story from *Raffles* to *Miss Blandish*; similar conclusions could be reached by comparing the progress of 'Romance' from the Victorian to the contemporary magazine story; or the evolution of humour from *Punch* to the *New Yorker*.

Finally, *Rhythm*. The rhythm of a narrative is a measure of its artistic economy; and economy is not brevity, but implicitness. Implicitness is a technique which forces the reader to work out for himself what is implied. Language itself is never completely explicit; words are mere stepping-stones for thoughts. When listening to speech, we have continuously to establish connections between the words; otherwise, as when our attention flags, they become a mere medley of sounds. Economy in art thus has its roots in the basic mechanism of communicating thought-contents by acoustic or optic signs, and is a purposeful development of it. The reader has to fill in the gaps by drawing his own conclusions and projecting his own emotions; economy compels the consumer to re-live the producer's creative effort. The artist rules his subjects by turning them into accomplices.

Civilisation accelerates the rhythm of art, not because cars run faster but because thoughts run faster. Newspapers, radio, mass-produced books, have beaten and smoothed our associative pathways, and established a network of fast-running association trains where the Victorian reader's imagination ambled in a mailcoach. This does not mean that the rhythm of the narrative must necessarily become hectic and jumpy like

Dos Passos' camera eye, or syncopated like a Hemingway dialogue. Nor should the narrator run after the thought-train like Joyce. His function is rather that of the pointsman's at the switchbox.

5

If one analyses any true novel, that is to say, a novel in which the conflict arises from the interplay of character and environment and bears the stamp of inescapability, one always arrives at a mythological core. The *leitmotifs* are timeless, but the orchestration is period-bound. The modes and moods of a given period form a pattern; the individual threads in it must be seen both in the light of their archetypal origin and of their social context. If one of these conditions is missing, the novel will be a failure. But if both are fulfilled, something strange will happen. As with every living organism, you will get more out of it than you put in. It will not only describe, it will point. The novelist should never aim at more than stating; but if his echo does not bear a message, he has failed. Every philosophical, scientific, or artistic statement which is true, not only describes the world but changes it.

The antithesis to art is propaganda, where the emphasis is not on stating, but on changing. Hence the paradoxical result that, in order to change the world, the artist must forget his desire to do so. Since most writers have strong feelings about politics or other matters, the above sounds like an injunction to walk the tight-rope—which it is; but it is attenuated by the artist's inborn or acquired skill at walking the tight-rope in his sleep.

A Rebel's Progress

TO GEORGE ORWELL'S DEATH*

To meet one's favourite author in the flesh is mostly a disillusioning experience. George Orwell was one of the few writers who looked and behaved exactly as the reader of his books expected him to look and behave. This exceptional concordance between the man and his work was a measure of the exceptional unity and integrity of his character.

An English critic recently called him the most honest writer alive; his uncompromising intellectual honesty was such that it made him appear almost inhuman at times. There was an emanation of austere harshness around him which diminished only in proportion to distance, as it were: he was merciless towards himself, severe upon his friends, unresponsive to admirers, but full of understanding sympathy for those on the remote periphery, the 'crowds in the big towns with their knobby faces, their bad teeth and gentle manners; the queues outside the Labour Exchanges, the old maids biking to Holy Communion through the mists of the autumn mornings . . .'

Thus, the greater the distance from intimacy and the wider the radius of the circle, the more warming became the radiations of this lonely man's great power of love. But he was incapable of self-love or self-pity. His ruthlessness towards himself was the key to his personality; it determined his attitude towards the enemy within, the disease which had raged in his chest since his adolescence.

His life was one consistent series of rebellions both against

* First published in *The Observer*, 29th January, 1950.

the condition of society in general and his own particular predicament; against humanity's drift towards 1984 and his own
drift towards the final breakdown. Intermittent hæmorrhages
marked like milestones the rebel's progress as a sergeant in the
Burma police, a dishwasher in Paris, a tramp in England, a
soldier in Spain. Each should have acted as a warning, and
each served as a challenge, answered by works of increasing
weight and stature.

The last warning came three years ago. It became obvious
that his life-span could only be prolonged by a sheltered
existence under constant medical care. He chose to live
instead on a lonely island in the Hebrides, with his adopted
baby son, without even a charwoman to look after him.

Under these conditions he wrote his savage vision of 1984.
Shortly after the book was completed he became bedridden,
and never recovered. Yet had he followed the advice of doctors
and friends, and lived in the self-indulgent atmosphere of a
Swiss sanatorium, his masterpiece could not have been written
—nor any of his former books. The greatness and tragedy of
Orwell was his total rejection of compromise.

The urge of genius and the promptings of common sense can
rarely be reconciled; Orwell's life was a victory of the former
over the latter. For now that he is dead, the time has come to
recognise that he was the only writer of genius among the
littérateurs of social revolt between the two wars. Cyril Connolly's remark, referring to their common prep-school days:
'I was a stage rebel, Orwell a true one,' is valid for his whole
generation.

When he went to fight in Spain he did not join the sham-
fraternity of the International Brigades, but the most wretched
of the Spanish Milicia units, the heretics of the P.O.U.M. He
was the only one whom his grim integrity kept immune against
the spurious *mystique* of the 'Movement', who never became a
fellow-traveller and never believed in Moses the Raven's Sugar-
candy Mountain—either in heaven or on earth. Consequently,
his seven books of that period, from *Down and Out* to *Coming up
for Air*, all remain fresh and bursting with life, and will remain
so for decades to come, whereas most of the books produced by

the 'emotionally shallow Leftism' of that time, which Orwell so despised, are dead and dated today.

A similar comparison could be drawn for the period of the war. Among all the pamphlets, tracts and exhortations which the war produced, hardly anything bears re-reading today—except, perhaps, E. M. Forster's *What I Believe*, a few passages from Churchill's speeches, and, above all, Orwell's *The Lion and the Unicorn*. Its opening section, 'England Your England', is one of the most moving and yet incisive portraits of the English character, and a minor classic in itself.

Animal Farm and *1984* are Orwell's last works. No parable was written since *Gulliver's Travels* equal in profundity and mordant satire to *Animal Farm*, no fantasy since Kafka's *In the Penal Settlement* equal in logical horror to *1984*. I believe that future historians of literature will regard Orwell as a kind of missing link between Kafka and Swift. For, to quote Connolly again, it may well be true that 'it is closing time in the gardens of the West, and from now on an artist will be judged only by the resonance of his solitude or the quality of his despair'.

The resonance of Orwell's solitude and the quality of his despair can only be compared to Kafka's—but with this difference: that Orwell's despair had a concrete, organised structure, as it were, and was projected from the individual to the social plane. And if 'four legs good, two legs bad', is pure Swift, there is again this difference: that Orwell never completely lost faith in the knobby-faced yahoos with their bad teeth. Had he proposed an epitaph for himself, my guess is that he would have chosen these lines from Old Major's revolutionary anthem, to be sung to a 'stirring tune, something between "Clementine" and "La Cucuracha" ':

> *Rings shall vanish from our noses,*
> *And the harness from our back . . .*
>
> *For that day we all must labour,*
> *Though we die before it break;*
> *Cows and horses, geese and turkeys,*
> *All must toil for freedom's sake.*

Somehow Orwell really believed in this. It was this quaint belief which guided the rebel's progress, and made him so very lovable though he did not know it.

Judah at the Crossroads

AN EXHORTATION*

THE martyrdom of the Jews runs like a jagged scar across
the face of human history. The resurrection of the State of
Israel offers, for the first time in two thousand years, the
possibility of solving the Jewish problem. Up to now the Jews'
fate lay in the hands of the Gentiles. At present, it lies entirely
in their own hands. The wandering Jew has arrived at a crossroads, and the consequences of his present choice will make
themselves felt for centuries to come.

The total Jewish population of the world is at present estimated at eleven and a half millions. On the European Continent the National Socialist régime nearly succeeded in
eliminating the previously strong and culturally significant
Jewish community. Out of a pre-war population of six million
Jews (excluding Russia), only one million, that is, approximately fifteen in a hundred, survived in 1946. In Berlin and
Vienna, in Warsaw and Prague, where Jews played an important and at times dominant part in cultural life, their influence
has completely disappeared. The first question which the Jews
now have to decide is whether it is desirable that the void
should again be filled. Should they flock back into these areas,
which have become the cemeteries of their kin, should they try
to regain their former positions in finance, industry, literature,
journalism, the arts and sciences, while retaining their separate
identity as Jews, and thereby resuscitate the 'Jewish problem'
in Europe? The question must be answered in the light of past

* This essay follows to their conclusion certain thoughts and suggestions
tentatively expressed in *Promise and Fulfilment* (1950); I have used passages
from that book, and from my earlier *Thieves in the Night*, without quotation
marks.

experience, and of the new reality created by the State of Israel.

In the United States, where the major part of contemporary Jewry lives, the problem arises in a different form: should the American Jews aim at maintaining their separateness as a religious and social community, or at gradually eliminating it?

In the third geographical area where Jews live in large numbers, the territories East of the Iron Curtain, the question is less acute. The pressure of the anti-religious totalitarian State (in spite of temporary oscillations of the line) is gradually eliminating the institutions and traditions on which Jewish separateness depended: the synagogue, the Yiddish language, Jewish residential districts and even Jewish surnames. If these régimes survive the next two or three generations, there will be little or no trace left of a separate Jewish community in the religious and ethnical sense.

But in Western Europe and America, and in every other part of the world where Jews exist in sizeable numbers, the dilemma arising out of the creation of the Jewish State is grave and acute, though the majority of them do not as yet realise its full implications, and the fateful choice it imposes on them. To put it bluntly, it is the choice between either becoming a citizen of Israel, or ceasing to be a Jew in the national, religious, or any other meaning of the word. The choice is imposed by historic circumstance and by the essential content of the Jewish tradition itself.

2

The ultimate distinguishing mark of the Jew (I shall come back to this point later) is not his race, language or culture, but his religion. It officially defines him as a Jew from the moment of his birth, it is the original source of his social and cultural peculiarities, and of his self-awareness as a Jew.

Unlike any other religion, however, the Mosaic religion is inseparably tied to the idea of a separate nation. One can be a Catholic or a Protestant, a Moslem or a Buddhist, regardless of nationality or race. But the Jewish faith implies membership of a historic nation with a land of its own, from which it has

been temporarily exiled. Christianity and Islam only demand
from their followers that they accept certain doctrines and
ethical rules which transcend frontiers and nations; the Jewish
believer professes to belong to a chosen race, the seed of
Abraham, Isaac and Jacob, with whom God made a covenant
including the promise of preferential treatment and of a
geographical home. 'Blessed be the Lord, our God, who led
our fathers out of the bondage in Egypt'—the person who
recites that prayer claims a racial ancestry (whether biologi-
cally he is right or not) which automatically sets him apart
from the racial and historic past of the people in whose midst
he lives. A comparison between Christian and Jewish festivals
reveals the significant fact that the former are sacred, the latter
nearly all secular in character. Christians celebrate mystical or
mythological events: the birth and resurrection of the Son of
God, the assumption of the Virgin; Jews commemorate landmarks in national history: the Maccabean revolt, the exodus
from Egypt, the death of the oppressor Haman, the destruction
of the Temple. The Old Testament is first and foremost the
history book of a nation; every prayer and ritual observance
strengthens the Jew's consciousness of his national identity. The
claim that Judaism is 'a religion like other religions, a private
affair which has nothing to do with politics or race' is either
hypocritical or self-contradictory. *The Jewish faith is nationally
and racially self-segregating*. It automatically creates its own
cultural and ethnic ghettoes.

At the end of the Passover meal, for the last two thousand
years Jews all over the world have lifted their glasses and drunk
a sacred toast to 'next year in Jerusalem'. Thus the Jewish
religion postulates not only a national past, but also a national
future. The Proclamation of Independence of the Jewish State,
issued on 14th May, 1948, declares: 'Exiled from the land of
Israel, the Jewish people remained faithful to it in all the
countries of their dispersion, never ceasing to pray and hope
for their return and the restoration of national freedom.' Jews
refer to the last two millennia of their history as the Diaspora,
or Age of Dispersion, and to all countries outside Palestine as
'the Galuth' or 'the Lands of Exile'. His faith thus compels the
Jewish believer to regard himself as a person with *a national past*

and future different from that of the Gentiles among whom he lives. The 'Englishman of Jewish faith' becomes a contradiction in terms. As a member of the chosen race, temporarily exiled from his promised land, he is not an English Jew, but a Jew living in England. This refers not only to Zionists, but to all members of the Jewish community who, whatever their attitude to Zionism and Palestine, are bound to regard themselves, by the articles of their faith, as members of a separate race with a separate national past and future. The fact that they are unaware, or only half aware of the secular implications of their creed, and that the majority indignantly reject 'racial discrimination' if it comes from the other camp, makes the Jewish tradition only more paradoxical and self-contradictory.

Racial discrimination does indeed work both ways. The tendency, even among liberal and enlightened Jews, to seek each other's company, to keep themselves to themselves in marriage and social life, is only partly due to the pressure of hostile surroundings. An equally important bond is tradition with an ethnic and national tinge. Catholic minorities in Protestant countries sometimes display an apparently similar tendency towards solidarity. But the analogy is misleading, for this solidarity—or cliquishness—is confined to Catholics with strong feelings about their faith, or at least about the position of their Church in the world. Jewish cliquishness, on the other hand, extends to members of the community who hold no religious convictions, are indifferent to Zionism, regard themselves as hundred per cent Americans or Englishmen, and yet cling together, tied by shared habits and tastes, by an inert tradition voided of all spiritual content which, to quote Arnold Toynbee, is merely 'the fossilised remnant of a once independent culture'.

A further symptom of the discriminatory character of Judaism is the Jewish attitude to the Gentile. That twenty centuries of persecution must leave their marks of suspicion and defensive hostility, we take for granted; the point is too obvious to need elaboration. But the Jewish attitude to the Stranger in Israel carries an element of rejection which is historically older than the ghettoes, which dates back to the tribal exclusiveness of the Mosaic religion. The Hebrew word

'Goy' which designates the non-Jews does not merely mean 'pagan' or 'unbeliever'; it does not refer to a soul capable of salvation or a body capable of being accepted into the community after acquiring the true faith. The 'Goy' corresponds rather to the Greeks' 'Barbarian', to our 'natives' and 'aborigines'. It refers not to a religious, but to a racial and ethnic distinction. In spite of occasional, and somewhat half-hearted, injunctions to be kind to the Stranger in Israel, the Goy is treated in the Old Testament with a mixture of hostility, contempt and pity, as not really quite up to human standards. In the centuries that have passed since, the concept of the Goy has lost some of its tribal emotionalism, but it has never entirely lost its derogatory echo. In the ghettoes of Poland, the young men sang mocking songs about the drunken Goy, which were no nobler in spirit than the anti-semitic jingles about Kikes and Yids. A persecuted minority certainly has good excuses for repaying hostility and contempt in the same coin, but the point I wish to make is that we are faced with a vicious circle: that a religion with the secular claim of racial exclusiveness must needs create secular repercussions. The Jew's religion sets him apart and invites his being set apart. The archaic, tribal element in it engenders anti-semitism on the same archaic level. No amount of enlightenment and tolerance, of indignant protests and pious exhortations, can break this vicious circle.

'Anti-semitism is a disease that spreads apparently according to its own laws: I believe the only fundamental cause of anti-semitism—it may seem tautological—is that the Jew exists. We seem to carry anti-semitism in our knapsacks wherever we go.' This was said by the late Professor Chaim Weizmann, first President of the resurrected Jewish State, in summing up the calvary of twenty long centuries. To expect that it will come to a spontaneous end in the twenty-first is to go against historic and psychological evidence, against the law of cause and effect. It can only be brought to an end by Jewry itself. But neither President Weizmann nor any of the Jewish leaders of our time had the courage to face this fact and to speak out openly.

To come back to my starting-point: the general distinguishing mark of the Jew, that which makes him a Jew on his documents and in the eyes of his fellow-citizens, is his religion; and the Jewish religion, unlike any other, is racially discriminatory, nationally segregative, socially tension-creating. Once this basic fact—supported by the evidence of the five volumes of the Old Testament, the hundreds of volumes of sacred commentaries, and the common book of Jewish prayers—is firmly and uncontroversially established in our minds, and the unconscious resistances against accepting it are overcome, then the first step towards solving the problem has been made.

The emphasis here is on the 'unconscious resistances' which, as we shall see later, are immensely and understandably strong among all who, by faith or tradition, claim to be Jews. For the moment, however, I shall leave the psychological aspect aside, and proceed with my argument.

3

Let us distinguish between three categories of Jews: (*a*) the minority of orthodox believers, (*b*) the larger group of the adherents of a liberalised and diluted version of the Mosaic religion, (*c*) the largest group of agnostics, who, for complex reasons of tradition or pride, persist in calling themselves and their children 'Jews'.

The orthodox believers outside the State of Israel are a small and dwindling minority. The stronghold of orthodox Jewry was Eastern Europe—Poland, Latvia, Lithuania, Ruthenia— where the Nazi fury reached its peak and wiped them almost completely off the face of the earth. The scattered survivors, and the small orthodox groups in the United States, are composed mostly of elderly people. Orthodoxy is dying out in the Western world, while the bulk of the strictly tradition-bound communities in North Africa, the Yemen, Syria and Iraq are emigrating to Israel.

Thus, as a social group the remnants of orthdox Jewry no longer carry much weight. But their position is symbolical of the dilemma that confronts Judaism at large. Since the burning down of the Temple they have never ceased to pray for the restoration of the Jewish State, for 'next year in Jerusalem'.

On 14th May, 1948, their prayer was suddenly fulfilled. Now
the logical consequence of the fulfilment of a prayer is that one
ceases to repeat it. But if prayers of this kind are no longer
repeated, if the mystic yearning for the return to Palestine is
eliminated from the Jewish faith, then the very foundations and
essence of that faith will have gone. No obstacle prevents any
longer any orthodox Jew from obtaining a visa at the Israeli
Consulate, and booking a passage on the Israeli Line. The alternative before him is either to be 'next year in Jerusalem',
or to cease repeating a vow which has become mere lip-service.

In fact the major part of Judaism's prayers, rites, and
symbols have become meaningless since the restoration of the
Jewish State. To persist in them in the future would be as
anachronistic and absurd as if Christians persisted in secretly
gathering in catacombs, or Lutherans continued reading their
Bible in secret. The Proclamation of Independence of the
State of Israel affirms that it 'will be open to Jews from all the
countries of their dispersion'. On the eve of Sabbath the ram-
horn sounds again in the streets of Jerusalem to call the faithful
to worship. The Lord of Israel has kept the Covenant and
returned Canaan to Abraham's seed. The orthodox Jew can
no longer refer to himself with the ritual phrase as living 'in
exile'—unless he means a self-imposed exile, based on economic considerations which have nothing to do with his religion.
If he refuses to obey the commandment to return to the land
of his fathers, he places himself outside the Covenant and
excommunicates himself according to his own terms of
reference—though of course he will never admit it.

The orthodox position typifies in an extreme form the
dilemma that is inherent in any liberalised and reformed
version of Judaism. I have dwelt at length on the essentially
racial and national character of the Jewish religion. Any
attempted reform, however enlightened, which aims at eliminating this specific content of Judaism would eliminate its very
essence. Take away the 'Chosen Race' idea, the genealogical
claim of descent from one of the twelve tribes, the focal interest
in Palestine as the *locus* of a glorious past, and the memories of
national history perpetuated in the religious festivals; take
away the promise of a return to the Holy Land—and all that

remained would be a set of archaic dietary prescriptions and tribal laws. It would not be the reform of a religion but its complete emaciation, and a turning back of the clock to the Bronze Age.

Let us now consider the position of that vast majority of contemporary Jewry who display an enlightened or sceptical attitude towards the faith of their ancestors, yet for a number of complex motives persist in confirming their children in that faith and impose on them the 'separateness' that it entails. Paradoxically, it is this type of 'nondescript' Jew, unable to define his Jewishness in either racial or religious terms, who perpetuates the 'Jewish question'.

In dealing with this central problem, I shall repeatedly quote from Isaiah Berlin's series of articles, 'Jewish Slavery and Emancipation',* which has come to be regarded as a classic treatment of the subject. Berlin starts by agreeing that 'there is no possible argument against those truly religious Jews to whom the preservation of Judaism as a faith is an absolute obligation to which everything, including life itself, must without hesitation be sacrificed', and later on endorses the view that for these full-blooded Jews, as it were, the only logical solution is emigration to Israel. He then turns to the 'nondescript' category and says:

'. . . But it is not so clear that those who believe in the preservation and transmission of "Jewish values" (which are usually something less than a complete religious faith, but rather an amalgam of attitudes, cultural outlook, racial memories and feelings, personal and social habits) are justified in assuming without question that this form of life is obviously worth saving, even at the unbelievable cost in blood and tears which has made the history of the Jews for two thousand years a dreadful martyrology. Once . . . unreasoning faith is diluted into loyalty to traditional forms of life, even though it be sanctified by history and the suffering and faith of heroes and martyrs in every generation, alternative possibilities can no longer be dismissed out of hand.'

* *Jewish Chronicle*, June, 1950.

The only alternative to the perpetuation of Jewish separateness for that nondescript majority who have outgrown Jewish nationalism and the Jewish religion, is to renounce both, and to allow themselves to be socially and culturally absorbed by their environment. All that I have said before leads up to this harsh but inescapable conclusion.

Yet the psychological resistances against it are enormous. The springs of this resistance are partly to be found in the general human tendency to avoid a painful choice. But equally important emotional factors are spiritual pride, civic courage, the apprehension of being accused of hypocrisy or cowardice, the scars of wounds inflicted in the past, the reluctance to abandon a mystic destiny, a specifically Jewish mission.

Let me concede at once that psychologically there is every excuse for Jews being emotional, illogical and touchy on the question of renunciation—even if they are unable to say what exactly they are reluctant to renounce. But let it be also clear that, while every man has a right to act irrationally and against his own interests, he has no right to act in this way where the future of his children is concerned. I would like to make it clear at this point that my whole line of argument, and the practical conclusions derived from it, are aimed not at the present, but at the next generation, at the decisions which men and women who were brought up in the Jewish community must take regarding not their own status, but the future of their children. Once this point is clearly established, a number of objections against the process of assimilation will be automatically removed.

I shall now consider some typical objections which were raised since, several years ago, I first proposed the solution advocated in these lines. They are well summarised in the questions put to me by an interviewer from the London *Jewish Chronicle* after the publication of my book *Promise and Fulfilment** in which I had tentatively broached the subject. The interviewer was Mr. Maurice Carr, and the interview, from which the following extracts are quoted, appeared in the official weekly paper of British Jewry under the headline

¹ London and New York, 1949.

'Arthur Koestler's Renunciation'.* It opened with a long introductory remark by Mr. Carr:

> '. . . I was anxious to obtain [the author's comments] to the Epilogue in his book Promise and Fulfilment whose message may be summed up in this one brief passage:
> "The existence of the Hebrew State . . . puts every Jew outside Israel before a dilemma which will become increasingly acute. It is the choice between becoming a citizen of the Hebrew nation and renouncing any conscious or implicit claim to separate nationhood."
> . . . If that was what Arthur Koestler really meant, then it seemed to me, willy-nilly, he was placing himself in the evil company of the professional anti-Semites, who, with the logic of violence, bedaub the walls with the slogan: "Jew go to Israel or into the crematorium!" . . . The ineffable quality of Jewishness, having weathered so many cataclysmic storms in the past, will no doubt resist Arthur Koestler's assault upon it.'

(Question): When you say categorically that the Wandering Jew must decide either to become an Israeli or to renounce utterly his Jewishness, are you thinking in ultimate or immediate terms?

(Answer): I think that the choice must be made here and now, for the next generation's sake. The time has come for every Jew to ask himself: Do I really consider myself a member of a Chosen Race destined to return from exile to the Promised Land? In other words: Do I want to emigrate to Israel? And if not, what right have I to go on calling myself a Jew and thereby inflicting on my children the stigma of otherliness? Unless one shares the Nazis' racial theories, one has to admit that there is no such thing as a pure Jewish race. The primary distinguishing mark of the Jew is his religion. But this religion becomes meaningless if you go on praying for the Return to Zion even while you are firmly resolved to stay away. What then remains of your Jewishness? Not much more than the habit of regarding yourself, and being looked upon by others, as an outsider.

* Jewish Chronicle, 5th May, 1950.

But you thereby condemn your children to unwholesome environmental pressures which at best create handicaps of varying severity for their inner development and public career, and at worst lead to Belsen and Auschwitz.

(*Q.*): Is your haste in proclaiming the choice between Israel and total abandonment of Jewishness attributable to the fear of new Belsens and Auschwitzes?

(*A.*): Anti-Semitism is growing. Even the British, for all their traditional tolerance, have recently been affected, otherwise they wouldn't have swallowed Mr. Bevin's Palestine policy. But, to my mind, it is not so much the danger of pogroms as the fundamental evil of abnormal environmental pressures from which the Wandering Jew must save himself and the coming generations.

(*Q.*): Does it not occur to you that in seeking the will-o'-the-wisp of 'normality' and security, runaway Jewry will be sacrificing the distinctive Jewish genius: and do you not consider, from the broadest humanist viewpoint, that such a loss of the Jewish heritage and of Jewish talents will more than outweigh any problematic gains?

(*A.*): It is undoubtedly true that the stimulus of environmental pressure has produced a greater porportion of intellectuals among Jews than among their host nations. This process of 'over-compensation' is familiar both to the psychologist and the historian—see in particular Adler and Toynbee. We also know that most great men in literature, art, politics, religion, had an unhappy childhood, were lonely and misunderstood, and that their creative achievements were partly due to their reactions to these pressure-stimuli. But would you recommend parents to give their children deliberately an unhappy childhood in the hope of breeding an Einstein, a Freud, or a Heine? Of course, abolish all suffering in the world and you would abolish the chance of producing outstanding personalities. But, after all, out of 1,000 individuals subjected to unhealthy environmental pressure, 999 will develop thwarted characters and only one will perhaps become an outstanding personality. I reject as wholly indefensible the vague Jewish sentiment: 'We must go on being persecuted in order to produce geniuses.'

As for the Jewish cultural heritage, the Scriptures and Apocrypha have become the common property of mankind. The Talmud is today of interest only to a narrow specialised group. To impose a study of it, and of Biblical exegesis, on Jewish children in general is as utterly absurd and sterile as it would be to compel all Christian children to study medieval scholasticism. By way of secular culture you have mainly modern Yiddish literature: but the Yiddish language was killed with the people who spoke it in Eastern Europe, and I don't suppose you would defend its survival in America any more than of Ukrainian. The only legitimate, natural home for the preservation and future growth of a specifically Jewish culture is Israel.

(*Q.*): How do you reconcile your dictum 'the means justify the end'* with your advice to the Wandering Jew to run away from himself? After the first cowardly step of abdication, surely the renegade Jew will have to stoop to gross deceitfulness, resolutely lying to himself, to his neighbours, and to his children about his Jewish origin. Otherwise if he chooses to be honest and disdains concealment, neither he nor his children will become thoroughgoing non-Jews. Rather will they merely become 'ex-Jews'. Will not then an ex-Jew be a new sort of freakish outsider, certainly spurned by the Jews, and in all probability still derided by the anti-Semites?

(*A.*): Today every Jew has the possibility of going to Israel, so it is no longer an act of cowardice to choose the alternative of renouncing one's Jewishness. It has become a voluntary renunciation, which before the rebirth of Israel it was not. . . . To cling to an outworn status of 'negative Jewishness' out of sheer stubbornness or from fear of being called a coward, is in itself an inverted form of cowardice for which helpless children will be made to suffer. As to the quality of honesty, that is the very thing I am advocating. It takes an equal measure of uncompromising honesty for one Jew to opt for 'next year in Jerusalem' and for another Jew to decide on renunciation. He who abandons Jewishness

* What Mr. Carr presumably meant was: 'Your rejection of the tenet that the end justifies the means.'

should not conceal anything from his children; nor on the other hand need he bother the children prematurely. After all, it is a question of tact and delicacy, rather like the problem of education on sexual matters.

(*Q.*): Of all the Jews persecuted by Hitler, none suffered such terrible despair as those who had thought to cast off all traces of their own or their father's or their grandmother's Jewishness. In one form or another, might not a similarly cruel fate—far worse than that which can ever befall a real Jew—overtake the would-be ex-Jews?

(*A.*): Whatever one does in life, there is always the chance that something will go wrong. But I am certain that by and large the Gentile world will welcome wholehearted Jewish assimilation. Individual complications may arise, especially in the first and second generations, but thereafter—what with mixed marriages—the Jewish problem will gradually disappear to the benefit of all concerned.

(*Q.*): What religious education, if any, would you suggest for the children of ex-Jews?

(*A.*): First let me make it clear that when I advocate the renunciation of the Jewish faith by those who are unwilling to live according to its tenets (that is, to return to the Promised Land) I emphatically do *not* advocate their conversion to any other religion—unless of course they feel spiritually and sincerely attracted to it. This would be contemptible hypocrisy. But I do advocate with equal emphasis that the *children* of these 'ex-Jews' who are not yet either spiritually or formally committed to the Jewish creed which their parents have abandoned, should be brought up like the other children of the environment in which they live. If the other children at their school go to church or chapel, let them go to church or chapel, and do not brand them as different. No new-born babe has a say in the question to which denomination it should belong, and the usual practice in the world today is that parents who have no specific religious convictions leave the religious formation of their children to the hazards of school and environment. I believe it is essential for a child to start his spiritual development with a belief in God, regardless whether this is a

Jewish, Calvinist, or Wesleyan God, and to be left to make his decision in matters religious when he reaches maturity. To put it bluntly, I regard it as an outright crime for parents who neither believe in Jewish doctrine nor live up to its commandments, to impose the stigma of 'otherliness' on a defenceless child who has not asked for it.

(Q.): Do you not feel that there is something abject, humiliating, in such a conformist surrender by the minority to the majority? Without any belief in, say, Catholicism, the ex-Jew is to send his children to a Jesuit school. He is to bury alive his own traditions and memories, and these memories, unfortunately, include bitter persecution at the hands of those whose ranks he is now joining uninvited. Is that not asking altogether too much?

(A.): To take your last question first, the memory of past persecutions: surely you do not suggest that resentment should be kept rankling and old hatreds perpetuated? It is, of course, never an easy thing to break with the past, to cast off traditions and memories. But millions of American immigrants have done just that without great effort. And if we accept the fact that anti-Semitism is not a transient phenomenon, then this sacrifice imposes itself to a much higher degree in the case of the Jews than, say, in the cases of Italian emigrants to the United States. While the Italians are fleeing from poverty alone, the Jews must get away from the spectre of extermination. It is imperative that the Jews should face up to their responsibilities to their children, whatever the wrench to their own feelings.

(Q.): Do you not think that the best, the most reasonable and most honourable policy for the Diaspora Jew is to carry on as in the past and at the same time to help build up the State of Israel as an eventual haven of refuge in a minority-baiting world?

(A.): No. That is the Jewish tragedy of wanting to have the cake and to eat it at the same time. That way lies disaster.

(Q.): Do you believe that Israel, as you say in your Epilogue to *Promise and Fulfilment*, is now so 'firmly established' that it can get along without further aid from the

Diaspora? Is not your cry 'Israel or renunciation' altogether premature, for even supposing that five million Galut Jews were to opt instantly for 'next year in Jerusalem', there just would not be any room for them there?

(*A.*): Israel is no less firmly established today than any European country which lives under the Communist menace. In view of the magnitude of the problem which Israel is facing in the absorption of immigrants, I would suggest that for a limited period of, say, five years, world Jewry should be encouraged to help finance the settlement of those Jews who desire, or are obliged, to migrate to Israel. After this transition period, there should no longer be any Zionist Organisation of America, no United Jewish Appeal, no Zionist movement, no fund-raising, in fact none of this paradox of a State proud of its sovereignty and yet going round with the begging-bowl.

As for your hypothesis of five million Jews wanting to go to Israel straight away, that is pure fantasy. The bulk of Jewry is in America. But only a few hundred American Jews have moved to Israel since its foundation. It would actually be a splendid thing for Israel if 50,000 American Jews with the right qualifications could be persuaded to go out at once. With their Western culture and technical ability they would transform Israel, and they would be ten times more valuable now than in the future.

(*Q.*): Do you still regard yourself as a Jew? Do you wish others to consider you as being no longer a Jew?

(*A.*): In so far as religion is concerned, I consider the Ten Commandments and the Sermon on the Mount as inseparable as the root and the flower. In so far as race is concerned, I have no idea and take no interest in the question how many Hebrews, Babylonians, Roman legionaries, Christian crusaders, and Hungarian nomads were among my ancestors. I consider it a chance occurrence that my father happened to be of the Jewish faith; but I felt that it committed me morally to identify myself with the Zionist movement, as long as there was no haven for the persecuted and the homeless. The moment that Israel became a reality I felt released from this commitment, and free to choose between becoming an Israelite in Israel or a European in Europe. My whole development and cultural allegiance made Europe the natural choice. Hence, to give a precise answer to your question: I regard myself first as a member of the European community, secondly as a naturalised British citizen of uncertain and mixed racial origin, who accepts the ethical values and rejects the dogmas of our Heleno-Judæo-Christian tradition. Into what pigeon-hole others put me is their affair.

That was the end of this long interview, followed by Mr. Carr's conclusion:

I do fear that a large number of lukewarm Jews are sub-consciously thinking along the lines formulated by Arthur Koestler; and his 'thinking aloud' on their behalf may prove extremely useful in drawing attention to an, as it were, submerged menace.

4

The publication of this interview aroused general indignation among the *Jewish Chronicle*'s readers. The protests were headed by a letter from the President of the Anglo-Jewish Association, the Hon. Ewen E. S. Montague, o.b.e., k.c., which was a beautiful example of question-begging:

The brilliantly written interview by Mr. Maurice Carr, in which the apostasy from Judaism of Mr. Koestler is reported, will have filled most of your readers with distress and dismay. . . .

Mr. Koestler . . . has sought to justify his action by stating that there are now only two courses that a Jew can take: to emigrate to Israel or to abandon his religion.

Many Jews have decided, or will decide, to take the former course, with the full respect, sympathy, and under-standing, as well as the good wishes, of their respective communities. But why should the thousands of others have to take the second course—the one adopted by Mr. Koestler?

The Anglo-Jewish Association numbers among its members many devout Jews of a piety that can be assailed by no one; they, in common with all our other members, find no difficulty in the present circumstances in reconciling Judaism, and an earnest and sincere wish that Israel may prosper, with a pride in their British citizenship and a full share in the duties, obligations, and rights of that status.

. . . It is vital, at this time in particular, to ensure that no one can doubt that one can still be a sincere Jew and a loyal citizen of the country in which he is living.

Together with the President of the Anglo-Jewish Association's letter, the paper printed another protest by a reader who declared in one paragraph:

Assimilation . . . solves nothing. The fault, dear Mr. Koestler, lies not in the Jews themselves, but in the intolerance of the people living around them. . . .

—and continued a few lines further on:

The Jew trying to assimilate is to me a pitiable figure lacking in sincerity. . . .

A week later the journal came out with an editorial:

The very provocative interview, published recently in *The Jewish Chronicle*, with Mr. Arthur Koestler, should remind us of the fact, apparent to most Jewish women, that the home is the citadel in which to defend the Jewish faith . . . And there has yet to be found any comparable system of daily home life. The dietary laws receive daily confirmation from leading medical authorities: the Jewish housewife down the ages knew how often they protected her and her loved ones from the scourges and plagues that raged around her. Is she, then, at a time when the world so badly needs good men and women, to abandon her faith and sink her own and her family's identity, in order that boys and girls may appear like robots in uniforms indistinguishable one from another?

Still in the same issue there were more letters of protest, all of them sadly illustrative of the manner in which religious fervour degenerates, unnoticed by the believer, into racial pride and perpetual resentment:

In common with the vast majority of my fellow-Jews, outside as well as inside Israel, I feel myself to be just one of a grand array of comrades-in-arms, clad in spiritual armour, scattered over the wide world, and engaged in a fierce and enduring defensive action for a world of freedom, truth, and justice. This struggle began on the day about 4,000 years ago, when the Children of Israel turned their backs on the slave-State of Egypt. . . . More than a thousand years ago a Hebrew poet or *paitan* gave us the answer in *Vehi She'amda*, that beautiful jewel embedded in the Hagada: 'This it is which has stood by our fathers and ourselves. For not one enemy alone has risen up against us to destroy us, but in every generation they rise up against us to destroy us, but the Holy One, blessed be He, delivers us from out of their hands' . . . Mr. Koestler seems to be unaware of the fact that the Sermon on the Mount has its origin in Rabbinic thought, that it is merely a rehash of Jewish doctrine. . . . Why does not Mr. Koestler turn his brilliant pen to a far nobler purpose? Let him fight, and urge others to fight, against intolerance and injustice, but let him not ask us obsequiously to crawl to our oppressors' camp, where these two evils have flourished for so long.

Another week later the paper came out with yet another editorial:

In actual fact, the dilemma which Mr. Koestler poses . . . is basically false. . . . While the Holy Land must always retain its unique significance for Jewry, the message of Judaism and the mission of the Jewish people are not confined to the Holy Land but are universalistic in character. . . . the undying Messianic hopes and aspirations of our Faith forbid us to withdraw from our world-wide mission in the service of mankind. More than ever in these days are we called upon to promote, in whatever country we may dwell, the Jewish ideals of righteousness and brotherhood among the nations. It is not easy to share Mr. Koestler's satisfaction that modern civilisation stands in no need of this Jewish contribution.

Apparently the official organ of British Jewry still regards 'the ideal of righteousness and brotherhood' as a Jewish monopoly; it actually drove its message home with the somewhat dated quotation: 'and ye shall be unto Me a kingdom of priests and a holy nation.' If the paper's claim were to be taken seriously, it would mean that Messrs. Ben Gurion and Mendès-France, Comrade Kaganovich and Henry Morgenthau, Albert Einstein and Louis B. Mayer of Metro-Goldwyn-Mayer, are all commonly engaged in carrying out a specifically Jewish mission. It is precisely this kind of turgid bombast which gave rise to the legend of the Elders of Zion, and keeps suspicions of a Jewish world-conspiracy alive. But the controversy served nevertheless a useful purpose by letting the cat of fierce racial pride out of the religious bag, and revealing the tragic contradiction of Jewish existence. For how is the world to reconcile the claim that an Englishman of Jewish faith is like other Englishmen, with the statement, printed in the same issue of the paper: 'To be a Jew means that you believe that the past of Jewry is your past, its present your present, its future your future . . .?'

It is remarkable that England's leading Jewish paper did not receive or print a single letter of even partial support for assimilation—which after all has been going on as a historic process for a few thousand years. The passages that I have quoted give only a feeble taste of the vehemence and abuse which the interview aroused in this, probably the most liberal, tolerant and enlightened Jewish community in the world. One can understand the true believer who exclaims with John Donne: 'Oh, for some, not to be martyrs is a martyrdom.' But to protest against martyrdom and yet ask for just a little more of it for one's children and children's children without knowing why, is a less defensible attitude.

5

I shall now elaborate some of the points raised in the controversy, and shall at the same time try to progress from abstract
argument to the field of practical measures. It will be simplest
to resort to the form of the imaginary dialogue (which in this
case is based on a series of actual dialogues in the past):

(*Question*): All previous attempts of Jewish communities to
become completely assimilated to their host nation have ended
in failure—see Germany for instance; why should it be
different this time?

(*Answer*): The reason for past failures and tragedies is that
so far all attempts at assimilation were half-hearted, based on
the faulty assumption that the Jews could become full-blooded
members of their host nations while retaining their religion and
remaining the Chosen Race. *Ethnic assimilation is impossible
while maintaining the Mosaic faith; and the Mosaic faith becomes
untenable with ethnic assimilation.* The Jewish religion perpetuates
national separateness—there is no way around that fact.

There is, on the other hand, at least one example of successful assimilation on a large scale: the Spanish Jews, who some
five centuries ago embraced the Catholic faith as an alternative
to expulsion, and who (with the exception of a heroically
stubborn minority who continued to practise Judaism in secret
until they were martyred) have been completely absorbed,
racially and culturally, by the Spaniards. To quote Toynbee
again: 'There is every reason to believe that in Spain and
Portugal today there is a strong tincture of the blood of these
Jewish converts in Iberian veins, especially in the upper and
middle classes. Yet the most acute psycho-analyst would find
it difficult, if samples of living upper- and middle-class Spanish
and Portuguese were presented to him, to detect those who had
Jewish ancestors.'

(*Q*.): Your arguments are based on the assumption that the
only, or at least the principal, distinguishing mark of the Jew
is his religion. What about race, physical features, and those
peculiarities of Jewish character and behaviour which are
difficult to define and yet easy to sense?

(*A.*): Racial anthropology is a controversial and muddy field, but there is a kind of minimum agreement among anthropologists on at least these two points: (a) that the Biblical tribe belonged to the Mediterranean branch of the Caucasian race, and (b) that the motley mass of individuals spread all over the world and designated as 'Jews' are from the racial point of view an extremely mixed group who have only a remote connection, and in many cases no connection at all, with that tribe. The contrast between the short, wiry, dark-skinned Yemenite Jew who looks like an Arab, and his Scandinavian co-religionist is obvious. Less well-known is the fact that even Jews from geographically close neighbourhoods (e.g. Russian and Polish Jews) differ markedly in physical type. Certain Italian and Spanish physiognomies are pronouncedly semitic in appearance, and some Spanish families have probably a higher percentage of semitic genes than those groups of European Jews whose ancestors got into the way of the Crusaders and other marauding hordes. But the most puzzling racial paradox of all is the quite un-Jewish appearance and mentality of the new native generation in Israel:

The Palestine-born young Jew's nickname, *sabra*, is derived from the prickly, wild-growing, somewhat tasteless fruit of the cactus plant. In physical appearance he is invariably taller than his parents, robustly built, mostly blond or brown-haired, frequently snub-nosed and blue-eyed. The young male's most striking feature is that he looks entirely un-Jewish; even his movements are angular and abrupt in contrast to the characteristic curvy roundedness of 'Jewish' gestures. The girls, on the other hand, seem as yet to remain physically closer to the Eastern-European Jewish type. On the whole, there can be little doubt that the race is undergoing some curious biological alteration, probably induced by the abrupt change in climate, diet and the mineral balance of the soil. It also seems that the female is slower in undergoing this transformation, more inert or stable in constitutional type. The whole phenomenon confirms in a striking manner that environment has a greater formative influence than heredity, and that what we commonly regard

as Jewish characteristics are not racial features, but a
product of sustained social pressures and a specific way of
life, a psycho-somatic response to 'the stimulus of penalisa-
tions'.

In his mental make-up the average young *sabra* is fearless
to the point of recklessness, bold, extroverted and little
inclined towards, if not openly contemptuous of, intellectual
pursuits. The children are particularly good-looking; after
puberty however, their features and voices coarsen and seem
never quite to reach the balance of maturity. The typical
sabra's face has something unfinished about it; the still un-
determined character of a race in transition. His diction is
abrupt and unmodulated, which sometimes gives the impression of rudeness. . . . What kind of civilisation he will
produce one cannot foretell, but one thing seems fairly
certain: within a generation or two Israel will have become
an entirely 'un-Jewish' country. *(Promise and Fulfilment.)*

When the fallacies of racialism have been discarded, all that
survives of the Biblical race is probably a statistically very small
'hard core' of genes which, in certain segregated, inter-
marrying Jewish communities kept 'Mendling out', as the
biologist says, in curved noses and wistful irises. But even
regarding such facial features it is extremely difficult to distinguish between true heredity and environmental influence. The
fairly uniform facial changes of priests living in celibacy, of
actors, of convicts serving long sentences, and other types of
'professional physiognomies' could easily be mistaken for racial
characteristics; and the growing likeness of ageing married
couples is an equally puzzling confirmation of the feature-
forming power of shared environment.

Turning from physical appearance to the mental habits and
peculiarities of Jews, these vary so widely from country to
country that we can only regard them as the product of social,
not biological inheritance. The typical Jewish abhorrence of
drunkenness, for instance, is the unconscious residue of living
for centuries under precarious conditions which made it
dangerous to lower one's guards; the Jew with the yellow star
on his back had to remain cautious and sober, and watch with

amused or frightened contempt the antics of the drunken Goy. Revulsion against alcohol and any other form of excess, recklessness and debauch, was instilled from parent to child in successive generations—down to the milk-drinking Prime Minister of France and the abstemious owners of Château-Laffitte.

Jewish casuistry, hair-splitting and logic-chopping, can be traced back to the Talmudic exercises which, until quite recently, dominated the Jewish child's curriculum in school; as one brilliant biographer of Marx has pointed out, the Dialectic owes as much to Hegel as to Marx's rabbinical background.* The financial and forensic genius of the Jew is obviously a consequence of the fact that until the end of the eighteenth century, and in some countries well into the nineteenth, Jews were debarred from most normal professions; the reasons why in the arts and letters Jews play an interpretative rather than a creative part has been exhaustively analysed in Isaiah Berlin's essay.

We thus have a small and somewhat hypothetical 'hard core' of Jewish characteristics in the sense of biological heredity, and a vast complex of physical and mental characteristics which are of environmental origin and transmitted through social inheritance. Both the biological and social features are too complex and diffuse to identify the Jew as a Jew with anything approaching certainty; the decisive test and official identification mark remains his religion.

(Q.): Your arguments may be logical, but it is nevertheless inhuman to ask people to discard, in the name of expediency, a centuries-old tradition as if it were a worthless garment.

(A.): Let us try to define what exactly we mean by 'Jewish tradition'. Do we mean the concept of monotheism, the enthronement of the one and invisible God, the ethos of the Hebrew prophets, the wisdom of Solomon, the Book of Job? They are all in the King James's Bible and have become the common property of the Western world. *Whatever came after the Bible is either not specifically Jewish, or not part of a living tradition.* Since the conquest of Jerusalem by Titus A.D. 71, the Jews have ceased to be a nation, and ceased to have a language and

¹ Leopold Schwarzschild, *The Red Prussian*, London, 1948.

secular culture of their own. Hebrew as a spoken language went out of use long before the beginning of the Christian era (at the time of Jesus, the language of Palestine was Aramaic); the Jewish scholars and poets in Spain wrote in Arabic, as their descendants wrote in Italian, German, English, French, Polish and Russian. It is true that certain segregated Jewish communities developed a vernacular or *patois* of their own, such as Sephardi and Yiddish, but none of these produced a literature of any consequence and even remotely comparable to the imposing 'Jewish' contribution to German, Austrian, English or American culture.

The only specifically Jewish intellectual activity of the post-Biblical centuries was theological. But Talmud, and Kabbala, and the endless volumes of rabbinical exegesis are unknown to 99 per cent of the general Jewish public, and are no more part of a living tradition than the exercises in casuistry of the medieval Schoolmen. Yet they were the *only* product of a specifically 'Jewish tradition', if that expression is to be given concrete meaning, during the last two thousand years.

In other words: since the first century A.D. the Jews have had no national history, no language, literature and culture of their own. Their philosophical, scientific and artistic achievements consist in contributions to the culture of their host nations; they do not constitute a common cultural inheritance or autonomous body of traditions. The fallacy of postulating a special Jewish 'mission' and 'tradition' becomes evident if we consider that in these terms Disraeli was part of the mission, Gladstone was not, Trotsky was part of it, Lenin was not; Freud was, Jung is not; and that Jewish readers ought to prefer Proust to Joyce, Kafka to Orwell, because the first in each pair is part of the tradition, the second is not.

To sum up: the Jews of our day have no cultural tradition in common, merely certain habits and behaviour-patterns, derived from a religion whose commandments they reject, and from the unhealthy environmental pressures on a segregated minority. The sooner all this is discarded, together with segregation and minority status, the better for all concerned.

(*Q.*): More logic-chopping. You carve up that indefinable entity 'tradition' into tidy categories as if it were a steak that you can cut into chunks. But when a Jew, even a hundred per cent agnostic American, hears the ancient injunction: 'Hark O Israel: the Lord our God, the Lord is one', then something stirs in him which makes all your arguments collapse.

(*A.*): That something that stirs in him is shared by all mankind. I reject the arrogant presumption of your witness who believes that the message is addressed to him and his kin alone. That, if you permit me to say so, is a metaphysical snobbery based on genealogical assumptions as untenable as Houston Stewart Chamberlain's myth of the Nordic Man.

(*Q.*): You are very impatient with Jewish emotionalism, but there are other minorities just as sentimental and tradition-bound—think, for instance, of the Irish Catholics in the United States.

(*A.*): The parallel is misleading. The Irish-American's ties to his old country date from a recent past and fade away in the second or third generation. The Jew's 'old country' is not the country of his parents or grandparents, but of a hypothetical ancestor who abandoned it two thousand years ago. The American Jew's sentimental allegiance to the State of Israel is not of the same kind as e.g. the Italo-American's feeling for Italy. Italo-Americans *come* from Italy. Jewish-Americans do not come from Israel but long to go there—or at least pretend to in their prayers.

There is a very serious practical problem involved in this. In both World Wars, Americans of German, Italian and Japanese descent fought in the American Army against their countries of origin. They had become assimilated and detached from their ancestral ties; whereas the Englishman or American who persists in regarding himself as a Jew by religion and tradition, remains attached to the State of Israel both in a mystical and a directly political manner. The imputation of 'split loyalties' is an old anti-semitic argument. The existence of the State of Israel and of the international Zionist organisation lends this imputation a measure of reality fraught with danger. I do not mean danger to England or America, but to the Jews themselves. Israel is no longer a mystic promise, but an independent state with an independent policy, and any political allegiance to a foreign country is bound to arouse suspicion in times of international crisis. The results to which such suspicions may lead we know only too well from the past.

(*Q.*): Even if all your arguments were granted, there would still remain a deep-felt reluctance, a spiritual and æsthetic revulsion in Jewish parents against the idea of bringing up their children in a faith in which they themselves do not believe.

(*A.*): My plea is addressed to parents who do not believe in the Jewish religion either; to that vast majority of agnostics and near-agnostics who accept the ethical values of our Judeo-Christian heritage and reject all rigid doctrine. The educational system in most countries requires that a child, on entering school, should receive religious instruction. The decision whether he will be instructed in Catholic, Protestant or Jewish dogma is not the child's, but depends on the hazard of his parents' denomination. The proper thing for parents who reject all dogma is to say: 'If my child must be brought up in a definite religion, then let it be the same in which his playmates are brought up, and not one which sets him apart by its archaic racial doctrine, marks him out as a scapegoat, and gives him mental complexes. Which particular doctrine he is taught does not matter very much, as with maturity he will make his own spiritual decisions anyway; what matters is that he should not start under a handicap.'

(*Q.*): Your arguments betray a utilitarian approach to religious questions which seems to me cynical and improper.

(*A.*): Only because you suffer from the guilt-complex of the agnostic who is unable to hold a dogmatic belief but wishes that he could. That, I suspect, goes for all of us, children of the post-materialistic era, filled with transcendental yearnings; once more conscious of a higher, extra-sensory order of reality, and yet intellectually too honest to accept any dogmatic version of it as authentic. If you belong to this category, then surely you too regard the historical accounts of the lives of Buddha, Moses, Jesus and Mohammed as eternal symbols, as archetypes of man's transcendental experience and spiritual aspirations, and it makes little difference which set of symbols will be taught to your child according to the hazards of his birth. In my personal opinion it is essential for the moral development of the child to start with some form of belief in a divine order, whose framework he will at first take for Gospel truth until the spiritual content matures into symbolic interpretation. From this point of view—which is the basis of our discussion since my argument is expressly *not* directed at the orthodox believer—it is quite irrelevant whether the child's imagination is centred on Moses bringing water forth from the rock or on the miracle of the water turned into wine at Cana.

Allow me to reverse the charge: I find it cynical on your part to turn your child into a potential victim by teaching him to believe in the miracle of the rock but not in the miracle of Cana, or by celebrating the Sabbath on Saturday instead of Sunday. Do you realise that this futile calendrical dispute, the Jew closing his shop on Saturday and working on Sunday, has been a major irritant and cause of martyrdom for countless centuries? Do you call it cynical if one deplores the holocausts of Jewish victims burnt, raped, robbed, chased and gassed in the name of a Lilliputian fanaticism regarding the question on which end to break the spiritual egg?

(*Q*.): Let us turn to the practical side of the problem. You advocate that non-doctrinaire Jews should bring up their children as members of the congregation of their neighbours; what about 'restricted' residential districts and schools, and similar obstacles, handicaps and embarrassments?

(*A*.): No doubt in the first generation there will be plenty of all that, plenty of bitterness, disappointment and failure in individual cases. But in the second generation there will be less of it, and in the third, what with intermarriage and the disappearance of all self-segregatory motives, the 'Jewish question' will gradually taper off and fade away. The obvious example of this process is the cultural and social homogeneity of third-generation Americans of heterogeneous origin. Immigrants of the first generation have a natural tendency to huddle together with their countrymen and to show suspicion and hostility to other groups; the second generation, once through American school, has an equally natural tendency to break away from parental traditions, to cast off their distinguishing marks, and become full-fledged Americans. The Jews alone among the varied European immigrant population have resisted this

'tapering off' process, and persist in their religious, social and
ethnic separateness generation after generation.

I repeat that in the past there were good excuses for this.
Before the resurrection of Israel, to renounce Jewry meant to
deny solidarity with the persecuted, and might have been
regarded as a cowardly capitulation. The Jews could not
vanish from the scene of history in an anti-climax. But with the
rebirth of the Jewish State, the climax is reached, the circle is
closed. It is no longer a question of capitulation, but of a free
choice. Hence the obligation of Jewry to pause on its long
journey, review its situation and face the facts which some time
ago it was excusable and even honourable to shun.

6

I shall now have to deal with one last objection which carries
more psychological weight than all the others, because it is not
based on logic but on the denial of logic as a guide in human
affairs. Isaiah Berlin has expressed this attitude with much
insight and eloquence in his essay. After explaining that he was
to a large extent in agreement with my position, Mr. Berlin
continued with a 'but':

But there are . . . many individuals in the world who do
not choose to see life in the form of radical choices between
one course and another, and whom we do not condemn for
this reason. 'Out of the crooked timber of humanity', said a
great philosopher, 'no straight thing was ever made.' Fearful
thinkers, with minds seeking salvation in religious or political dogma, souls filled with terror, may wish to eliminate
such ambiguous elements in favour of a more clear-cut
structure, and they are, in this respect, true children of the
new age which with its totalitarian systems has tried to
institute just such an order among human beings, and sort
them out neatly each to his own category. . . . To protest
about a section of the population merely because it is felt to
be an uncosy element in society, to order it to alter its outlook or get out . . . is . . . a kind of petty tyranny, and derives
ultimately from the conviction that human beings have no

right to behave foolishly or inconsistently or vulgarly, and that society has the right to try and rid itself by humane means, but rid itself nevertheless, of such persons although they are neither criminals nor lunatics nor in any sense a danger to the lives or liberties of their fellows. This attitude, which is sometimes found to colour the views of otherwise civilised and sensitive thinkers, is a bad attitude because it is clearly not compatible with the survival of the sort of reasonable, humane, 'open', social texture in which human beings can enjoy those freedoms and those personal relationships upon which all tolerable life depends.

Mr. Berlin is as sceptical as I am regarding the possibility of normalising the social status of Jews so long as they insist on calling themselves and being called Jews. Half of his essay is devoted to a penetrating analysis of the psychological factors inherent in the Jewish condition, which make anti-semitism past, present and future, unavoidable. He also agrees that the rebirth of the State of Israel puts every individual Jew in a dilemma. His argument is simply that you should neither expect nor encourage people to act logically, and that unreason, however irritating or maddening, must be tolerated.

I fully agree that nothing could be more unreasonable than to expect people to behave reasonably. But if you argue that Jews have a right to be guided by irrational emotion and to behave 'foolishly, or inconsistently, or vulgarly', you must grant the same right to their adversaries, and I need not enlarge upon the result. It seems to me that if you have a voice and a pen, it is incumbent on you to advocate that course of action which you believe to be in the public interest, and thereby to influence the precarious balance between reason and passion in people's minds. It also seems to me, as I said before, that people have an inalienable right to mess up their own lives, but no right to mess up the lives of their children, just because being a Jew is such a cosy mess. The pressure of totalitarian forces from outside and inside our Western civilisation has led to a tendency among liberals like Mr. Berlin to call any attitude of non-complacency 'totalitarian'. If you try to sort out logically a complex situation and to point out that it demands a choice between alternative lines of action, you will promptly be accused of painting in black-and-white. A certain amount of administrative and ideological muddle, a margin of tolerated confusion are indeed as essential to the functioning of a democratic society as lubricants and safety valves are to a machine. But the harsh, inhuman precision of totalitarian ideologies makes the liberal mind inclined to believe that the oily lubricants are all that matter, whereas pistons, pressure and energy are totalitarian as such. Words like 'blueprint', 'planning', and even 'order' have acquired a derogatory meaning ever since various forms of a 'new order' were looming on the horizon. The understandable human weakness for evading painful decisions and responsibilities has come to be regarded as a virtue and the essence of democracy. The liberal in retreat does not ask for freedom of choice, but for freedom from choice.

If my saying that we must decide whether we belong to the Chosen Race or to the nation whose citizen we are, if the revolutionary discovery that we can't eat our cake and have it, are figments of a totalitarian mind, then I must confess to a totalitarian mind. If 'out of the crooked timber of humanity no straight thing was ever made', I still think it more honourable to try to straighten the timber than to make it more crooked for sweet crookedness' sake. Or shall we rather fall back on the ancient adage:

> When in danger or in doubt,
> Turn in circles, scream or shout?

7

In summing up, I may be allowed to quote from the closing page of *Promise and Fulfilment*:

Orthodox Jewry is a vanishing minority. It is the well-meaning but confused majority which, through inertia, perpetuates the anachronism by clinging to a tradition in which it no longer really believes, to a mission which is fulfilled, a pride which has become inverted cowardice. Let them stop to think whether they have the right to place the burden of the ominous knapsack, now void of contents, on their children who have not asked for it.

To break the vicious circle of being persecuted for being 'different', and being 'different' by force of persecution, they must arrive at a clear decision, however difficult this may be. They must either follow the imperative of their religion, the return to the Promised Land—or recognise that that faith is no longer theirs. To renounce the Jewish faith does not mean to jettison the perennial values of Judaic tradition. Its essential teachings have passed long ago into the mainstream of the Judeo-Christian heritage. If a Judaic religion is to survive outside Israel, without inflicting the stigma of separateness on its followers and laying them open to the charge of divided loyalties, it would have to be a system of faith and cosmopolitan ethics freed from all racial presumption and national exclusivity. But a Jewish religion thus reformed would be stripped of its specifically Jewish content.

These conclusions, reached by one who has been an active supporter of the Zionist Movement for a quarter-century, while his cultural allegiance belonged to Western Europe, are mainly addressed to the many others in a similar situation. They have done what they could to help to secure a haven for the homeless in the teeth of prejudice, violence and political treachery. Now that the State of Israel is firmly established, they are at last free to do what they could not do before: to wish it good luck and go their own way with the nation whose life and culture they share, without reservation or split loyalties.

The mission of the Wandering Jew is completed; he must discard the knapsack and cease to be an accomplice in his own destruction. The fumes of the death chambers still linger over Europe; there must be an end to every calvary.

The Boredom of Fantasy*

Note to the Danube Edition. The first half of this broadcast, omitted from the present edition, described the rise of the new craze for science fiction in the United States and its grotesque by-products, from space operas to nuclear blasters for junior. It continued:

Bᴜᴛ a craze of such vast dimensions is never entirely crazy. It always expresses, in a distorted way, some unconscious need of the time. Science-fiction is a product of the atomic age. The discoveries of that age weigh like an undigested lump on the stomach of mankind. Electronic brains which predict election results, lie-detectors which make you confess the truth, new drugs which make you testify to lies, radiations which produce biological monsters—all these developments of the last fifty years have created new vistas and new nightmares, which art and literature have not yet assimilated. In a crude and fumbling fashion, science-fiction is trying to fill this gap. But there is perhaps another, hidden reason for this sudden hunger for other ages and other worlds. Perhaps, when they read about the latest hydrogen bomb tests, people are more aware than they admit to themselves, of the possibility that human civilisation may be approaching its end. And together with this may go a dim, inarticulate suspicion that the human race may be a biological misfit doomed to extinction like the giant reptiles of an earlier age. Some apocalyptic intuition of this kind may be one of the reasons for the sudden interest in life on other stars.

As a branch of literature, science-fiction is, of course, not new. As early as the second century Lucian wrote a story of a

* Broadcast on the BBC Home Service, May, 1953.

THE BOREDOM OF FANTASY

journey to the moon. Swift wrote science-fiction; so did
Samuel Butler, Jules Verne, H. G. Wells, Aldous Huxley,
George Orwell. But while in the past such exercises were
isolated literary extravaganzas, they are now mass-produced
for a mass audience. Moreover, modern science-fiction takes
itself very seriously. There are certain rules of the game which
every practitioner must observe, otherwise he will be torn to
shreds by the critics. Some of the best-known science-fiction
authors in America are actually scientists, several of international repute, who write under pen-names. The most recent
and distinguished recruit to their ranks is Lord Russell. All
this is a guarantee of scientific accuracy, but unfortunately not
of artistic quality.

Mr. Gerald Heard has recently expressed the opinion that
science-fiction is 'the mark of the dawn of a new vision, and
the rise of a new art', and simply *the* future form of the novel.
Other well-known critics overseas also believe, in all seriousness, that science-fiction, now in its infancy, will grow up and
one day become the literature of the future.

I do not share their opinion. I believe that science-fiction is
good entertainment, and that it will never become good art.
It is reasonably certain that within the next hundred years*
we shall have space-travel, but at that stage the description of
a trip to the moon will no longer be science-fiction but simple
reportage. It will be fact, not fantasy, and the science-fiction
of that time will have to go even further to startle the reader.
What Mr. Heard's claim really amounts to is the replacement
of the artist's disciplined imagination by the schoolboy's
unbridled fantasy. But day-dreaming is not poetry, and fantasy
is not art.

At first sight one would of course expect that imaginative
descriptions of non-human societies on alien planets would
open new vistas for the somewhat stagnant novel of our time.
But most disappointingly this is not the case, and for a simple
reason. Our imagination is limited; we cannot project ourselves into the distant future any more than into the distant
past. The historical novel is practically dead today. The life of
an Egyptian civil servant under the Eighteenth Dynasty, or

[1] *Sic!* This was broadcast in 1953.

even of a soldier in Cromwell's army, is only imaginable in dim outline; we are unable to identify ourselves with the strange figure moving through such a strange world. Few Englishmen can really understand the feelings and habits of Frenchmen, much less of Russians, much less of Martians. And without this act of identification, of intimate understanding, there is no art, only a thrill of curiosity which soon yields to boredom. The Martian heroes of science-fiction may have four eyes, a green skin and a foreign accent stranger than mine—we just couldn't care less. We are tickled by them for a few pages; but because they are too strange to be true, we soon get bored.

For every culture is an island. It communicates with other islands but it is only familiar with itself. And art means seeing the familiar in a new light, seeing tragedy in the trivial event; it means in the last resort broadening and deepening our understanding of ourselves. Swift's *Gulliver*, Huxley's *Brave New World*, Orwell's *Nineteen-Eighty-Four*, are great works of literature because in them the gadgets of the future and the oddities of alien worlds serve merely as a background or pretext for a social message. In other words, they are literature precisely to the extent to which they are *not* science-fiction, to which they are works of disciplined imagination and not of unlimited fantasy. A similar rule holds for the detective story. Georges Simenon is probably the greatest master in that field, yet his novels become works of art precisely at the point where character and atmosphere become more important than the plot, where imagination triumphs over invention.

Thus the paradoxical lesson of science-fiction is to teach us modesty. When we reach out for the stars, our limitations become grotesquely apparent. The heroes of science-fiction have unlimited power and fantastic possibilities, but their feelings and thoughts are limited within the narrow human range. Tom Corbett, Space Cadet, behaves on the third planet of Orion exactly in the same way as he does in a drugstore in Minnesota, and one is tempted to ask him: 'Was your journey really necessary?' The Milky Way has become simply an extension of Main Street.

Travel is no cure for melancholia; space-ships and time-machines are no escape from the human condition. Let Othello subject Desdemona to a lie-detector test; his jealousy will still blind him to the evidence. Let Oedipus triumph over gravity; he won't triumph over his fate.

Some twenty years ago the German writer, Alfred Döblin, wrote a novel in which humanity discovers the secret of biological self-transformation: by a click of their fingers people can change themselves into giants, tigers, demons, or fish— much like Flook in the *Daily Mail* cartoon. At the end of the book the last specimens of this happy race sit, each on a solitary rock, in the shape of black ravens, in eternal silence. They have tried, experienced, seen and said everything under the sun, and all that is left for them to do is to die of boredom— the boredom of fantasy.

The Shadow of a Tree

The article which follows may serve as an illustration of the period-bound character of science-fiction. It shows that all Utopias, including horror-Utopias, tell us more about the time when they were written than about the future they purport to predict. I must explain the circumstances which caused it to be written.

In October 1951 – the date is relevent – Collier's came out with a special issue of 125 pages, called Preview of the War We Do Not Want. *The editorial preface declared: 'We believe that this is the most important single issue that any magazine has ever published.' The issue did in fact create a stir in Europe as hardly any American magazine before, though not in the way it was intended.*

From the journalistic point of view it was an unprecedented enterprise. Its preparation took ten months. During that time the contributors were constantly kept informed, by the editorial board, of each other's contributions, suggestions and ideas, so that the whole issue assumed a planned and co-ordinated character. The contributors were a team of the strategic, economic and Eastern experts of the New York Times, New York Herald Tribune, *and* Christian Science Monitor; *of radio commentators, authors and politicians, including Hanson Baldwin, Stuart Chase, Marguerite Higgins, Edward Murrow, Professor Allan Nevins, J. B. Priestley, Walter Reuther, Robert Sherwood, Lowell Thomas, Walter Winchell, Philip Wylie, and others.*

The idea behind it all was explained in the editorial, which said:

'We do not think that war is inevitable. We are emphatically opposed to any suggestion of a "preventive" war. We believe that each day of peace and preparation makes the free nations stronger

*and lessens the chance of world conflict. Yet such a conflict could
start tomorrow, through design or miscalculation or desperation.
This issue of* Collier's, *written as of* 1960, *shows how that war
would be fought and won, and reports on the programme of
reconstruction that would follow victory.*

'*We have no illusions about the fearful cost of victory. If the
unwanted war does come, we feel that the peace which follows
should not repeat the pattern of unconditional surrender, repara-
tions and trials of war criminals. The liberated people could be
left to choose the political forms of freedom which would flourish
best in Russian soil.*

'*Implicit in all that you will read in the pages that follow is the
means by which the catastrophe of another war can be avoided.
That means rests with the Soviet government. They can believe the
truth—that the West has no aggressive intentions and is willing to
live at peace with Russia. Or they can continue to delude their
people and themselves with their own propaganda, start a war, and
see enlightenment brought to their people by armed might.*

'*An appeal to the reason of Joseph Stalin and the men around
him is the ultimate purpose of this issue of* Collier's. *And we
earnestly pray that its effect will be to help establish and maintain
an enduring peace.*'

*The issue caused a storm of protest, especially in France—so
much so that the editors hurriedly dropped the project of its re-
publication in book form. This reaction was typical of the public's
passionate rejection of any warning which brings out people's
repressed fears and compels them to face, if even for an instant, the
hideous and threatening reality around them—(see* A Guide to
Political Neurosis). *As such bursts of irrational passion must
always be covered by some rational pretext, the attackers turned
the contents of the issue and the intention behind it upside down.
The* Preview of the War We Do Not Want *was unmistakably intended to act as a warning and deterrent from war; the
critics in the French press described it as an encouragement to war
and an act of provocation.*

*My contribution was meant to outline the task of social re-
construction and rehabilitation in post-war Russia. I have no
reason to apologise for its content—except for its datedness. For*

this piece of Utopia was written in 1951, the good old days of the atom bomb, before the hydrogen bomb. At that time one could still hope that an atomic war would cause terrible, yet nevertheless limited, damage; and that when the war was over humanity, with a gigantic effort, could find its feet again. Today this hope no longer exists.

*   *   *

THE SHADOW OF A TREE*

Our correspondent has recently returned from a three-month journey through Russia. He travelled extensively through the Ukraine, the Moscow region, and was the first correspondent to be admitted to the 'Convicts' Republic' (Kolymskaya Respublika Osoozhdyonnykh) on the Kolyma Peninsula in Siberia, about which, since the liberation began, only vague and fantastic rumours have reached the outside world. Mr. Koestler's visit was sponsored by UNIHOPE—the United Nations Housing and Providing Enterprise. The following are edited extracts from his diary.   THE EDITORS

Kharkov, 30th June, 19..

From the air all the towns in the Ukraine, Kiev, Voronesh, Kharkov, Poltava, look the same, seem to have been designed according to one pattern. Near the centre you see two or threehuge circular patches; their diameters vary between half amile and three miles. These patches are the areas of total destruction, which have been cleared and ploughed up by UNIHOPE's flying bulldozer squads and converted into vegetable plots. 'Later on' public buildings and parks are supposed to replace them, but this 'later on', which is incessantly on every Russian's lips, still belongs to the distant future.

In the past, at any rate, the potatoes and cabbages grown on these plots saved the lives of thousands of citizens in the devastated towns during the famine-years after the war. From the air, the circular potato and cabbage plots look like huge greenish-brown discs. Between and around them sprawl the 'old cities' or what remains of them; buildings are propped and patched up by improvised means, windows boarded up for lack of glass and shattered balconies shaved off the scarfaced façades—the whole very dreary and depressing.

Then, outside the 'old cities' you see the new quarters of prefabricated houses—five, ten, twenty thousand mass-produced

* First published in *Collier's Magazine*, October, 1951.

little dwelling cubes, laid out in geometrical patterns by UNIHOPE's building trust. These 'Woolworth villages', as æsthetically sensitive visitors call them because they look as if they had been assembled in the Five and Ten Cents Stores, are nevertheless colourful and gay—from the air you get the impression of huge polka-dot ties and ribbons fanning out of the old cities into the surrounding steppe. The living space provided is only sixty square feet per individual, which means that there are two people to a medium-sized room, but for most Russians this is a luxury which they had never known before.

Food and housing were the two nightmare problems which faced the United Nations in liberated Russia. So long as these were not solved, the world 'liberation' remained a mockery. The historic achievement of our Atlantic civilisation was not that we won the war, but that we were able *to transform the greatest Army ever known into the greatest welfare organisation ever known.*

The Berlin airlift had proved that the transformation of a destructive force into a providing force was not only technically possible, but also produced quicker results than any philanthropic welfare organisation could achieve. UNIHOPE was an enlargement of the Berlin airlift on a scale of approximately 1,000,000 to 1. The flying Bulldozer Squads, 'Operation Harvest', 'Operation Vitamin C', and 'Operation Housing', saved not only the vanquished Russians; they also saved the victors from the moral disasters which previous wars had brought in their wake. The first World War had been followed by an irresponsible Jazz Age; the second, by half of Europe falling from Hitler's frying pan into Stalin's fire. The third produced UNIHOPE—and restored the shaken self-confidence of our civilisation.

Kharkov, July 5th (Election Day)

The elections to the Kharkov Municipal Council—the first free elections since 1917—were a disappointing affair with touches of crude comedy. No fewer than twenty-two parties and 'programmes' competed; among them:

The Unified Monarchist Great-Russian Party.
The Ukrainian Separatist Party.
The Peasant Party (individual farmers and small-holders).
The Agrarian Co-operative Party.
The Liberal Democratic Party, and
The Democratic Liberal Party. (The programmes of these two parties of the urban middle-classes are indistinguishable, but their leaders are involved in a mortal personal feud.)
The Democratic Workers' Party (free Labour Unionists).
The Syndicalist Workers' Party (followers of Kropotkin's theory of ideal anarchism).
The 'Amerikansky Party' (founded by a locally famous black marketeer in the hope of getting on the U.S.A. payroll).
The 'Genrik Adamchiki' (Ukrainian spelling of Henry Adamite, founded by a professor who happened to read Adam's work on Progressive Land Taxation).
The Avengers of Trotsky. (This group preaches that Communism was a good thing under Lenin and Trotsky, and only became a bad thing under Stalin. They are a minor headache for our security service.)
The 'Kontriky' (former political prisoners and deportees; derived from the abbreviation of 'counter-revolutionary element', which was their designation under the Soviet régime. This influential group is held together by a kind of *esprit de corps*; no definite political programme).

These twelve are the 'political parties' as we understand the term. The remaining 'independent candidates'—cranks, religious sectarians and world reformers—who, since the liberation, are sprouting like mushrooms after rain, might be classed as 'religious and miscellaneous'. They include:

The Pupils of Tolstoy (a pacifist and vegetarian Christian group, rejecting religious dogmatism).
The Theocrats (followers of the Orthodox church, who hold that Russia should be ruled by the Patriarch Sergei).
The 'Old Believers' (a traditionalist sect of religious zealots).
The Servants of God (who refuse to have family names).
The Doukhobor (who refuse to wear clothes).

The Starosti (who preach and sometimes practise self-castration, because mankind is evil and should be brought to an end).

The Esperantists (who hold that introduction of a universal language would solve all problems).

The Pavlovites (who hold that the whole of mankind should be made to have uniform opinions through controlled reconditioning of their reflexes by Professor Pavlov's famous method of training dogs).

The Barankavitzi (have never been able to find out what they want).

The remaining party, called *The World Redeemers*, was founded by an escaped inmate of a mental home, who started raving and had to be locked up on the night before the elections.

In short, Russia is having its exuberant honeymoon with Democracy. The spectacle may seem strange to the Western mind, but I witnessed a similar phenomenon some thirty years ago in Tel Aviv when, during the first municipal election, not less than twenty-four parties were competing for a total of 150,000 votes. There a people was granted political self-determination for the first time in two thousand years; here for the first time in fifty years—provided that we call the Czarist régime a democracy. So it is only natural that after the terrible pressure which they endured, the Russians are having a rollicking time with the new, super-democratic electoral system.

The most remarkable thing about the electoral campaign was its atmosphere of nearly complete calm. Only one or two minor clashes occurred between Monarchists and Separatists. Owing to the shortage of printing facilities, electoral propaganda was in the main confined to hand-printed leaflets, stencilled posters and such-like. Measured by the standards of American or French electoral campaigns, it was an idyllic affair.

This is probably due to the fact that the man-in-the-street is still unable to take elections seriously. As far back as he can remember, they were a kind of compulsory ritual which resulted in 99·8 per cent of the population casting its vote for the only existing party. He simply cannot believe that elections have any influence in determining his and the nation's future. What really interests him is the next draw of the Great Lottery, scheduled for the coming Sunday.

Kharkov, July 8th

The final results of the elections were announced yesterday. They are, to say the least of it, unexpected.

The counting of the votes started with a solemn ceremony in Freedom House, in the presence of the local authorities. The first sealed ballot-box was opened by Colonel Dalcroix who is the local C.O. of UNITOC (United Nations Temporary Occupation Command). Next to him sat Krupnik, Mayor of Kharkov, a broad-faced, impassive man of Ukrainian peasant stock. All went well at the beginning; the Colonel made a short speech, and after the clapping had subsided, pulled the first ballot-paper from the box and handed it solemnly to the Mayor to read the vote. I must explain that each ballot-paper contained a list of the twenty-two parties, each preceded by a little square in which the voter was to mark by a cross the party he had chosen. There was a tense silence, for everybody felt that the first vote had a kind of symbolic significance. Krupnik looked at the paper and announced the vote: '*Da*.'

'*Comment?*' asked the Colonel. 'What does he mean by "*da*"?'

' "*Da*" means "yes",' the translator explained amiably.

'*Mais comment?* For which party did the person vote?'

'The citizen voter voted for them all. He just wrote "*da*" at the top of the paper.'

There was a pained silence.

'Well, well,' said the Colonel, 'let's try the next one.' He pulled out a second ballot-paper and handed it to the Mayor.

'*Da*,' Krupnik read impassively.

The female representative of the Peasant Party began to giggle; this exploded the tension, and the whole room burst into laughter. Every second or third vote turned out to be a '*da*'; other voters had obediently marked all the twenty-two little squares with crosses. Krupnik continued to read out stolidly the '*da-da*'s' with a kind of unconscious approval on his square face. It sounded strangely reassuring, like a child's babbling: '*Da-da-da.*'

The result was announced last morning. The largest number of votes went to the Monarchists and to the Ukrainian Separatists, with the Peasant Party, the former deportees, the Theocrats and the 'Amerikanskys' as runners-up. Over fifty per cent of the votes were '*da*'s', and had to be invalidated. According to the radio it was the same story everywhere: fifty, sixty, and up to seventy per cent invalid votes.

July 9th

Dinner at the UNIHOPE canteen with Isakoovich, the translator. He is a wizened little man of fifty, a former school-teacher from Minsk, who lost his whole family in the pogrom-years (the famous Jew-killings organised as a diversion during the Red Army's retreat). He is an intelligent, well-read man, so I was surprised when he said that he had voted for the Pavlovites.

'What do you want?' he said with a shrug. 'The elections were the best proof of the truth of Pavlov's theory. You give a dog a series of electric shocks and sound a gong with each shock; after a while the sound of the gong alone will send the dog into convulsions. Similarly, when you speak to a Russian the word "election" he will twitch and yell "*da*".'

Had I myself made this remark, Isakoovich would have rightly been offended, for he loves Russia; but he spoke with a melancholy detachment. What he said brought home to me that this is an age of science-fiction come true. Not because of the war—on the whole, the war was fought with more conservative weapons than had been previously expected. The fascinating novelties are those of mass-psychology. The confessions at the show trials were only a small foretaste of the unholy miracles which a determined modern tyranny can produce by processing the minds of its subjects.

July 10th

Item: Who are the best-paid people, the biggest profiteers in contemporary Russia? The translators of foreign books. When the Curtain rose after forty years, the hunger for books, magazines, for every form of printed material which contained information on the mysterious world in the West was enormous. Nobody wants to read a book by the erstwhile Russian writers; they have for too long played the part of literary prostitutes. The translators, these former pariahs of the arts, have stepped into the shoes of the poets and novelists. Top of the best-seller list is still a Russian translation of the Sears Roebuck catalogue (complete and unabridged) with explanatory footnotes.

Moscow, July 14th

One question that people always ask at home is never asked here: 'What happened to Communism in Russia?' Everybody yawns when a visitor brings it up, because the answer is so obvious to every Russian. The answer is that there never was Communism in Russia; there were only Communists. When the Communists disappeared, Communism disappeared.

Why is this so self-evident to every Russian, and so difficult to understand for people abroad? Because people outside Russia thought of Soviet Communism as a political system in the Western sense; or as some miscarried attempt to establish social justice; or as a kind of secular religion. It was, of course, nothing of the sort—except for a short period in the beginning, long since forgotten. For the last decades—as far back as the memories of the present generation can reach—it had ceased to be a political movement, for it had no opponents in Russia against which it could measure itself in terms of ideas or power. It could not teach the masses any programme or philosophy, for the line changed incessantly in a dizzy zigzag; yesterday's truth became today's heresy, and the very foundations of faith and belief were destroyed in the process.

In a primitive community you can sometimes replace political thinking by a kind of simple loyalty to the government. But that loyalty too was destroyed when again and again men who were one day members of the Government confessed the next that they had always been traitors, spies and enemies of the people.

When in the early years of the Revolution the priests vanished from the Russian scene, religion did not vanish with them; it remained alive in the people. But when the Communists vanished from the scene, Communism vanished with them because as a faith it had never existed among the Russian people.

Communism as a faith had, during the last generation, only existed among people outside Russia. It existed because large parts of the population of the world lived in squalor and misery, and wanderers in the desert are always ready to believe in a mirage. The rulers of Russia kept the country hermetically closed to keep up the illusion, and to hide the reality behind the mirage. It was so cunningly done that in the Western world even opponents of the Communist régime had no idea of the full extent of horror which it contained. The truth about Russia was the best kept secret in history.

When I say that Communism in Russia has vanished with the Communists, I do not mean that the results of forty years of indoctrination from cradle to grave have vanished with it. The mental ravages caused by that indoctrination are visible at every step here. But that indoctrination did not teach the people Communism. It taught them one word: '*da*', to achieve a 99·8 per cent unanimous, roaring '*da*' for Comrade Ivan's promotion, and the same roaring '*da*' for his execution; '*da*' for the crusade against the Nazis and '*da*' for the pact with the Nazis; '*da*' for everything which the omniscient leader decided. This feat was achieved not by propaganda as we understand it, but by mental processing. The régime did not want Communists; it wanted robots. It will take at least a generation to change them back into humans again.

Moscow, July 17th

Three days in bed with 'flu, plagued by *klopy*, the famed Russian bed-bugs. The Russians say it is a new strain of super-*klopy*—a mutation caused by radio-activity, like the red forget-me-not. At any rate, they are formidable beasts and they seem to thrive on DDT.

Being ill I could not attend the drawing of the Lottery, but I am told it was, as always, a huge success, with the usual speeches, concert recitals, dancing, etc. The Lottery is an institution which has come to stay. As people at home seem to have some misconceptions about it, here is a brief history of this most popular feature of contemporary Russian life:

THE STORY OF THE GREAT LOTTERY

Next to food and housing, the third vital post-war problem was the *Bezprizornye*—the locust-plague of waifs and strays turned into juvenile delinquents. These hordes of little savages of every age from seven upward have been a recurrent feature of Soviet life ever since the Revolution. After the Civil War in the early 1920s, their number was estimated at over a million. The mass-deportations in the 'thirties produced new waves of the plague, and the collapse of the Soviet régime led to a resurgence of it on a scale never equalled before. Gangs of juvenile criminals, who had reverted to a stage of primitive savagery, roamed the countryside. Martial law was ineffective against them, for soldiers won't shoot at children. No effective steps could be taken against the black market so long as the racketeers were able to use hordes of corrupted children as their agents and informers. The *Bezprizornye* were the yeast on which crime, drunkenness and prostitution thrived during the famine-years. The most appalling symptom of the plague were the child-brothels, of which Moscow alone counted about a score.

The occupation authorities fought a losing battle against the *Bezprizornye*. They were rounded up, sheltered and fed in improvised camps during the winter. But when spring came, they escaped in droves and swarms from the camps and took to the roads again. The authorities were faced with the loathsome necessity of putting barbed wire, watch towers and armed guards round the children's camps.

The effects of this measure were disastrous. The Soviet régime had deported juvenile delinquents to remote labour camps in Siberia, where they could perish out of sight. The new prison camps for children, which the liberators were forced to establish in the vicinity of every large town from the Black Sea to the Baltic, were sores on their conscience; to Russian eyes they were a hideous reminder of the past, and a proof that the future would be no better. By the autumn of the second post-war year, the number of children in the camps was approaching the one-million mark.

On October 15th, the 'United Nations Commission of Inquiry into Conditions in the Children's Camps in Russia' published its report. It described with complete frankness a situation which was heart-breaking and hair-raising to Western public opinion. In spite of the efforts of a host of pediatricians, psychiatrists, nurses and teachers, the camps were a hotbed of every form of vice and juvenile corruption. The report concluded that no reasonable hope for improvement could be entertained by the forcible herding together of child delinquents behind barbed wire in a desolate country of famine and chaos. The only hope of saving and rehabilitating the children was 'to disperse them and transplant them into a healthy environment in countries where life was relatively normal'.

It seemed a fantastic proposal. But the outcry which the report caused in Europe and America put an end to red tape and procrastination—particularly after the 'Battle of Downing Street', when a swarm of incensed English spinsters broke the windows of the Foreign Office, penetrated into the building and all but lynched the Foreign Secretary. Similar events in other capitals at last forced the United Nations to act. The action, once started, was on a grandiose scale.

'Operation SKID' ('Save the Kids') was entrusted to the newly founded UNIHOPE. By Christmas, the plan for dispersing the Russian waifs and strays to Australia, New Zealand, Canada and the United States was blueprinted in detail. Threequarters of the children were to be billeted with foster parents who had volunteered to take them; the remainder in boarding schools, sanatoria, school farms, etc. The air

transport fleet of UNIHOPE, which carried food and prefabs
for the 'Woolworth towns' to Russia, made their return trips
loaded with children—the gallant air-crews' nightmare. By
the summer of next year, six months after the start of 'Operation SKID', eighty per cent of the children had been eva-
cuated; the remaining twenty per cent, hardened young
criminals of over fifteen, were sent to specially created refor-
matory schools in Russia. Another year later, the last camp
was closed down.

But that was not the end of the story. In the famine areas,
despairing Russian, Ukrainian, Armenian mothers disguised
their children as *Bezprizornye* and sent them out on the roads
to be picked up and sent to the lands of plenty—determined to
save them from starvation even at the price of never seeing
them again. The flood had diminished to a trickle, but even so
several thousand children were shipped every month overseas.

These pseudo-orphans became later on the cause of a
dramatic turn of events. It was discovered that nearly all
parents, before taking the desperate step of parting with their
children, had banded them like migrating birds by some
identification mark: amulets, neck-chains, even tattooed
initials. A year or so later, as conditions gradually improved,
they began to flood the authorities with applications for getting
their children back. UNIHOPE had to broadcast and adver-
tise several thousand 'wanted' lists over three continents.
Eventually the children began to come back.

The return of these formerly starved little wretches, their
changed physical appearance and mental outlook, their
manners and clothes, were a miracle in the eyes of the Russians
—and one of the greatest feats of political propaganda brought
about unintentionally. UNIHOPE was now swamped with
pathetic requests from parents to send their children for a
year's health cure abroad. (One should remember that even
today the average ration is under 1,800 calories per head, and
that in many areas these rations exist only on paper.) It was
obvious, however, that UNIHOPE could not go on indefinitely
carting children over the world. That is how the idea of the
Lottery was born.

Instead of selecting children for the limited number of

available places by investigating the economic situation of the parents—which would have been a hopelessly cumbersome procedure leading to jealousies and complaints—the selection of applicants was made by lottery. Each town and administrative district had it small quota, and the lucky ones' names were chosen in public at the quarterly draws. These draws, followed by the distribution of consolation prizes in the shape of toys, picture books and huge quantities of ice-cream, became extremely popular not only among children but among grown-ups as well. The programme soon included musical recitals, Punch and Judy shows, and was wound up by a dance. In every town 'Draw Day' became a kind of popular festival, replacing the traditional Russian fair.

As the Lottery craze grew, the planning committee of UNIPROD (United Nations Political Re-education Department) had the inspiration to extend the scheme to adults. Having lived cut off from the rest of the world for nearly half a century, the one overwhelming desire of every Russian was to visit the mysterious countries abroad—if only for a month, a day, or an hour. The returning children's tales had been the most effective propaganda for the ways of the free world—each of them worth a million dollars spent on UNIPROD's vapid broadcasts and tons of its tedious pamphlets. Obviously, the most effective method of political re-education was to try the same thing with adults—journalists, doctors, teachers, industrial managers, farmers.

The project now consists in guided three-months tours for 100,000 professional men per year, in those countries where they are able to learn most in their speciality. The 'quotas' are apportioned both by geographical regions and professional groups. In this way we may hope to destroy within a few years the last vestiges of the Curtain, and the tenacious psychological after-effects of the past. Although the average citizen's chances of having his name drawn is less than one in a thousand, the national craze is still unabated today. The Russians are gamblers at heart, and the '*Lotereya*' appeals more to their imagination than lectures and arguments.

Already most towns and rural centres have their nucleus of lottery-winners whose eyes have seen our way of life, whose minds have been re-awakened by the shock of contact with a different reality. They have become missionaries of the free world, but in their own manner, their own uniquely Russian way; and it is prehaps not too optimistic to assume that they will gradually succeed to the defunct 'Party' in the intellectual leadership of the country.

THE CONVICTS' REPUBLIC

Magadan, Kolyma Peninsula, August 1st

On the road to the settlement at 'Kilometer 64', Berzin' Temporary Administrator of the Convicts' Republic of Kolyma, explained:

'There are three basic facts about Kolyma. It is the region where the lowest temperatures on earth have been recorded. It is the richest gold-mining region in the world. It is a region, six times the size of France, which was for twenty years administered as a single Forced Labour Camp, with ninety per cent of its population convicts . . .'

He did not speak again for a few miles, when he stopped the car near a group of labourers working on a cabbage-patch. We got out in the sweltering heat—for a hundred days, from June to August, the sun does not set over Kolyma. The workmen, like ourselves, wore mittens and mosquito nets to protect their faces against the swarms of insects which were buzzing around them in a dense cloud. These gnats, midges and gadflies are the scourge of Kolyma in summer, as scurvy, frost-bite and gangrene are in winter.

Berzin borrowed a spade from the workmen and marched our party across the cabbage field. He halted at the edge of the swamp which filled the bleak landscape until it merged into the dark hue of the *taiga*—the virgin forest, stretching for a thousand miles to the Arctic Ocean. He handed me the spade and said: 'Try it.'

Sweating under the thick net and unable to wipe the sweat from my eyes, I dug into the soft, squashy earth. About ten inches down the spade suddenly struck a hard surface which felt like rock. Berzin smiled with the non-paralysed half of his face. 'What do you think it is?'

'I don't know. Gold?'

'No. Ice.'

He explained that even during the summer the earth only thaws to a depth of nine or ten inches; underneath, covering the whole Peninsula, lies a stratum of 'geological ice', several hundred feet thick.

During the ten weeks of the Polar night the temperature here often drops below minus fifty degrees Fahrenheit. The blizzards reach such a savage fury that even in Magadan, the capital, ropes have to be stretched from house to house to which people can cling when forced to go outdoors—otherwise they would be swept into the sea. In the winter camps, far inside this land of white death, less than half of the slaves used to survive the Polar night. In some of the camps not a single living being was found when the roads opened in spring— convicts, guards and dogs were buried under the same indifferent blanket of snow.

During the first years of colonisation, in the early 1930s, only one in five of the convicts survived eighteen months in Kolyma. Towards the end, the mortality was thirty per cent per annum. That gave a man an average expected life-span of three years; but the average spans of their sentences were ten, twenty and twenty-five years.

There is a cliché about our times reverting to 'dark medieval days'. But the Middle Ages had no horrors comparable in extent to the slave-continents of Kolyma, of the Baikal-Amur region, of the Vorkuta and Pechora camps, with their fifteen to twenty million starving, freezing, tattered, vermin-ridden inmates, condemned to slow death after the last inch of labour had been squeezed out of them. Even in antiquity, even among primitive and barbarian civilisations, such an ocean of suffering was never inflicted on such a mass of human lives. Here human evolution had touched the bottom—and it looked as if it would never recover again.

The men and women of Kolyma developed a special mentality. A few had lived in the camps for five, ten or fifteen years; some had been sent to the camps as children, others were born in the camps and had never been past the barbed-wire fence and the machine-gun turrets. This special mentality has to be borne in mind if one tries to understand the developments in Kolyma and in some of the other vast convict districts since the war.

Here, in a nutshell, is what happened in Kolyma.

The Peninsula lies at a distance of six thousand miles from the centre of European Russia. In peacetime, the unwilling travellers reached Kolyma by the Trans-Siberian Railway from Moscow to Vladivostok, and continued the journey by boat, past Sakhalin and across the Sea of Okhotsk. Since the war, all land and sea communications had been cut off, and the sparse supplies which reached Kolyma came by air. Even now, three years after the end of the war, with guerilla fights still raging in the Urals and around Lake Baikal, the region can only be approached by a somewhat hazardous air journey. Thus, for the approximately two million deportees on Kolyma, return home has so far been impossible.

I should mention here that for the majority of them the word 'home' is an abstraction. The deportee was cut off from communication with his family, which was not even informed of his death. Besides, all members of a deportee's family were themselves automatically liable to deportation to different camps. As a measure of mental self-protection, the convict had to erase all hopes of a happy reunion, and to banish the very word 'home' from his mind.

This was particularly true of the Chinese, Mongolian, Tibetan and Korean prisoners who, since the beginning of the Great China Purge, arrived in growing numbers, until they formed more than fifty per cent of the slave population.

The slaves of Kolyma were not allowed to read newspapers, but prisoners employed in clerical jobs snatched up bits of information from the radio. After the flight of the Government from Moscow, the collapse of organised resistance could no longer be concealed. It led to mass-desertions among the guards and a break-down of discipline.

The first mutiny occurred at the camp of Elgen on the Taskan River, a hundred and fifty-five miles north-west of Magadan. The slaves got hold of an amount of high explosives used on road-building, blew up the machine-gun towers, over-powered and killed the remaining guards. The heaviest losses were inflicted upon them, not by the demoralised guards, but by the pack of wolfhounds which were a standing feature of every Kolyma camp. That is how Berzin, the leader of the mutiny, had half his face lacerated and permanently paralysed.

From Elgen the insurgents set out in trucks and jeeps, armed with the garrison's weapons, for Yagodnoye, the next big camp, thirty miles away. The guards at Yagodnoye were taken by surprise and surrendered. After a summary trial by the prisoners, all guards, with the exception of two who had a reputation for humanity, were driven into the marshes and shot.

After Yagodnoye, it was the turn of Talon, Balagannoye and finally of the capital, Magadan. Left without authority or directives, and fearful about their own future, the MVD detachments accepted their fate with resignation and only resisted sporadically. The small minority of free citizens in Magadan and the other centres were quick to turn their coats when the wind changed. After the fall of Magadan, the whole huge territory, from the Lena and Aldan Rivers to the Amur and the Pacific Ocean, became an administrative No-Man's Land.

The second and much bloodier phase of the struggle was fought between the nascent Convicts' Republic and the common criminals who represented one-fourth of the population of the camps. In all civilised countries, including Czarist Russia, political prisoners enjoyed preferential treatment over criminals. The totalitarian régimes reversed this procedure. In Nazi and Soviet concentration camps the common criminals were put in charge as barrack elders and foremen of the labour gangs. The *urki*, as the Russian criminals call themselves, had a free hand to rob, brutalise and denounce the political prisoners, and to work them to death in the brigades under their command. The *urki* were worse than the wolfhounds, and hardly more humane.

After the rebellion, an attempt was made to integrate them into the new community, but it failed. The criminals remained a disruptive element who, through theft, drunkenness, rape and murder, made life intolerable. During the Polar night of 1957, a ghastly civil war was fought all over Kolyma which ended with the eviction of the *urki* from the cities and camps. Most of them perished in the *taiga*; a few went over to the politicals and were accepted; several thousand are said to have made their way to the inaccessible regions of the north where they live by preying on the native hunting and fishing tribes—the Yakuts and Chukchi.

After that, Berzin and his colleagues could start bringing some semblance of order into the vast kingdom which had so unexpectedly fallen into their lap—a kingdom of two million starved convicts who found themselves in temporary possession of the richest gold deposits on our earth.

At the outbreak of the second world war, the Kolyma mines produced four to five million ounces of gold per year, while the total output of the rest of the world was thirty-two million ounces. Between the second and third war, the Kolyma output rose further, while production in the rest of the world declined; so the Convict Republic was in potential control of twenty to thirty per cent of the world's gold resources.

Nobody had foreseen this turn of events. In the general blue-print for the occupation period, all natural resources, mines and industries were to be administered by the provisional Russian Government under the supervision of UNITOC. But UNITOC's authority still ends roughly at the Urals; in Asiatic Russia it only controls certain key regions, such as Kamchatka, Sakhalin and the towns along the Trans-Siberian Railway. The only way of getting control of Kolyma would have been to land allied troops—a step which was fraught with the danger of international complications. The future of the Kolyma gold was already the subject of jealousies and intrigues among the Allies; besides, a sudden influx of a quarter of the world's gold production would have a disrupting effect on world economy. The God-forsaken Peninsula on its layer of geological ice became one of the worst headaches for the victors.

The solution of the dilemma—and of a number of related problems—came with the founding of UNIHOPE. In retrospect, the decision to use the Kolyma gold for financing UNIHOPE's gigantic rehabilitation enterprise seems only logical; but to have taken this logical step at the time was a considerable feat of imagination and statesmenship—and one of the truly great decisions which shaped the future of mankind.

Once the decision was taken, the problem of administering the Peninsula ceased to be political dynamite, and became a question of technical efficiency. Evidently, the gold could only be mined by the men on the spot. The men had constituted themselves an Autonomous Convicts' Republic, 'pending the election by the Constituent National Assembly of an all-Russian central government, and until such time as this elected government is capable of exercising effective control'. Their proclamation was in accordance with Point Seven of the United Nations Temporary Occupation Charter, which encouraged the formation of *de facto* local administrations in liberated Asia. In other respects too, the proclamation was reasonable and businesslike. It was mainly the work of Dr. Hsiao, a former Professor of International Law at the University of Peking, who had been sentenced to twenty years for 'counter-revolutionary, Trotskyite-Maoist propaganda', and had survived five years of Kolyma as a latrine cleaner.

The main points of the proclamation were that the 'Temporary Administration' of the Republic should function under the supervision of UNITOC but enjoy local autonomy under Point Seven of the Charter; that the total amount of gold mined should be surrendered to UNIHOPE in exchange for food, housing, clothing, medical supplies, and the gradual repatriation of those desiring to return to their countries of origin, as soon as conditions permitted.

Three days after the first radio communication had been received by UN headquarters on Sakhalin, the first mission of UNIHOPE landed at the airport of Magadan. It was headed by Brigadier-General Sir Robert Manningham-Ward, D.S.O., C.B.E., who had looked at this mission with some misgivings, and was agreeably surprised by the reception he met. In his first letter to Lady Manningham-Ward, he wrote:

'These convict leaders are not only eminently reasonable, but some of them, like Professor Hsiao, are delightful chaps. What's more, Hsiao has been to Eton and has managed to preserve his tie, but had to use it, I am sorry to say, for foot rags. He says it saved his remaining six toes.'

Kolyma, August 5th

Berzin owed his reputation to the fact that he was one of the handful of inmates of Elgen camp really guilty of the charge which led to his conviction. He was convicted at the age of sixteen under Articles 7, 10 and 11 of Paragraph 58 of the Soviet Criminal Code: Sedition; Counter-revolutionary Agitation and Propaganda; and Organisation of Counter-revolutionary Groups. As a schoolboy in Odessa he had participated in the short-lived activity of a group of adolescents whose parents had fallen victims to the purge. The group called itself 'Revenge for our Parents' and was promptly rounded up after issuing its first stencilled leaflet. He got fifteen years which, after he had served them, were automatically extended by another ten. The irony of Berzin's story is that his own parents had not been purged; he had joined the organisation for the sake of his girl-friend, Màsha. After he was caught, his parents, both respected Party members, were of course arrested too; he has never heard of them since. He is now forty-one years old, twenty-five of which were spent in the camp; an unparalleled record of longevity in Kolyma which made him into a legendary figure.

He is short, stocky, has immense physical strength and a mask-like face, half of which is paralysed. He speaks little and listens impassively to others; it is quite impossible to form an idea of the mental world in which he lives—the private universe of a man who for a quarter-century has been a slave, and has yet preserved his dignity and remained a man.

They say he is an 'anarchist', though he himself never talks about politics. In this respect Berzin is not an exception. Hardly anyone among the ex-convicts is interested in politics; most of them confess somewhat dubiously that they are 'anarchists' and 'followers of Tolstoy and Prince Kropotkin'. If pressed for an explanation, they will say hesitantly that the source of all evil and the main enemy of man is the State; if the State were abolished all would be well and all men would become brothers. If you try to argue with them, they become confused, and subside into silence. Their notion of 'anarchism' is entirely vague, and based on nebulous hearsay. The Chinese majority is illiterate, and the others nearly so. From the moment of their arrest they were deprived of any kind of reading matter—in Berzin's case since the age of sixteen. It is impossible for them to form any clear political idea; politics, like most questions beyond their narrow horizon, make them feel bored and mentally helpless. Their minds, starved of contact with the outside world, have become sluggish; their intellect has atrophied for lack of exercise. Those who have spent more than ten years here are afraid of going back into a world from which they have become estranged. Before their liberation, they worked twelve to fourteen hours a day on starvation rations, under unimaginable conditions of hardship. Now they work six to seven hours, are well-fed, clad, and housed in a manner which seems to them undreamed luxury. But their physical and mental rehabilitation is a slow process, and many are past recovery.

Immediately after the liberation, as food, medicaments and warm clothing began to pour in, the death-rate, for a few weeks, rose steeply. Many convicts who previously had kept a precarious hold on life by sheer power of will, died when the tension in them snapped and their will relaxed. A short while later, a wave of alcoholism swept Kolyma, until Berzin and his colleagues were forced to resort to prohibition. Other fashions and crazes followed. To be constantly hurried by the guards and *urki* had become second nature to the convicts, so that they did not know what to do with the long hours of leisure which were suddenly theirs. Boredom and restlessness, particularly during the months of the Polar night, led to a variety of crazes—for gambling, knitting and embroidery; the men also took to keeping strange animal pets and to inventing complicated culinary dishes—the longer they took to prepare, the better.

Kolyma, August 6th

One of the curiosities of Kolyma is the immense popularity of the 'story-tellers' who, in the absence of books, had become a standing institution in all Soviet prisons and labour camps. The story-teller rarely invented his yarn; mostly he gave his own version of novels and stories which he had read in bygone days. The age of slavery had led to a revival of the bards.

In the camps, the story-teller was the only person whose life and possessions were safe, even from the criminals. In the free Convicts' Republic he has become a highly paid professional. Having lost the reading habit, large numbers of the workers prefer to gather in the evenings in the recreation room and to listen to the bard's condensed, but all the more colourful version of *Anna Karenina*, *Hamlet* or *The Arabian Nights*'

The main problem, and an unsolved one, which prevents return to full normality, is the absence of women. The porportion of female to male prisoners in the camps was about one to a hundred. Here in Kolyma, the poet's praise of the woman 'who is worth her weight in gold' has come unexpectedly true, regardless of the lady's age and appearance. This led to certain developments otherwise only found in primitive societies. One of them is polyandry—several husbands sharing one woman.

Kolyma, August 9th

. . . Four years have passed since the mutiny of Elgen brought liberation to the slaves of Kolyma. Even this sketchy report may convey an idea of the deep injuries which the bodies and souls of these men have suffered, of the slowness of the process of recovery, and the great number of those in whom the human substance has deteriorated beyond repair.

All tyrannies carry the seed of their own destruction—but at what price, at what terrible price for humanity.

Kolyma, August 10th

Hsiao gave a small party in his house; Berzin was there, and two other members of the Temporary Administration. One was a tall, fidgety man, a former school-teacher from Latvia, who is in charge of the public re-education programme; he made a somewhat dispirited impression. The other was Mother

Seraphimova, an old Russian peasant-woman with a wrinkled face and young eyes, who hardly said a word during the whole evening and probably understood little of what was said, but whose presence radiated a feeling of peace. Seraphimova is illiterate and has no particular function in the Government; but she was unanimously elected because of this indefinable quality which seems to have a purifying effect on everybody who comes in contact with her. She is perhaps as nearly a saint as people can be at this time and in this place. I ought to mention that every slave camp had its 'saint', just as it had its story-teller.

We drank tea and talked; the conversation was rather halting. Towards the end of the evening I asked Hsiao what lesson Kolyma had taught him. He smiled embarrassedly; it was then that Seraphimova spoke for the first time. She said:

'Show him your pictures.'

Hsiao rose and came back after a little while with some ink drawings he had made. They were landscapes in the classic Chinese tradition: a few of the sad, sparse larch trees of Kolyma; tattered men being marched to work; in the background the monotonous skyline of the *taiga*, and the desolate cliffs which close in the harbour of Magadan.

'They are quite unworthy,' said Hsiao, actually blushing. 'But this is what Kolyma taught me.'

He pointed a thin, yellow finger at the figures in the foreground; and then I saw what he meant. The men and the trees in the landscape had shadows. From time immemorial, Chinese painters had made their pictures without shadows in them.

'You see,' he explained, 'for three months in summer the sun never sets in Kolyma. The light is almost horizontal; so a tree throws a very long shadow. One day I suddenly *saw* the shadow of a tree and I decided that my picture would not be complete without it; so I put it in. For a painter grown up in the classic Chinese tradition, this was a very daring thing to do. All real revolutions happen in the minds of people. They will happen as long as there are men—even in Kolyma. Everything else is of little importance.'

Moscow, August 15th

Back from Kolyma.

I must have caught some kind of fever in the gnat-infested swamps, for last night I was plagued by a nightmare. I dreamt that UNIHOPE, and the free Convict Republic, and the rescue of the children, and the Great Lottery, only existed in my own imagination—a dream born out of frustration and despair; and that in reality vengefulness, rapacious greed and blindness of heart have made the victors repeat the blunders of the past, and throw away humanity's last chance of salvation. I woke up among the crawling bugs.

III. THE FAILURE OF RESPONSE

The Right to Say 'No'

FOUR CONTRIBUTIONS TO THE
CONGRESS FOR CULTURAL FREEDOM

The Congress for Cultural Freedom, an international meeting of writers, scholars and scientists under the patronage of Bertrand Russell, Benedetto Croce, John Dewey, Karl Jaspers, and Jacques Maritain, was held in June, 1950 in Berlin. Its opening session coincided with the beginning of the Korean war. It served a double purpose: as a kind of intellectual airlift, a demonstration of Western solidarity with the brave and battered outpost of Berlin, a hundred miles behind the Iron Curtain; and as an attempt to dispel the intellectual confusion created by the totalitarian campaigns under the slogan of peace. Out of the deliberations of the Berlin Congress arose an international movement with branches and publications in a number of European, American and Asiatic countries, among them Encounter, *London, and* Preuves, *Paris.*

I. MANIFESTO OF THE CONGRESS FOR
CULTURAL FREEDOM*

1. We hold it to be self-evident that intellectual freedom is one of the inalienable rights of man.

---

* This manifesto, which I drafted by request of the steering committee, was unanimously adopted at the closing session of the Congress on 30th June, 1950. The words in square brackets were added to the draft by the British members of the editorial committee, Professor A. J. Ayer and Mr. Hugh Trevor-Roper.

2. Such freedom is defined first and foremost by his right to hold and express his own opinions, and particularly opinions which differ from those of his rulers. Deprived of the right to say 'no', man becomes a slave.

3. Freedom and peace are inseparable. In any country, under any régime, the overwhelming majority of ordinary people fear and oppose war. The danger of war becomes acute when governments, by suppressing democratic representative institutions, deny to the majority the means of imposing its will to peace.

Peace can be maintained only if each government submits to the control and inspection of its acts by the people whom it governs, and agrees to submit all questions immediately involving the risk of war to a representative international authority, by whose decision it will abide.

4. We hold that the main reason for the present insecurity of the world is the policy of governments which, while paying lip-service to peace, refuse to accept this double control. Historical experience proves that wars can be prepared and waged under any slogan, including that of peace. Campaigns for peace which are not backed by acts that will guarantee its maintenance are like counterfeit currency circulated for dishonest purposes. Intellectual sanity and physical security can only return to the world if such practices are abandoned.

5. Freedom is based on the toleration of divergent opinions. The principle of toleration does not logically permit the practice of intolerance.

6. No political philosophy or economic theory can claim the sole right to represent freedom in the abstract. We hold that the value of such theories is to be judged by the range of concrete freedom which they accord the individual in practice.

We likewise hold that no race, nation, class or religion can claim the sole right to represent the idea of freedom, nor the right to deny freedom to other groups or creeds in the name of any ultimate ideal or lofty aim whatsoever. We hold that the historical contribution of any society is to be judged by the extent and quality of the freedom which its members actually enjoy.

7. In times of emergency, restrictions on the freedom of the individual are imposed in the real or assumed interest of the community. We hold it to be essential that such restrictions be confined to a minimum of clearly specified actions; that they be understood to be temporary and limited expedients in the nature of a sacrifice; and that the measures restricting freedom be themselves subject to free criticism and democratic control. Only thus can we have a reasonable assurance that emergency measures restricting individual freedom will not degenerate into a permanent tyranny.

8. In totalitarian states restrictions on freedom are no longer intended and publicly understood as a sacrifice imposed on the people, but are on the contrary represented as triumphs of progress and achievements of a superior civilisation. We hold that both the theory and practice of these régimes run counter to the basic rights of the individual and the fundamental aspirations of mankind as whole.

9. We hold the danger represented by these régimes to be all the greater since their means of enforcement far surpasses that of all previous tyrannies in the history of mankind. The citizen of the totalitarian state is expected and forced not only to abstain from crime but to conform in all his thoughts and actions to a prescribed pattern. Citizens are persecuted and condemned on such unspecified and all-embracing charges as 'enemies of the people' or 'socially unreliable elements'.

10. We hold that there can be no stable world so long as mankind, with regard to freedom, remains divided into 'haves' and 'have-nots'. The defence of existing freedoms, the reconquest of lost freedoms [and the creation of new freedoms], are parts of the same struggle.

11. We hold that the theory and practice of the totalitarian state are the greatest challenge which man has been called on to meet in the course of civilised history.

12. We hold that indifference or neutrality in the face of such a challenge amounts to a betrayal of mankind and to the abdication of the free mind. Our answer to this challenge may decide the fate of man for generations.

13. [The defence of intellectual liberty today imposes a posi-

tive obligation: to offer new and constructive answers to the problems of our time.]

14. We address this manifesto to all men who are determined to regain those liberties which they have lost, and to preserve [and extend] those which they enjoy.

II. TWO METHODS OF ACTION*

Since the earliest days, the teachers of mankind have recommended two diametrically opposed methods of action. The first demands that we should refuse to see the world divided into black and white, heroes and villains, friends and foes; that we should distinguish nuances, and strive for synthesis or at least compromise; it tells us that in nearly all, seemingly inescapable dilemmas there exists a third alternative which patient search may discover. In short, we should refuse the choice between Scylla and Charybdis and rather navigate like Odysseus of the nimble wits. We may call this the 'neither-nor' attitude.

The second, opposite advice was summed up two thousand years ago in one single phrase: 'Let your communication be, Yea, yea, Nay, nay; for whatsoever is more than these, comes from evil.' This we may call the 'either-or' attitude.

Obviously humanity could not have survived without taking both methods into account. By neglecting the first advice, men would long ago have torn each other to pieces. By neglecting the second, man would have forsaken his dignity and moral backbone, and lost his capacity to distinguish between good and evil.

It is equally obvious that each of the two tenets has a different field of application. To enumerate these would be a tedious and pedantic undertaking, and frequently there is conflict between both methods within the same field. Our concern here is with action in the political field. And there it seems that the first method is valid for long-term planning with a certain elbow-room in space and time, and that the second is valid in

* Address delivered (in German) at the opening session of the Congress for Cultural Freedom, 25th June, 1950.

immediate and vital emergencies when, in Beethoven's words, 'Fate knocks at the gate of existence'.

In such an emergency, the threatened individual or group or civilisation can only survive if it acts with the unhesitating assurance of an organic reflex. The nerves of all living organisms function according to the so-called all-or-nothing law; they either react to a stimulus for all they are worth or do not react at all. And it is not by chance that the calculating machines called electronic brains are constructed according to the same 'either-or' principle. They perform immensely complex functions, but each time a decision is required of them, they act according to the Gospel of Matthew.

In vital emergencies like the present, when man stands at a crossroads which only leaves the choice of this way or that, the difference between the very clever and the simple in mind narrows almost to vanishing point, or even turns to the latter's advantage. It is amazing to observe how in a crisis the most sophisticated often act like imbeciles. Imbued with the mental habits of the 'neither-nor' attitude, of looking for synthesis or compromise—a profoundly human attitude of essential value in its proper field—they are incapable of admitting, even to themselves, that there are situations in which an unambiguous decision is vital for spiritual and physical survival. Faced with destiny's challenge, they act like clever imbeciles and preach neutrality towards the bubonic plague. Mostly they are victims of a professional disease: the intellectual's estrangement from reality. And having lost touch with reality they have acquired that devilish art: they can prove everything that they believe, and believe everything that they can prove. Their logic reminds one of the German students' old nonsense-song:

The elephant has his tail in front and his trunk is at his rear;
But when he turns round his trunk is in front and his tail is at his rear.

Don't misunderstand me: I know that many of those who are not here with us today cherish freedom too, and are rather frightened of the fate which might befall them if everybody imitated their attitude of contemplative detachment. It is only that they haven't yet learnt that there is a time to speak in relative clauses, and a time to speak in terms of Yea and Nay. For destiny's challenge to man is always couched in simple and direct language, without relative clauses—and requires an answer in equally simple terms.

III. AN OUTGROWN DILEMMA*

The thesis which I wish to put before you is that the anti-
monies 'Socialism and Capitalism', 'Left and Right', are
rapidly becoming meaningless, and that so long as Europe
remains bogged down in these false alternatives which obstruct
clear thinking, it cannot hope to find a constructive solution
for its problems.

I

The term 'Political Left' originated, as you know, with the
distribution of factions in the French National Assembly after
the Revolution in 1789. At the beginning of the nineteenth
century it spread over the Continent and was applied to that
section of a country's legislature which sat to the left of the
President's chair and was traditionally associated with liberal
and democratic opinions. Gradually, the word came to mean
the radical or purist or extremist wing of any ideological
school or movement, whether liberal and democratic or not.
Later on it was used in an even more vague and metaphorical
way; and the more it was drained of meaning, the stronger
became its emotional appeal. At the beginning of the last war
there existed about half a dozen political parties in France, all
of them conservative to reactionary in their programme, all of
them seated in the right wing of the Chamber, and all of them
carrying the word 'Left' in their names.

I mention this development as a semantic curiosity and
because of its relevance to the present situation. For to this day

* Edited version of a talk to the political panel session of the Congress for
Cultural Freedom, June, 1950.

European Liberals and Social-Democrats refer to themselves as 'the moderate Left' which, if words are to be taken seriously, must mean that they differ only in degree but not in kind from their neighbours of 'the extreme Left'. And 'the extreme Left' is still regarded as synonymous with the Communist Party, in spite of the fact that virtually every tenet in the Communist *credo* is diametrically opposed to the principles originally associated with the Left. In short, the term 'Left' has become a verbal fetish whose cult sidetracks attention from the real issues. It is at the same time a dangerous anachronism, for it implies the existence of a continuous spectrum between liberal progressives and the worshippers of tyranny and terror. And such is the magic power of words over the mind that European Socialists who think of themselves as 'men of the Left' were unconsciously led from a fallacious verbal identification to a real feeling of solidarity with the Communists. They may feel critical or even hostile towards their 'extreme' neighbours of the Communist Party; they retain nevertheless an ambivalent neighbourly feeling for them, a conviction of 'having the same historical roots', of being, after all, 'on the same side of the barricades'.

A good many American liberals fell into the same emotional trap during the 'thirties and even later. The victim of the witch-hunt supplied the whip which scourged him and became an accomplice in his own perdition. However, the relative safety and prosperity of that continent made the confused American liberal gradually accessible to reality and enabled him to get out of the trap, while a major portion of the French and Italian Left, and a smaller portion of the British, exposed to the neurosis-forming climate of Europe, have remained in it.

In the past it was always 'the Left' who protested loudest against tyranny, injustice, and infringements of human rights. The failure of European 'Leftists' and American liberals to lead the fight against the worst régime of terror and despotism in human history created a strategic vacuum on the ideological battlefield. This vacuum was filled by the Christian Democrats in Italy, the Gaullists in France, by Senator McCarthy and his associates in the U.S.A. McCarthyism represents the wages of

the American liberals' sins. If today everywhere in the world
the parties who claim to represent the 'moderate Left' are
beaten or in retreat, it is because they were found wanting on
the most crucial issue of our time.

2

Europe has developed a political climate in which words are
no longer taken seriously. The ideological chaos created a
semantic inflation and a semantic black market where words
are traded at a meaning-value entirely different from their
official quotation: where war is prepared by peace petitions,
police states are labelled popular democracies, and 'Leftism'
means benevolent neutrality towards despotism.

At first sight the alternative 'Capitalism or Socialism'
appears much more concrete and meaningful than 'Right or
Left'. But on closer inspection it will be found that the term
'Socialism' has suffered a semantic decay similar to that of the
'Left'. German National Socialism, Russian Soviet Socialism;
French Socialism which is Marxist with a pinch of salt, British
Socialism which is Christian, non-Marxist, Fabianist, and
heaven knows what, all derive their emotional dynamism from
the fetish-power of the same word, attached to quite different
meanings.

However, let us leave semantics aside, though it is an
essential branch of political hygiene. If we are not too pedantic,
we may hope to agree at least on some rough-and-ready
definition of what Socialism really means, and on some
common denominator for the aspirations of the various existing
Socialist parties.

Let us turn first to the field of *international* politics. One of the
basic elements of Socialist thought, from Spartacus's slave
revolt to Thomas More's *Utopia*, from the primitive Christian
communities to Marx, is the brotherhood of man. In the past,
Socialists have always fought against parochialism, chauvinism, aggressive nationalism and have preached internationalism, cosmopolitanism, the abolition of ideological and political
barriers among nations. But do they still?

In the Union of Soviet Socialist Republics the word 'cosmopolitan' has become a term of abuse, and chauvinism has reached a hitherto unprecedented peak. At the same time at the recent Paris Congress of the French Communist Party a banner was stretched across the hall which read: 'The true internationalist is he who is prepared unreservedly, unhesitatingly, and unconditionally to defend the U.S.S.R.' So much for the Russian version of Socialist internationalism.

In the *Western* world the only great power with a Socialist Government is Great Britain. The Labour Party won the elections a few weeks after the end of the war in the still strongest country of Europe, and just at the decisive moment when it no longer needed a Socialist training to understand that Europe must unite or perish. Never before in history was Socialism offered such a chance. Yet from the moment it came to power, the Labour Government has deliberately obstructed every effort towards European unity. The non-Socialist Governments of France, Germany and Italy have proved themselves more internationally-minded than the Socialist Government in England.

Of course Britain has a particularly difficult position between the Continent and the Commonwealth; and there are always plausible arguments for avoiding decisions which would require a certain amount of historical imagination. But the essential point is that the victory of British Socialism has not abolished British insularity; it has, on the contrary, strengthened and deepened it. It was Churchill the Conservative, not Attlee the Socialist, who started the United Europe movement which led to the Council of Strasbourg; and when the movement got under way, the Labour Party's attitude to it remained consistently hostile. The reason for this was explained in a statement by the National Executive Committee of the Labour Party issued in June, 1950. 'No Socialist government in Europe,' the decisive phrase in the statement runs, 'could submit to the authority of a [supranational] body whose policies were decided by an anti-Socialist majority.'

What this amounts to is simply a mild British version of the Russian 'Socialism in One Country' policy. The Russian veto in the United Nations finds its equivalent in the British veto against the political and economic unity of Europe.

It need not be emphasised that there is a world of difference between the British and the Soviet régimes. My comparison refers merely to one specific aspect; the collapse of the cosmopolitan *élan* in the Socialist movement. This process started almost a generation ago, in 1914, and has now reached a stage where we can see the paradoxical phenomenon of capitalist America being prepared to make sacrifices in national sovereignty which Socialist Russia refuses, and of British, French, and German Conservatives pursuing a more internationally-minded policy than their Socialist opposite numbers. In other words, *Socialism has lost its claim to represent the internationalist trend of humanity.* As far as the integration of our world is concerned, the Socialist-Capitalist alternative has become void of meaning.

Is it more meaningful when applied to *domestic* policy?

As regards political and intellectual freedom, there is no relevant difference bewteen Socialist Britain and the capitalist United States. And in the domain of unfreedom there is little to choose between Socialist Russia and Fascist Spain. Again the real division cuts across the abstract frontiers between Socialism and Capitalism. Only one field remains where the alternative is apparently still relevant: the economic field.

Theoretically there is an unbridgeable gulf between nationalisation of the means of production on the one hand, and private ownership, profits, and exploitation on the other. But in fact recent developments have abolished the static trench-warfare between the classes and have transformed it into a fluid war of movement. As the question is too complex to be treated here in any systematic manner, I must confine myself to a few remarks in shorthand, as it were.

First, even Marx and Engels knew that nationalisation itself is not a panacea. It is useful to recall Frederick Engels' remark that if nationalisation were identical with Socialism, then the first Socialist institution must have been the regimental tailor. In fact, the Soviet workers do not own their nationalised factories any more than a sailor of the Royal Navy owns the battleship in which he serves. The people's control over the battleships, railways, factories, coal mines, which they theoretically own, depends entirely on the political structure of the state. In Russia, where the Trade Unions have ceased to be an instrument of the working class and have become an instrument for the coercion of the working class, the theoretical owners of the factories and of the land have less influence over management, and work under worse conditions, than their comrades in any Western country. On the other hand, trust managers, factory directors, and 'proletarian millionaires' (an official Russian term) form a privileged class, just as much as and more so, than in capitalist countries. To be sure, their income is called salary and not profit, but again this distinction is mainly abstract. Nor is, on the other hand, the factory owner in capitalist countries any longer able to draw unlimited profits from his enterprise or do with his workers what he likes. I refer you to James Burnham's analysis of the relevant changes in the meaning of the term 'ownership' in recent times.

Generally speaking, nationalisation without an appropriate change in political structure leads not to State Socialism but to State Capitalism. The difference between the two cannot be defined in economic terms; it is a matter of democratic controls, of political freedom, and cultural climate. A nationalised economy in itself may serve as a basis for a totalitarian autocracy of the Russian type or even for a Fascist régime.

Equally problematic is the question just *how much* nationalisation makes a country socialist or capitalist? British Socialism nationalised the railways, but France and Germany had state-owned railways long before. The total nationalisation of all means of production and distribution has been recognised as unworkable even in Russia. The alternative is no longer nationalisation or private economy in the abstract; the real problem is to find the proper balance of state ownership, control, planning, and free enterprise. And the search for this delicate balance is again not an abstract but an empirical pursuit. Apparently each nation has to work out its own formula, for there are many imponderabilia which enter into the equation.

As an example of the complex reality masked by the 'Capitalism versus Socialism' slogan, one may quote food-rationing. Food-rationing—which means state control of distribution—worked very satisfactorily in puritan England under

Conservative and Socialist governments alike. But it broke down completely in Italy and France, both countries with a highly individualistic and resourceful Latin population. Obviously, far-reaching inferences must be drawn from this fact concerning the balance of state control and free enterprise appropriate to each of these countries. In short, even in the purely economic sphere we are not dealing with a clear-cut alternative between Capitalism and Socialism, but with a kind of continuous rainbow spectrum whose shape and colour are largely determined by psychological and other factors not contained in Socialist theory.

3

What I have said should not be misinterpreted as an apology for Capitalism or as an attack on Socialism. My point is that this alternative is rapidly becoming as antiquated and meaningless as the dispute between Jansenists and Jesuits or the Wars of the Roses. Nor did I mean to say that it always *was* meaningless. I said it is *becoming* meaningless, because it operates with rigid nineteenth-century conceptions, and does not take into account new realities which have emerged since, and new conflicts which cut across the conventional boundaries.

It is not a novelty in history that a real dilemma which once seemed all-important is gradually drained of its meaning and becomes a pseudo-dilemma as new historical realities emerge. People lost interest in waging wars of religion when national consciousness began to dawn on them. The conflict between republicans and monarchists went out of fashion when economic problems became all-important. The examples could be multiplied. Every period seems to have its specific conflict which polarises the world and serves as an ideological compass in the chaos—until history passes over it with a shrug; and afterwards people wonder what they were so excited about.

It is a further fact that some of these great ideological conflicts are never decided; they end in a stalemate. In successive centuries it looked as if the whole world would either become Islamic or Christian, either Catholic or Protestant, either republican or monarchist, either capitalist or socialist. But instead of a decision there came a deadlock and a process which one might call *the withering away of the dilemma*. The withering, or draining of meaning, always seems to be the result of some mutation in human consciousness accompanied by a shift of emphasis to an entirely different set of values— from religious consciousness to national consciousness to economic consciousness and so on.

This 'and so on' poses a problem which we are unable to answer with certainty. We cannot foretell the nature of the next mutation in the consciousness of the masses, nor the values which will emerge on the next higher level. But we may assume on the strength of past analogies that the battle-cries of economic man will appear to his successor just as sterile and pointless as the Wars of the Roses appear to us.

Two short remarks in conclusion. First, it is necessary to qualify the statement that the apparently decisive conflicts of a given period tend to end in a stalemate and wither away. This did indeed happen in the past, but only in cases where the forces in the conflict were fairly balanced. Europe remained Christian because the Arabs never got to Paris and the Turks were beaten back at the ramparts of Vienna. There are other, less edifying examples of history solving its dilemmas. The conclusion is obvious.

In the second place, though we cannot foresee the values and spiritual climate of post-economic man, certain conjectures are permissible. While the majority of Europeans are still hypnotised by the anachronistic battle-cries of Left and Right, Capitalism and Socialism, history has moved on to a new alternative, a new conflict which cuts across the old lines of division. The real content of this conflict can be summed up in one phrase: total tyranny against relative freedom. Sometimes I have a feeling in my bones that the terrible pressure which this conflict exerts on all humanity might perhaps represent a challenge, a biological stimulus as it were, which will release the new mutation of human consciousness; and that its content might be a new spiritual awareness, born of anguish and suffering, of the full meaning of freedom. And I don't mean by that, freedom from want, freedom from fear and the rest. Since the dawn of civilisation people have fought under the slogan of freedom; but it was always freedom *from* some particularly irksome oppression, freedom in a restricted, negative sense. I mean freedom in a much deeper and fuller sense than any we can conceive today, or see realised anywhere in organic nature. If that is the case, then we are indeed living in an interesting time, and the answer which we shall give to destiny's challenge is not without import for the future of our species.

A Guide to Political Neuroses*

Most contemporary theories regarding political behaviour are based on a curious paradox. It is common knowledge (a) that crowds tend to behave in an irrational manner ('mass hysteria', 'mass obsessions', etc.). It is equally common knowledge (b) that individuals often react in an irrational manner to the problems of sex and in their relations to family, superiors, and subordinates. Yet, while we admit that crowds behave like neurotics in public affairs, and that individuals display complexes in their private affairs, we still cling to the strange illusion that the average citizen, when not in a crowd, is a politically rational being. Our whole manner of running a democracy is based on this implicit assumption. This unwarranted, dogmatic belief in the political rationality of the individual is the ultimate reason why democracies are always on the defensive against totalitarian opponents, not only physically but also psychologically. For the evidence suggests that twentieth-century man is a political neurotic.

The totalitarians have understood this. They are the forces of death assailing our civilisation; and as death thrives on disease, he is a good diagnostician. If we want to survive, we must be equally good diagnosticians. But one cannot arrive at a correct diagnosis if one starts with the assumption that the patient is sane. The belief in the basic political sanity and rationality of the individual has been implanted in us, during the Age of Enlightenment, by a ·long succession of French, German, and English philosophers—by Encyclopædists, Marxists, Benthamites, Owenites, and Progressives of all shades. Freud and his successors have demolished one corner of this optimistic belief in man as a rational being: we accept

* First published in *Encounter*, November, 1953.

the fact that our sexual libido is thwarted. It is time for us to recognise that our political libido is just as complex-ridden, repressed and twisted, if not even more.

The Mental Curtain

At first sight it may seem that talk of a 'political libido', a political unconscious' and its 'repressed memories', is merely a new intellectual pastime, a juggling with metaphors and analogies. But any detached study of the contemporary scene will show that the neurotic entanglements of the political instinct are as real, and no less profound, than those of the sexual instinct.

A neurotic may be described as a person who has faulty contact with reality, and whose judgments are based, not on hard facts, but on his wishes and fears. Facts which are likely to upset the patient's wish-and-fear universe are not admitted to conscio1sness; they are 'censored' and become repressed complexes. If this simplified schema is applied to political behaviour, it will be seen to cover the whole range of political pathology, from the 'controlled schizophrenia' of a Klaus Fuchs, through the wish-dream world of the Stockholm peace campaigner, to the flight from reality of the 'neutralist'. The political clichés which serve as rationalisations of his unconscious fears are as irrelevant as a neurotic's explanations of why he won't eat fish. When Harold Laski wrote to Mr. Justice Frankfurter in 1941 that 'the U.S.S.R. has its roots in popular opinion more profound than any other system', argument had become pointless against such vagaries of the political libido, and the professor had become an obvious case for the psychotherapist.

Into the neurotic's distorted universe no facts are admitted which may upset its inner consistency. Arguments cannot penetrate the buffers of casuistry, the semantic shock-absorbers, the emotional defences. The inner censor—in the full psychiatric sense of the word—that protects the patient's illusions against the intrusion of reality, is incomparably more effective than any totalitarian state censorship. The political neurotic carries his private Iron Curtain inside his skull.

The unpalatable facts which have been rejected by the inner censor are subsequently repressed, and cluster into complexes. The political subconscious has its own logic, symptoms, and symbols. Alger Hiss and Whittaker Chambers have become such symbols in a Punch-and-Judy show or dream-fantasia, where guilt is attributed, not on the strength of evidence, but according to the dream-logic of the unconscious. If 'censored' facts are mentioned in the presence of the political neurotic, he will react either with vehemence or a superior smile, either with straight abuse or with devious double-think, according to the nature of the defence-mechanism which protects him against his deep uncertainty and unconscious fear. Otherwise, the precarious balance of his dream-world would collapse and leave him defenceless against the stark world of reality—a reality so terrifying that even the sane can only face it with a shudder.

Repressed Guilt

In the gas chambers of Auschwitz, Belsen, and other exter-mination camps, around six million human beings were put to death during the closing phase of the Second World War. It was the greatest organised mass-killing in history. At the time it happened, the majority of the German people did not know what was going on. Since then, official documents, books and films have publicised the facts to such an extent that it has become impossible for any educated person to ignore them. And yet the average German does manage to ignore them. The truth has not penetrated the nation's consciousness, and probably never will—because it it too terrifying to face. If admitted to consciousness, the load of guilt would be too heavy to carry, and would crush the nation's pride, frustrate its effort to rise again as a great European power. Many intelligent and well-meaning Germans react, when Auschwitz and Belsen are mentioned in their presence, with a stony silence and the pained expression of a Victorian lady confronted with a rude reminder of the Facts of Life: that they happen to be facts, never enters her head; they are just unmentionable, and that is all there is to them. Others will either deny the facts, or call them vastly exaggerated, or will, in the same breath, use several mutually contradictory arguments without being aware of the contradiction.

The remarkable thing about this reaction-pattern is that it betrays an unconscious guilt-complex even among those who had no share in the killings—and these are the vast majority of the Germans. Before the law, and as far as their conscious knowledge goes, they are innocent. To make a nation collectively responsible for the deeds of a criminal minority is both legally and morally unjust. But the 'political subconscious' approaches the matter in a different way. It automatically assumes a shared collective responsibility in the nation's triumphs and defeats, in its honour and guilt. In fact, the most outstanding characteristic of the political libido is its tendency to identify the self with a nation, tribe, church, or party. The political libido can be defined as the individual's need to feel himself as part of a community, his urge to belong.

Now when this unconscious tendency towards identification produces pleasurable results, these are willingly admitted to the conscious self: every German feels proud of 'our Goethe' as if he had a share in creating him, every American feels satisfaction about the War of Independence as if he had fought in it. But the less pleasurable products of the tendency towards identification occupy no such place of honour in the conscious ego. And still others may act as a traumatic shock, and therefore must be quickly forgotten and repressed. *Our* Goethe, *our* Beethoven, *my* country are part and parcel of the ego. But *our* Auschwitz, the children whom *we* gassed, the war which *we* started, must be forced into the mental underground.

Repressed political complexes have a thwarting effect, just as repressed sexual complexes have. A lasting cure can only be effected if the repressed experience is brought back to memory, however painful the process may be. In the case under discussion, this operation of mental hygiene could only be accomplished by the leaders of the German people. Punishment and humiliation inflicted from outside only make things worse. For the victors it is right to forget; but the vanquished must learn to remember.

Collective Amnesia

The French suffer from a repressed complex of a different kind, of which the manifestations are even more conspicuous. When the legitimate government of France, after the collapse of its armies, capitulated in June, 1940, the majority of Frenchmen accepted the defeat and tried to reach some kind of *modus vivendi* with the German victors. With Europe gone and England hopelessly isolated, this was for the average, non-political Frenchman the only reasonable course to take. When General de Gaulle proclaimed from London that 'France had lost a battle but had not lost the war', the people trapped in France understood that this was a nice propaganda slogan, but had little relation to the facts. For approximately two years they went about their business as best they could, and enjoyed relative peace. Only a small number among them followed de Gaulle's call and escaped to England to enlist in his volunteer army, or joined the resistance movement. This again is only natural, for at the time resistance seemed sheer madness or quixotry, and at all times in all nations the heroic madmen have been a tiny minority.

The turning of the tide of war, the forced enlistment of Frenchmen for labour service in Germany, and a number of related factors gradually swelled the ranks of the resistance movement until, at the time of the Allied landing, some 20,000 to 40,000 Frenchmen were seriously engaged in sabotage, espionage, and armed resistance. Even at that time they were a small minority, and their bravery and self-sacrifice did not materially affect the course of the war. France was liberated not by the *maquis* but by the power of the Anglo-American war-machine, by British and American aircraft and tanks.

This hard fact was slurred over by the Anglo-American leaders who, for reasons of courtesy, vastly over-emphasised the French contribution to the war. It is only natural that French generals and politicians took the same line, in order to bolster up the nation's shaken self-respect and save it from the humiliating awareness of having been liberated by foreigners. Thus, within less than a year, the average Frenchman became honestly convinced that France had never been defeated, that she had been saved by her own effort, and moreover that he, Monsieur Dupont, had always been a valiant *résistant* and had only been lacking in opportunity to prove it. The memories of his own thoughts and acts during the dark interlude between 1940 and 1943 have been so successfully repressed that those years have become a kind of gap or hole in the texture of French history. This explains how it became possible for the French Communists, who from 1939 to 1941 had openly preached treason and surrender, and had called resistance to the German aggression an 'imperialist adventure' and a 'rich man's war', to merge four years later as the strongest party in France. They benefited from the collective amnesia; their record was swallowed by the gap in the nation's memory.

Thus the mental structure of present-day France is built on delusion and self-delusion. The legend of the undefeated, victorious nation was first maintained by mutual tacit consent, then quickly grew into an act of faith. The former collaborator not only wears the ribbon of the *résistance* in his buttonhole; he also honestly believes that he is entitled to wear it. Because he admires the heroes of the resistance movement, and because he feels that they represent the true spirit of the nation, he is unconsciously led to believe that he belongs to them. It is *our* Goethe, *our* Jeanne d'Arc, *we* the nation of heroic *maquisards* all over again.

We see here a similar process at work as in the case of the Germans—the process of unconscious identification with a representative minority—but with opposite results. In the case of the Germans, identification resulted in shared guilt, which had to be repressed. In the case of the French, identification leads to shared glory, and allows the political libido to expand with a flourish. But the repressed memories exert their steady, poisonous influence on the nation's morale. The fiction of the past can only be maintained by evading the reality of the present. France, so the legend goes, owed nobody anything in the past, and will owe nobody anything in the future. If Marshall Aid is sent to her, this is done to serve some obscure scheme of Wall Street. If arms and troops are sent it is to further the interests of American imperialism. The only war-

time memories connected with Americans which have remained vivid and undistorted are that the bombers often
missed their targets, destroying French cities and lives; and
that G.I.s often got drunk and traded cigarettes for the passing
favours of women. Hence: no more liberation à l'Américaine.
We want to be left alone. We want none of your alms, and none
of your coca-cola, and none of your atom-bombs. If you leave
us alone, the Russians will leave us alone too.

Elaborate variations of this theme can be read every day in
French newspapers of all shades. The one subject never mentioned is the tragic but crucial fact that the physical survival of
France depends on the American atomic potential. If it were
admitted, the whole fictitious structure would collapse. And if
one were to take away the wishful element from the patient's
wish-and-fear world, only fear would remain—the unbearable,
repressed terror of a Europe still virtually defenceless against
the Russian threat.

So the fiction has to be maintained, and reality evaded at all
cost. Any nation which has suffered three invasions within one
century and lost at least one male member per family, would
develop the same neurotic pattern.

Escape from Reality

Escape from reality is a basic feature of contemporary
Europe, but has for a long time been a specific British vice. It
almost seems as if the British had paid for their remarkable
immunity from hysteria by imperviousness to reality; a short-
coming craftily hidden by the art of making their follies appear
as sweet reasonableness.

In the days of the London blitz, the P.E.N. Club had asked
Louis Golding to give a talk comparing the American to the
British novel. Golding had just finished when the air-raid
warning went, but the discussion was continued, business as
usual. The second or third speaker was a crumpled, tweedy,
lovable little man who, I believe, had written a biography of
an obscure Wiltshire naturalist of the seventeenth century. He
was attacking Hemingway, Dos Passos, Faulkner, and others.

'It seems to me,' he gently explained, 'that these modern

American novelists suffer from a morbid preoccupation with violence. When you read their books you would think that the ordinary man spends his life punching people's noses or being hit on the head. Now, as a matter of fact, ordinary people rarely meet with violence in their lives. They get up in the morning, potter in their gardens . . .'

A bomb whistled and crashed some blocks away, and the anti-aircraft batteries started their infernal hollering. The little man waited patiently for the next lull, then calmly continued:

'What I mean to say is, violence rarely plays a part in ordinary people's lives, and it is positively indecent for an artist to devote so much time and space to that kind of thing. . . .'

One of the outstanding features of neurotic behaviour is the patient's inability to learn from his past experiences. As if acting under a spell, he gets himself over and again into the same type of entanglement and repeats the same errors. British foreign policy towards European union, and French internal politics during the last thirty years, seem to be dictated by this kind of repetition-compulsion.

The trigger which set off the Second World War was Germany's claim to a town that formed an enclave in Polish territory and could only be reached through a corridor. That war was not yet over when Allied statesmen agreed to create a new enclave of exactly the same type, only accessible through a corridor across foreign territory. The name of the first enclave was Danzig; the name of the second is Berlin. Behind the shallow truism that 'History repeats itself' hide the un-explored forces which lure men into repeating their own tragic errors.

The obvious and outstanding example of such a compulsion is the so-called policy of appeasement. The lesson of the 'thirties: that an aggressive, expansive power with a messianic belief in its mission will expand as long as a power-vacuum exists; that improvement of social conditions, however desir-able in itself, is no deterrent and no protection against attack; that the price of survival is the sacrifice of a distressing part of the national income for defence over a distressingly long period; and that appeasement, however seductive and plausible its arguments sound, is not a substitute for military strength but a direct invitation to war—all this should be still only too fresh in our memories; yet an astonishing number of politicians, not to mention the millions of common men, seem determined to commit the same errors, and re-live the same tragedy again.

'From the danger of war one cannot protect oneself by weapons, one can achieve this only by moving forward into a new world of law. . . . Armaments cannot be fought by piling up armaments; that would be like getting Beelzebub to drive out the Devil.'

This sound like a speech by Mr. Aneurin Bevan in 1953. In fact it is a speech by Mr. Clement Attlee, delivered on 11th March, 1935 in the House of Commons in protest against the Government's proposal of a modest increase in rearmament.* When he suggested 'disbanding the national armies' as a brilliant idea to save peace, he was interrupted by shouts 'Tell that to Hitler'. He brushed the interruption aside, as Mr. Bevan brushes similar irrelevancies aside eighteen years later. In the same year, 1935, a 'Peace Ballot' obtained eleven million signatures in England—more than half the English electorate. All this is forgotten today, repressed and relegated to the political subconscious.

Even the slogans by which the aggressor hypnotised the victim were the same. Hitler sponsored Peace Congresses of German and French war veterans who protested against the conspiracy of the 'cannon merchants' and the pluto-democratic warmongers of Wall Street. Anti-Nazi refugees who talked about Hitler's concentration camps and aggressive intentions were regarded as atrocity-mongers, persecution maniacs, and fomenters of hatred between nations, as their successors, Russian refugees and ex-Communists, are regarded today. If only the Cassandras and Jeremiahs would shut up, all would be well! After each act of aggression, Hitler made a gesture of peace which was as eagerly taken at face value as are similar gestures by Stalin and Malenkov; men who warned against

* Obviously, one could find similar statements by Conservative spokesmen of other periods.

such gullibility were accused of deliberately sabotaging the chances of peaceful settlement. When Hitler marched into the Rhineland (and immediately afterwards offered a twenty-five years' peace pact), the French Prime Minister came to London, and had the same type of welcome that American generals have nowadays in France. Detached political experts who did not like the Nazi régime warned against exaggerating its dangers by pointing out that the Germans only wanted to annex German territories such as the Rhineland and the Saar, but were 'far too intelligent' to swallow a foreign body like Czechoslovakia, which they could never digest. Since 1945, we hear precisely the same argument regarding Russia's intentions in Central and Western Europe.

The result of all this was that by 1936 the Belgians, Rumannians, Yugoslavs, etc., had become 'neutralists' and the system of collective security disintegrated as N.A.T.O. is disintegrating today.

The neurotic who each time commits the same type of error and each time hopes to get away with it is not stupid; he is just ill.

Some Minor Aberrations

For nearly every aberration of the sexual drive we can find a corresponding type of disturbance of the political libido. I shall mention only a few of the most prevalent patterns of political neurosis.

A person may both love and hate another person, and experience these emotions either simultaneously or in alternation—as in the case of temperamental couples, or of difficult child-parent relations. A typically ambivalent relationship of this kind exists between Britain and the U.S.A. Americans both love and deride English aristocrats, fashions, accents, and the stuffiness of British traditions in general. The British, for different reasons, view America with equally mixed feelings of admiration and mockery, envy and contempt. About once in every six months Anglo-American relations get poisoned and there is a minor crisis—mostly caused, not by any real conflict of interests, but by the mutual exasperation typical in an ambivalent partnership.

It also happens in neurotic case-histories that an emotion is succeeded in a lasting fashion by its opposite: blind infatuation by blind hatred, fervent admiration by shuddering revulsion. Many ex-Communists, ex-Catholics, and ex-patriates fall into this attitude of the disappointed lover towards the party, church, or country which once meant everything to them.

Fetishism

In psychiatric parlance, this means an aberration whereby the sexual instinct becomes attached to a symbol, or accessory, or part, of its natural object. Women's locks, or corsets, or riding-boots, may become the object of fetishist worship. The same fate may befall the political libido.

The fetish-character of such symbols as flags, uniforms, emblems, songs, and anthems is too obvious to need emphasis. In an equally obvious way, propaganda exploits such characteristic features as Hitler's forelock, Churchill's cigar, Stalin's high-necked tunic. Though the existence of such mass-infatuations is known, they are rarely recognised as the pathological symptoms they are. They not only mean a regression to primitive idolatry and totem-worship, but also that the symbol or part which has become the object of the fetishist cult replaces the thing which it stands for, and thus deflects the social energy from its original aim. The political drive of millions of idealists who started on the quest for a better world has thus been perverted, the striving for progress turned into worship of 'the Party', which is no longer regarded as an accessory to the original purpose, but as an object of worship in its own right.

Eternal Adolescents

The young radical intellectual of Bloomsbury, St. Germain des Près, or Greenwich Village is a relatively harmless type. Often his radicalism is derived from adolescent revolt against the parents, or some other stereotyped conflict which makes him temporarily despair of the world. But some of the young radicals never grow up; they remain the eternal adolescents of the Left.

One variety of this type is frequently found both in the

United States and in France, though rarely in England.
Young X starts as an enthusiastic Communist, is soon disillusioned, founds a Trotskyite opposition group of ten people,
discovers that six out of the ten form a secret 'opposition *bloc*'
within the group, is disillusioned, founds a 'little mag' with a
hundred per cent anti-capitalist, anti-Stalinist, anti-pacifist
programme, goes bankrupt, starts a new little mag, and so on.
All his struggles, polemics, victories, and defeats are storms in
a teacup, confined to the same small circle of radical intellectuals—a kind of family which thrives on quarrels and mutual
denunciations, and yet coheres by virtue of some unique
dialectical glue. A classic example is the group of Marxist-
Existentialists around Sartre's *Les Temps Modernes*, with their
perennial quarrels and schisms. The sectarian may be said to
suffer from the *incestuous* type of political libido.

A different type is Y, the busybody, whose name is on every
'progressive' committee, whose voice is raised in protest against
every injustice, who has embraced every good cause under the
sun, and has never achieved anything on earth. Y is the
political equivalent of a *nymphomaniac*; he suffers from an excess
of political libido. This kind of neurosis, too, flourishes chiefly
in the climate of the Left—for, generally speaking, the Left is
politically over-sexed.

Finally there is Z, the political *masochist*. With him, the
parable of the mote and the beam has been reversed. The
slightest injustice in his own country wrings from him cries of
anguish and despair, but he finds excuses for the most heinous
crimes committed in the opposite camp. When a coloured
tennis-player is refused a room in a London luxury hotel, Z
quivers with spontaneous indignation; when millions spit out
their lungs in Soviet Arctic mines and lumber-camps, Z's
sensitive conscience is silent. Z is an inverted patriot, whose
self-hatred and craving for self-punishment has turned into
hatred for his country or social class, and a yearning for the
whip that will scourge it.

The Desire to Belong

It is truism of psychiatry that nobody is perfectly sane. The difference between a normal person and a neurotic is a difference in degree, not in kind. But in specific periods of history, the social and cultural climate favours specific trends towards neurosis and aberration. In golden-age Greece, male homosexuality was an almost general phenomenon. In the 1920s, promiscuity reached unprecedented proportions. The political libido has similar ups and downs, ranging from relative normality to near-insanity. For a considerable time now we have been witnessing a steady deterioration towards the latter.

The possible causes of this process can only be briefly alluded to. While the sexual drive serves to perpetuate the race, the political libido represents the individual's urge to identify himself with an idea, or a set of values embodied in a community—in other words, his need 'to belong'. Both are basic human instincts, though !during the last few decades the importance of the second has been somewhat obscured by the Freudians' exclusive emphasis on the first.

In medieval days, despite wars, famines, and epidemics, man lived in a relatively stable universe. The formidable authority of the church, the fixed hierarchy of the medieval state, the belief in providence and divine justice, gave people a feeling of security and belonging. Then came a series of earthquakes, starting with the Renaissance, continued during the Reformation, and culminating in the French and Russian Revolutions, which gradually but completely shattered man's outlook on society and the universe. Medieval life had been regulated by unchallengeable commands, each ending with an exclamation mark; now all these were turned into question marks. The whole earth, formerly the stable centre of the universe, was transformed into a swirling experimental laboratory; values crumbled, ties snapped, the political libido of man was turned loose like an adolescent's erotic cravings. But up to this day the quest for a new, comprehensive order and creed which would embrace man's relations *both* to the universe and to society, has remained without result. Twentieth-century man is a political neurotic because he has no answer to the question of the meaning of life, because socially and metaphysically he does not know where he 'belongs'.

According to circumstances, a frustrated instinct may mani-

fest itself in a great variety of forms, and contradictory
symptoms are often found in the same person. Prolonged
frustration and defeat may lead to an atrophy of the instinct—
the patient becomes socially apathetic, his disappointments
turn into political cynicism and anti-social behaviour.
Symptoms of this process, of the political libido turning sour,
can be most strikingly observed in contemporary France.

Even more dangerous is the opposite process. The unfulfilled
urge 'to belong' may lead to 'political oversexedness', expressing itself in blind, self-sacrificing devotion to some unholy
cause. In our age those who felt most deeply that paradise was
lost, were the first to be attracted by the *ersatz*-kingdoms of
heaven: the World Revolution, Soviet Russia, or the Thou-
sand-Year-Reich. In psychiatric language, they developed
'fixations' of their political libido towards these gory substitutes
for Utopia.

All this does not mean that one should underestimate the
importance of economic factors and social pressures. No psychiatrist can cure poverty and disease among the vast populations of Asia. But the crucial point is that before the economic
needs of people express themselves in political action, a mental
process intervenes; and this mental process, as often as not,
initiates action directly *opposed* to the original need. The
optimistic thinkers of the nineteenth century thought that, by
and large, the actions of the masses coincided with their
interests; the twentieth century reminded us that even highly
civilised people like the Germans are capable of committing
collective suicide, driven by some neurotic obsession, and
regardless of economic reality.

Reasoning alone does not help against such obsessions. It is
in the nature of totalitarian creeds that they provide the
believer with emotional saturation, a complete experience of
belonging. Politicians are supposed to have a smattering of
history and economics; it is time they were obliged to learn the
elements of psychology, and to study the strange mental forces
which compel people to act with such stubborn determination
against their proper interests.

The Trail of the Dinosaur

L ET us imagine a kind of temperature-chart on which the growing power of *homo sapiens* over his environment is represented by a curve. For something of the order of half a million years, from Java Man to about 5000 B.C., the curve would remain nearly static, represented by a roughly horizontal line. With the invention of the pulley, the lever, and a few simple mechanical devices, the muscular strength of man would appear amplified, say, fivefold; after that, the curve would again remain nearly horizontal for the next five or six thousand years. But in the course of the last three hundred years, the curve would, for the first time in the history of the species, rise steeply in leaps and bounds, until it pointed almost vertically upward. To draw this chart true to scale, we would have to use graph paper several miles long; even so we would have only an inch or less of the paper left to plot the sudden, dramatic lifting of the curve's head—like a cobra stabbing upward.

Another, more specific chart, representing the destructive potentialities of the growth of power, would look even more dramatic—one merely has to remember that after the first world war, only forty years ago, statisticians reckoned that on the average ten thousand rifle bullets or ten artillery shells were needed to kill one enemy soldier.

Now let us contrast these two charts with a third one, on which we plot the progress of the species Man in moral philosophy, in cosmic awareness and spiritual clarity. This curve will show a slow rise during the prehistoric miles of nearly-flat stretch; then, when the Power-curve (P) starts rising, the Spiritual curve (S) will begin to undulate with indecisive ups and downs; finally, on the last, dramatic one-millionth part of the chart, where the P-curve shoots skyward with insane acceleration, the S-curve goes into a steep decline. The spiritual void at the end of the chart is less obvious than the accumulation of power: I shall come back to the 'S-curve' later on.

The point of these imaginary charts is that they show a very unusual type of curve, a geometrical freak which forces us to measure time at first in units of hundred thousands, then of thousands of years, then in centuries and decades until, towards the end, a single year weighs more than ten thousand years did before. A process which, once past a critical limit, shows this type of catastrophic acceleration, is called, in Physics, an explosion. A dispassionate observer from another world, to whom centuries are as seconds, able to survey the whole curve in one sweep, would have to come to the conclusion that our civilisation is either on the verge of, or in the process of, exploding.

I would like to labour the geometrical aspect of human evolution a little further by suggesting two more curves, the first representing progress in communication (C), the second, progress in understanding (U). The C-curve, which would comprise travel, and communication by visual and acoustic means, would again remain nearly flat for aeons; then, with the invention of the printing press, the steamship, railway, motor car, gramophone, telegraph, telephone, cinema, aeroplane, radio, video, radar and jukebox (all, except for the printing press, crowded into a single century) the curve would rise steeply to near-saturation—the point where the whole surface of the planet is visually and acoustically interconnected. One should have expected that this shrinking of the terrestrial surface in terms of communication would lead to a proportionate increase in its intellectual cohesion; but this did not happen. The shrinking of the distance between nations did not bring them 'nearer' to each other; three-dimensional travel did not abolish Chinese Walls and Iron Curtains, but merely extended them into atmospheric space; the unifying medium of the aether was split up by censorship and jamming. Even between such close neighbours and allies as the people of England and France, mutual comprehension and human sympathy is not markedly greater now than at a time when they were days, instead of hours, apart.

Nor did the extension of the range of the sense-organs through radio and television increase the intellectual range of the human mind, its powers of abstraction and synthesis. It seems rather that the reverse is true: that the stupendous amplification of vision and hearing caused a rapid deterioration of the intellectual and moral content of communication. In the new generation born into the age of television, not only the habit of reading, but the faculty of thinking in abstract, conceptual terms seems to be weakened by the child's conditioning to easier and more primitive forms of visual perception. The dangers of this regression from the conceptual to the perceptual, from abstract language to picture-strip language, are less obvious and immediate, but in the long run no less grave, than the spectacular increase in destructive power.

To sum up, our diagrams show an unprecedented increase in the range and power of the species' sensory and motor organs, coincident with a marked deterioration of the integrative functions which determine spiritual maturity and social ethics. There are frequent instances in history of moral slumps followed by a new upward trend; the alarming thing is the coincidence of a period of unprecedented spiritual decline with an equally unprecedented increase of power. The Promethean myth seems to be coming true with a horrible twist: the giant reaching out to steal the lightning from the gods is morally insane. Hence the difficulty as Betrand Russell wrote a few years ago, 'to persuade mankind to acquiesce in its own survival'.

2

Any attempt at such persuasion must take both the short-term and the long-term aspects of the situation into account. The first is political, the second transcendental in nature; and the two interact more directly than we realise. The politician unaware of the transcendental background of the crisis can offer only makeshift measures; and the saint who remains aloof in an emergency sins by omission.

On the level of practical policy, it is essential to distinguish between the desirable and the possible. We know by now that atomic war would be tantamount to a collective suicide of the species. To abolish the threat of atomic war is certainly desirable, but not in the realm of the possible. The banning of atomic weapons can only be effective if both parties agree to international supervision under conditions which include permanent inspection—the throwing open of the locked doors of secret laboratories, factories, plants, mines and military installations. But such a policy runs counter to the tradition of secrecy and distrust which Russia and the Asiatic nations have practised for centuries past; and it also runs counter to the basic principles and political structure of all dictatorial régimes, Communist or other. A dictatorship that accepted democratic controls, internally or internationally, would cease to be a dictatorship. The Chinese Wall and the Iron Curtain are not accidents of history, but massive symbols of national traditions and social régimes whose existence depends on their ability to block the movement of people and ideas.

Even if the present rulers of Russia desired to submit to genuine international control and inspection, they could not afford to do so any more than they could afford to abolish censorship, the one-party system, the political police and other essential requisites of dictatorship. Whether the dictatorship is good or bad, whether it is a dictatorship of the workers, peasants or dentists, of a bureaucracy or a theocracy, is irrelevant in this context.

It is equally irrelevant under what pretexts the Soviet Government evades the issue of genuine inspection and control—whether by procedural subterfuges, or by rejecting 'infringements of national sovereignty', or by spurious peace campaigns and the demand for a platonic ban on atomic weapons which would work against the side that manufactures and tests its bombs openly, and which would set a premium on secrecy. Oak Ridge, Harwell, Bikini, are widely discussed subjects in the West, while the corresponding places and events in the East are shrouded in complete secrecy.

I repeat: the abolition of atomic weapons under effective international control is entirely desirable, and by the nature of things just as impossible as it proved impossible to enforce disarmament in the defunct League of Nations' days. From this realistic starting point, three courses are open to the West. To continue developing nuclear weapons in full awareness of the danger to the human species; to renounce nuclear weapons one-sidedly, in full awareness of the decisive advantage thereby accorded to the opponent; or, finally, to start a 'preventive' war (which is of course a contradiction in terms), based on the assumption that the West still possesses a decisive superiority in atomic weapons, that this advantage is being lost, and that war at the present level of atomic developments would be less devastating than war in five or ten years' time and would impose a lasting peace on a unified world.

The third possibility we must reject out of hand, on the grounds that it is based on the old Ends and Means fallacy (cf. 'The Challenge of our Time'). All social progress, all human justice, requires a certain amount of ruthlessness; all surgical cures, the infliction of a certain amount of pain. But this justification of the means by the end is confined to very narrow limits, to situations where all the factors are of a manageable order and the results predictable with reasonable certainty—otherwise 'the surgeon's lancet turns into the butcher's hatchet'. With regard to preventive war, none of the above conditions is present. The amount of damage that would be inflicted on humanity is incalculable, the factors in the equation are unmanageable, and the results unpredictable. Even on the inadmissible premise that morality should be sacrificed to expediency, and the present generation sacrificed in the interest of future ones—even on these premises preventive war must be ruled out on the grounds that the magnitude and complexity of factors are beyond the computing capacity of the human brain.

Unfortunately, the premises that we reject are not rejected by the philosophy of dialectical materialism which is the *credo* of our opponents; and our scepticism regarding the limits of man's ability as a computing machine, is not shared by them.

Thus the possibility that our opponents may start 'preventive' war at a moment which they judge 'historically favourable' and under any convenient pretext, cannot be ruled out.

I would like to make this point clearer. In the previous paragraph I was not concerned with the question whether certain members of the Politbureau think it practicable to start a war in six months or six years, or whether they think that the inevitable Communist World-State can be realised without war. My point was that their philosophical approach to, and their terms of reference regarding, the problem of war are different from ours. The West has no unified philosophy, but it has a long and continuous ethical tradition which more or less articulately, more or less consciously, permeates the thinking of both leaders and people and limits the formers' freedom of action. The leaders of the other side are not subject to such limitations either by the philosophy to which they adhere, or by the machinery of democratic control. It is an unequal contest where one side believes in its historic mission which justifies all means including war, whereas the other does not; where one party is bound by certain rules of the game, the other party is not.

This difference ought to be constantly present to the mind of all responsible politicians, Left or Right, and guide their decisions, large and small. But psychologically, this is a rather difficult thing to ask for, because the tactical oscillations of Soviet policy, the occasional easing of surface tensions, and the frequent unmannerliness of American politicians, tend to obscure and blur the basic difference in philosophy. Wishful thinking, infatuation with pious platitudes, and the tempting road of least resistance are constantly lessening the West's chances of survival.

3

Marxist theory teaches that the proletariat must exploit to the full the constitutional freedoms which bourgeois democracy is obliged to grant (for the bourgeoisie is bound to be 'its own gravedigger') until an 'objectively revolutionary situation' occurs. At that moment the proletariat will rise and inter its

opponents in their self-prepared grave. *Mutatis mutandis* the
same theory applies to the international scene, where the
notion of the 'objectively revolutionary situation' is replaced by
the 'historically favourable situation' for adding another vassal
nation to the existing ones. One-sided atomic disarmament
would automatically create a 'historically favourable situation'
for Russia's bid to unify the world after its own fashion in the
interest of mankind.

There is nothing new about the argument that the only
deterrent against atomic aggression is an atomic stockpile. But
there is a new development regarding the value of an atomic
stockpile against non-atomic, local aggression. The theory that
the atomic superiority of the West could prevent local aggression by the threat of massive retaliation has become obsolete
for two reasons: firstly, Western atomic superiority is on the
wane; secondly, the destructive power of the new weapons is
now so monstrous that the punishment of limited and camouflaged aggression by the unleashing of open atomic war has
become politically and morally impossible. A policeman,
armed with an atom bomb and nothing else, could not prevent
the escape of a couple of housebreakers without blowing the
whole town to glory, himself included. We are faced with a
new paradox: the superior power of a weapon may reduce its
bearer to helplessness.

The policeman's part is made even more difficult by the fact
that political crimes are easier to camouflage than common
burglaries. Russia has conquered one half of Europe and a
large portion of Asia through acts of aggression in varying
disguises of varying plausibility, none of which presented a
clear-cut *casus belli*. The possibilities of veiled aggression are
inexhaustible; and it is unrealistic to believe that we can stop
it by the threat of 'massive retaliation'—which, if taken
seriously, would mean that we ought to have reacted to the
defenestration of Masaryk, or ought to react to the next
People's Rising in Afghanistan, by unleashing the nuclear
nightmare.

The upshot of this argument is that policing the world and
guaranteeing collective security never was, and never will be,
possible through reliance on the West's industrial superiority

and dreams of push-button retaliation. To put it in a nutshell: *atomic weapons are necessary as a deterrent against atomic aggression, but ineffective as a deterrent against local and camouflaged aggression.* The security of our streets cannot be guaranteed by tanks, only by police constables in sufficient numbers, armed with conventional weapons to cope with conventional ¡crimes. The practical conclusions are distressingly simple. The most conventional of all weapons, and the one which no nation can dispense with, is a people determined to fight on the beaches and to fight in the streets in defence of their freedom. However brave they are, they will never be able to stand up against an aggressor using the methods of total war. But if they are strong enough, and brave enough, they will survive because of the aggressor's reluctance to engage in open, total war. The oft-heard argument: 'What is the good of arming a few more divisions when we know that in the case of a showdown Europe cannot be defended anyway?' is both cowardly and false. Any European Defence Community can never aim at more than to make Europe unconquerable *short of total war.* But it can never aim at less than this. If, in the early post-war period, Czechoslovakia and Poland had been equipped with the number of divisions and the unbroken spirit of Finland in 1939, the Russians could not have deposed the Polish Government, nor pulled their Prague *coup.* They would have been forced to show their hand and engage in open warfare—and the odds are that they would not have dared to take the risk. It is indeed distressingly simple: free men must be prepared to defend their freedom or lose it.

4

The rearming of Western Germany is a side-issue which will probably be settled by the time this appears in print; but the passions raised by it will persist for some time and be exploited by the conscious and unconscious enemies of Western survival. The emotional resistance of the former victims of German militarism is understandable, but unfortunately beside the point; without German divisions Europe cannot be defended. The fear that the rearming of Western Germany may lead to a repetition of 1914 and 1939, reflects a humiliating inferiority complex and implies that Europe and the United States will repeat the mistakes which made German aggression possible. If the Atlantic Community cannot trust itself to keep under control a limited number of German divisions under unified command, then it has no chance to survive. It would of course be much preferable to have a European Army united 'at the base', not 'at the top'. A quasi pan-European army with a pan-European spirit and flag is, I believe, not only desirable, but still in the realm of the possible.

5

At the beginning of this essay, I made a distinction between the short-term and long-term aspects of the present crisis. All that I have said so far, refers to the short-term aspect and to short-term measures. The best we can hope to achieve by these measures is to gain time. Even if courage and reason prevail to a much greater extent than in recent years, the result cannot be more than a strategic and economic patchwork on a divided planet.

And yet by gaining time, by prolonging this misery of co-existence, mankind may hope for a reprieve. The nature of this tenuous hope I have tried to explain in 'An Outgrown Dilemma'. It is based on the possibility of some unexpected mutation in man's dominating passions and interests. Whenever history became polarised between two competing power-centres, roughly one of two things happened. Either one of the contestants was subjugated (the Rome-versus-Carthage pattern); or a stalemate was reached (the Christianity-versus-Islam pattern). Such stalemates have always started as unstable and precarious forms of 'co-existence', spotted with local outbreaks which threatened to grow into a total conflict. But under certain favourable conditions the stalemate became a permanent one, co-existence gradually changed into collaboration, and the crisis was over.

The conditions for this to happen are partly of a physical, partly of a psychological nature. The physical basis of the stalemate is balance of power, both 'central' and 'peripheral'.

By 'central' power I mean the total strength which each side would be capable of throwing into a total showdown, and which acts as a mutual deterrent from risking such a showdown. By 'peripheral' strength I mean the physical and moral capacity of exposed outposts and enclaves to defend themselves and hold out, if only for a limited time. This 'peripheral' strength is essential to the balance, because it makes the potential aggressor realise that he cannot have his way *in a swift and discreet manner*, and thus multiplies the risks attached to aggression. The Christian enclaves in Jaffa and Acre during the Crusades, the Protestant enclaves in Catholic countries and *vice versa* after the Thirty Years War, seem to prove that a stalemate may extend to the oddest geographical patchwork if the above-mentioned conditions are fulfilled. The Night of St. Bartholomew carries such vivid memories because it was an exception, and not the rule. On the other hand, the fate of the Jewish minorites in Europe, and of the Armenian enclaves in Turkey, was a kind of St. Bartholomew in permanence, because there was neither a 'central' power nor any peripheral strength to defend them.

However, a stalemate based on the balance of physical power is in itself not enough to prevent an ultimate showdown. The second condition is a change of the spiritual climate, a spontaneous mutation of interest, which blunts the horns of the dilemma. While the process of polarisation is at its height, it looks as if the whole world must either go Moslem or Christian, either Catholic or Protestant, either Monarchist or Republican, either Socialist or Capitalist. But if the deadlock lasts long enough, an unexpected mutation of the mass-mind may occur, the inevitable choice no longer appears inevitable, passion drains away and people simply become interested in something else. Religious consciousness yields to national consciousness, the fight for space to the fight for markets, the struggle between 'Left' and 'Right' to the struggle between East and West. The word 'heretic' has now gone into metaphorical use, but once it meant torture and the stake; and whether we live under a King or a President, is the least of our worries. Over and again it happened in history that the dynamo which generates the light and the sparks was switched off just before the fuses blew.

But in order that this may happen, some new dynamo must enter into action producing a different type of current, a shift of interest to a different set of values, conflicts and predicaments.

Every branch of human activity—literature, the arts, philosophy, even medicine—seems to be subject to these unpredictable periodic mutations; see the sudden shifts of emphasis in painting from narrative to composition, from contour to surface, from the sculptural to the dynamic, from representational to geometrical. It is not fashion that changes but the focus of the eye and the mind, concentrating its attention on different aspects, in due turn, of the complex entity, man—religious man, economic man, *homo politicus, homo faber, homo liber*.

One of these changes of spiritual climate, which is of particular relevance to us, seems to have occurred somewhere half-way through the Thirty Years War. I am quoting from Miss Wedgewood's classic work on the subject:*

'Never had the Churches seemed stronger than in the opening decades of the seventeenth century. Yet a single generation was to witness their deposition from political dominance. The tragic results of applied religion had discredited the Churches as the directors of the State. A new emotional urge had to be found to fill the place of spiritual conviction; national feeling welled up to fill the gap. The terms Protestant and Catholic gradually lose their vigour, the terms German, Frenchman, Swede, assume a gathering menace. A new standard of right and wrong came into the political world. Insensibly and rapidly after that, the Cross gave place to the flag, and the "Sancta Maria" cry of the White Hill to the "Viva España" of Nördlingen.'

Admittedly, by the time this great change came into the world, the war had run half its course and taken its toll of death and devastation; and it took another thirteen years to end. But perhaps the Russian conquest of Eastern Europe and the wars in Greece, China, Korea and Indo-China constitute the first half of our thirty years' war; and perhaps the second half need not be repeated—at least it may be argued, that the

* C. V. Wedgewood: *The Thirty Years War*, London, 1938.

conflict between Bourbon and Hapsburg had little relation to the original religious issue.

6

The age of religious conflict was superseded in the course of the seventeenth century by the emergence of two apparently unrelated factors: the rise of national consciousness, and the rise of a new philosophy. The latter, based on the discoveries of Copernicus, Galileo and Kepler, was gradually penetrating wider and wider strata of the public mind. If the earth no longer stood firmly planted by God in the centre of His universe, and was merely a small planet hurtling through space, then, though religious belief did survive, it could no longer command the exclusive interest of man. The sky around him had remained the same, but the focus of his eyes had radically changed since he had learnt that the fixed stars of the firmament did not dance attendance to him, and were blinking down with detached irony at the tiny creature on his spinning cannon ball. Within a century, more or less, the mind of European man had undergone a mutation more radical and fraught with consequences than if he had acquired a third eye or an additional limb.

It was a historic turning-point—the point where religion and science, religion and art, logics and ethics, began to part company and go their own separate ways. From the beginnings of civilised life, man's fate had been determined, and his conscience guided, by some super-human agency; from now on this function was taken over by sub-human agencies. The deities of the past may have been coarse or sublime, scandalous Olympians or a pure God of love; yet they were wiser, more powerful and on a higher plane of existence than man himself. The new determinants of man's fate—mechanical laws, atoms, glands, genes—which gradually took over, were of a lower order than man himself; they defined his condition but could provide no guidance whatsoever for his conscience.

The consequences of this shift of 'destiny from above' to 'destiny from below'* became only gradually apparent. Before

* Cf. *The Yogi and the Commissar*. London, 1945, p. 227 et seq.

the shift, the various religions had provided man with explanations of a kind which gave to everything that happened to him meaning in the wider sense of a transcendental causality and a transcendental justice. But the explanations of the new philosophy were devoid of meaning in this wider sense. The answers of the past had been varied, contradictory, primitive, superstitious or whatever one likes to call them, but they had been firm, definite, imperative. They satisfied, at least for a given time and culture, man's need for reassurance and protection in an unfathomably cruel world, for some guidance in his perplexities. The new answers, to quote William James, 'made it impossible to find in the driftings of the cosmic atoms, whether they work on the universal or on the particular scale, anything but a kind of aimless weather, doing and undoing, achieving no proper history, and leaving no result'.* In a word, the old explanations, with all their arbitrariness and patchiness, answered the question after 'the meaning of life' whereas the new explanations, with all their precision, made the question of meaning itself meaningless.

Our thinking habits are so entirely conditioned by post-Copernican developments that we automatically assume thinking always to have followed the same method. We take the ethical neutrality of our 'natural laws', the split between 'religious' and 'scientific' truth so much for granted that we assume they must have always existed. It requires a great imaginative effort to realise the full significance of the 'shift of destiny' of three hundred years ago; and that it constitutes a new departure, a break in the curve of man's spiritual evolution as unprecedented and unique as the sudden vertiginous rise of his physical power. We don't know how many tens of thousand years ago man for the first time asked the question about the meaning of life; but we do know at what point, so close to us in time, he lost the answer to it.

7

For a long time the majority of mankind remained unaware of the implications of the new philosophy. Its pioneers talked

* William James, *The Varieties of Religious Experience*.

in a timid and tentative voice, without quite realising what they were saying and doing to the mind of man, and often frightened of facing the consequences of their own theories. There were exceptions, men far-sighted enough to realise that the twilight of the gods was at hand, and foolish enough to shout it from the tree-tops—like that *enfant terrible*, Giordano Bruno, the Bertrand Russell of his age, who was burned alive. But when Copernicus set the earth spinning, he did so with a timid and apologetic gesture; Kepler saved his faith by declaring that God was a mathematician by profession; Galileo's career was a life-long walk on a tight-rope; Newton wrote a treatise on the locations of Paradise and Hell; and at the end of the long chain Professor Toynbee claimed that the Catholic Church, possessing the ultimate truth, was quasi-exempt from the laws of history.*

Thus the new philosophy, with the exception of some of its more brutal propounders in the eighteenth and nineteenth centuries, made no frontal attack on religious beliefs; but it gradually undermined their foundations, on which all previous civilisations had been based. In the old days, man hoped to influence, through magic and prayer, the superior powers which decided his fate; now he could manipulate the mechanical components of his destiny, glands and humours, atoms and genes, and determine his own determinants. Prayer did not fall into disuse but its function, the influencing of fate, was taken over by the laboratories. Slowly but inevitably, divine providence was replaced by the drift of cosmic weather, ethical guidance by the ethical neutrality of science, humility before the supernatural by a feeling of arrogant, unlimited power.

Religion did not die, nor was it driven underground by the new philosophy—it was merely relegated to an airtight compartment of the mind, and sealed off from contact with logical reasoning. The incompatibility between the two halves of the split mind was smoothed over by the Churches' diplomatic appeasement of Science, and by the believers' psychological resistance against admitting the split. Yet in spite of these mental shock-absorbers, religion gradually lost its power,

* *Civilization on Trial*, London, 1948, p. 238 ff. More recently, Professor Toynbee seems to have changed his view on this point.

became brittle and fragmentary; once the controlling force of daily life, it became a spiritual luxury. The 'oceanic feeling' could no longer fill man's horizon; it was preserved in a neat reservoir whose level kept steadily falling through drainage, leaks and evaporation.

Life was so exciting during these hectic, unprecedented centuries, that man did not realise what was happening to him. The navel cord through which he received his spiritual nourishment was shrivelling up, but there were plastic substitutes for it, and various forms of artificial nourishment. For a while the words *Liberté, Egalité, Fraternité*, produced a new magic, a seemingly apt substitute for the holy Trinity. There were breathtaking attempts to create a Humanist creed, and attempts to worship the Goddess of Reason; political movements and secular religions succeeded each other, exerting their immensely dynamic, but short-lived, appeal. The vertiginous rise of the power-curve was accompanied by mass-upheavals, ideological crusades and fanatical pursuits of Utopian mirages. Each of them promised a secular millennium, born out of a revolutionary apocalypse. Yet all the time, throughout these toxic excesses and spurious illuminations, there was a muffled feeling of uneasiness, of growing frustration, of spiritual desiccation. The explanations of science became more and more formal, non-committal and meaningless as answers to man's eternal question. As his science grew more abstract his art became more esoteric, and his pleasures more chemical. In the end he was left with nothing but 'an abstract heaven over a naked rock'.

8

With the beginning of the twentieth century, signs appeared which seemed to indicate an impeding turn of the tide. The descendants of Galileo and Newton found that they had been too optimistic in believing that the universe could be reduced to a mechanical model. The perfected measuring instruments signalled the presence of quantities and processes which not only eluded measurement, but by their very nature would always elude it. At nearly the same time, similar crises broke out in the other sciences: cosomology, biology, genetics, psychology. Physical determinism was shaken, rigid causality yielded to the elastic laws of probability; science had to admit that it can never predict, only guess, what will happen next. The living whole asserted its primacy over the measurable aspects of the parts; medicine had to lay increasing stress on the power of mind over matter. The most fashionable school of psychotherapy reverted to the Jamesian view that a trans-cendental faith was a biological necessity for man and that 'the total absence of it leads to collapse'—the dark, feverish night of the soul.

Slowly, hesitatingly, the pendulum seemed to start swinging back; man seemed to be getting ready for a new shift of focus, a new mutation. But so far this has failed to materialise; and all attempts at a spiritual revival within the framework of the established Churches proved artificial and abortive. History may move in a spiral, but it never moves in circles, never returns to a previous point of departure. The physicist who has witnessed the collapse of his mechanical model of the universe has become a humbler and wiser man, but he cannot be expected to return to Aristotle's four elements and to Ptolemy's sky rotating on hollow crystal spheres; nor will the physician, who has learnt to accept his limitations as a healer, revert to a pre-Harveian view of the body. Yet the established Churches demand from all of us who shiver in the darkness, precisely that kind of intellectual suicide and surrender of the critical faculties. To ask twentieth-century man to believe in a loving God who condemns half his children to eternal damnation without hope of an amnesty, is really a bit thick. The reassur-ing statements of some modern theologians that Hell does exist but is empty, or that it merely means exclusion from grace without overheating, are hardly on a more adult level; and Mr. Greene's defence of the bodily ascent of the Virgin in the pages of *Life* Magazine would embarrass even a saint. John Donne's 'with a great, sober thirst my soule attends' was the statement of a perennial faith in the language of his time; 'The Cocktail Party' in 'The Living Room' is a parody of it.*

* Note to Danube Edition: titles of religiously inspired plays by T. S. Eliot and Graham Greene respectively, which were much discussed at the time.

Perhaps if Luther had been born after Newton, the gulf between faith and reason would be less disastrous. As it is, the established Churches are venerable anachronisms. They are capable of giving a limited number of individuals a limited reassurance and a limited, sporadic uplift; but the Sunday driver does not answer the need for public transportation, and a Sunday faith is no answer to the peril threatening our race. We may postpone the atomic Sodom for a few years, but we cannot indefinitely prevent it. Only a radical change of the spiritual climate could prevent it.

Unfortunately, changes of this kind, the next mutation, the next jump ahead, are not only unpredictable but beyond the power of imagination. The causes which lead to these extra-ordinary transformations of the global mood—the springtide of Christianity, the ground-swell of the Renaissance, the hurricane age of Science—are equally obscure, even in retro-spect. Hegel's dialectic, Spengler's cycles, Toynbee's challenge-and-response patterns are beautiful prophecies in reverse—and as doubtful as all prophecies are, though they merely predict the past. The more we realise the infinite complexity of historic causation, the Nostradamus-in-reverse character of all philosophies of History, the more helpless we feel in trying to predict the next mutation. We can point to certain analogies, abstract certain patterns from the Persian carpet, isolate certain trends and chart their curves; the rest is guesswork, hope and prayer.

My own guess and hope, which I have indicated before, is the spontaneous emergence of a new type of faith which satisfies the 'greater sober thirst' of man's spirit without asking him to split his brain into halves, which restores the navel cord through which he receives the saps of cosmic awareness with-out reducing him to mental infancy; which relegates reason to its proper humble place yet without contradicting it. It all sounds very vague and irreverent, partly because we can imagine the machines, but not the beliefs of the future, and partly because we have become so accustomed to religion occupying one half of the split mind, that the idea of restoring its unity appears blasphemous. Is it really too much to ask and hope for a religion whose content is perennial but not archaic,

which provides ethical guidance, teaches the lost art of contem-
plation, and restores contact with the supernatural without
requiring reason to abdicate?

Clearly, the devout will regard this question as presumptuous
and betraying a lack of comprehension for the revealed, or
symbolic, or mystic essence of faith, according to his notion of
it. 'After all,' he will say, with indignation, or contempt, or
pity, 'you cannot expect a religion made to measure like a suit,
to satisfy your specific requirements.' The answer, I submit in
all humility, is that the indignation of one's Catholic, Protestant, Jewish and Moslem friends mutually cancel out; and
secondly, that the objection is historically untrue. For every
culture and every age *did* have its faith 'cut to measure', and
did restate the perennial content of all religions on its own level,
and in its own language and symbols. It is neither an irreverent
nor an impossible hope that this will happen again in the
future. But it *is* impossible to turn back to the language and
symbols of a past epoch, of a mental climate which is no
longer ours.

9

My starting-point was an imaginary chart, which showed a
vertiginous rise of the power-curve coinciding with an equally
unprecedented decline of the spiritual curve of living faith. It
is this coincidence of the two curves which makes the present
crisis so grave, which makes us feel that we are travelling at
breakneck speed through the night with the throttle open at
full and the steering broken down.

The decline of the spiritual curve remained for a long time
hidden or obscured by more dramatic events; and its consequences have only become fully apparent in our day. When,
a century and a half ago, the sailors at Spithead and the Nore
started their famous mutiny, they took pains to assert their
loyalty to the King, and to point out that they were merely
rebelling against certain Admiralty rules. They continued to
take the supreme authority for granted, and regarded themselves as His Majesty's loyal rebels. In a similar manner, the
founders of new and reformers of old religions always took the

existence of God for granted; they all were the Lord's loyal heretics. This seems to hold true for any period of human culture as far back as the beam of History is able to penetrate into the dark, and as far up towards the present as the beginning of the eighteenth century. At this point, the unique break occurs. God is dethroned; and although the incognisant masses are tardy in realising the event, they feel the icy draught caused by that vacancy. Man enters upon a spiritual ice age; the established Churches can no longer provide more than Eskimo huts where their shivering flock huddles together, while the camp-fires of rival ideologies draw the masses in wild stampedes across the ice. Yet even this desolate state of affairs is preferable to the threat of the medicine men to remedy the climate by turning the frozen waste into a blazing furnace.

The horror of it is that they have the power to do it. If only half the official statements about the new nuclear and bacteriological weapons are true, then the next few decades, or the next half century at the outmost, will decide whether *homo sapiens* will go the way of the dinosaur, or mutate towards a stabler future.

We shall either destroy ourselves or take off to the stars. Perhaps the conquest of interplanetary space will cause a Copernican revolution in reverse, the emergence of a new type of cosmic consciousness. Perhaps the creation of artificial moons and similar toys will prove such an absorbing diversion that the old passions will be deflated, and their causes forgotten. Perhaps some unexpected discovery in the field of extrasensory perception will provide us with a new spiritual insight, a new basis for our metaphysical beliefs, a new intuition of our ultimate responsibilities.

All this is vague and wild speculation, yet less wild and fantastic than what will happen to man if the near-miracle fails to materialise and the giant mushrooms start sprouting into his sky and lungs. The trouble with all near-miracles, such as our ancestors rising on their hind legs, or the rise of the new star over Bethlehem, or Galileo's climbing the tower of Pisa, is the unpredictability of their timing. Once we hoped for Utopia, now, in a chastened mood, we can at best hope for

a reprieve; pray for time and play for time; for had the dinosaur learnt the art of prayer, the only sensible petition for him
would have been to go down on his scaly knees and beg 'Lord,
give me another chance'.

Reflections on Hanging

The Light of Lights
Looks always on the motive, not the deed,
The Shadow of Shadows on the deed alone.

W. B. YEATS

To the Memory of
ROY CALVERT

ACKNOWLEDGEMENTS

My grateful acknowledgements are due in the first place to the editors of *Hansard* from 1808 to the present; next, to the Parliamentary Select Committee on Capital Punishment of 1929–30 and the Royal Commission on Capital Punishment of 1949–53. These two monumental documents I regarded as the Old and the New Testament of my text, with the Select Committee Report of 1819 and the Royal Commission Report of 1866 playing the part of the Apocrypha. With one exception, their admirable and moderate recommendations were never implemented, the governments who appointed them having taken the view of the Pasha in a novel of Mr. P. H. Newby: 'Monsieur Perry is a fanatic. I can see that he is the sort of man who prepares a report and then thinks it ought to be carried out.' Next in documentary value come Leon Radzinowicz's *History of English Criminal Law* and Messrs. G. Gardiner's and N. Curtis-Raleigh's pioneer work on *The Judicial Attitude to Penal Reform*. I am indebted to Mr. C. H. Rolph for his advice on procedure at identification parades, and to Mrs. Cynthia Paterson Jefferies for her patient help with the manuscript and proofs.

Preface to the First Edition

In 1937, during the Civil War in Spain, I spent three months under sentence of death as a suspected spy, witnessing the executions of my fellow prisoners and awaiting my own. These three months left me with a vested interest in capital punishment—rather like 'half-hanged Smith', who was cut down after fifteen minutes and lived on. Each time a man's or a woman's neck is broken in this peaceful country, memory starts to fester like a badly healed wound. I shall never achieve real peace of mind until hanging is abolished.

I have stated my bias. It colours the arguments in the book; it does not affect the facts in it, and most of its content is factual. My intention was to write it in a cool and detached manner, but it came to naught; indignation and pity kept seeping in. This is perhaps just as well, for capital punishment is not merely a problem of statistics and expediency, but also of morality and feeling. Fair pleading requires that one's facts and figures should be right, that one should not distort or quote out of context; it does not exclude having one's heart and spleen in it.

Some of the learned friends who helped with the material for this book, warned me against offending certain venerable prejudices and traditional susceptibilities concerning judges and juries, the notion of a fair trial, the handling of the prerogative of mercy, and so on. I have disregarded their warnings because appeasement never pays, and because I believe that the case for abolition has been weakened by lack of outspokenness. Others advised silence regarding the physiological facts about executions, past and present. That amounts to saying that the Queen of Spain has no legs and the hanged man has no neck. We hang on an average one person each month; if this thing is done in the name of the people, they have a right to know what is being done.

The reason why, twenty years ago, I made the acquaintance of the condemned cell was the hopeful belief in the salvation of mankind by world revolution; this book aims, more modestly, at saving thirteen wretches a year the pain and terror of going through the same experience. Apart from that, there is also a larger issue involved, for the gallows is not merely a machine of death, but the oldest and most obscene symbol of that tendency in mankind which drives it towards moral self-destruction.

A.K.

London
  October 3rd, 1955

Part One

TRADITION AND PREJUDICE
I. The Heritage of the Past

The charge is prepar'd; the lawyers meet;
The Judges all rang'd (a terrible show!).

JOHN GAY: *The Beggar's Opera*

1. The Jack-in-the-Box

GREAT BRITAIN is that peculiar country in Europe where people drive on the left side of the road, measure in inches and yards, and hang people by the neck until dead. To most Britons it never occurs that there may be something odd about this custom. Every nation takes its traditions for granted, and hanging is as much part of the British tradition as counting in shillings and pence. Generations of children have squeaked with delight at the appearance of the puppet hangman in the Punch and Judy show. Four executioners are included in the *Dictionary of National Biography*; Jack Ketch, Calcraft, and 'William Boilman'* were as popular figures in their time as film-stars are today. There seems to be a jolliness about the procedure as if the victim twitching at the end of the rope were not a real person but a dummy burnt on Guy Fawkes' Day. The present hangman, Pierrepoint, runs a public house called 'Help the Poor Struggler'; his former assistant, Allenby, ran one called 'The Rope and the Anchor';[1] and the present Lord Chief Justice delighted a Royal Academy banquet with the story of a judge who, after passing sentence of death on three

* Nickname for the executioner, derived, according to Macaulay, from the custom of publicly boiling the entrails of traitors after they were disembowelled alive.

men, was welcomed by a band playing the Eton Boating
Song's refrain: 'We'll all swing together.' This was printed in
an amiable 'Profile' of Lord Goddard in *The Observer*,[2] which
continued:

> There is a story of his boyhood, which even though it be
> apocryphal, may illustrate the Goddard legend. When he
> first went to Marlborough, it was apparently a school cus-
> tom to make every new boy sing or recite in his dormitory.
> Called upon to sing, the future Lord Chief Justice is said to
> have surprised the other boys by chanting in a piping voice:
> 'You will be taken from here to a place of execution and
> hanged by the neck until you be dead. And may the Lord
> have mercy on your soul.'

It all goes to show that hanging has a kind of macabre
cosiness, like a slightly off-colour family joke, which only
foreigners, abolitionists and other humourless creatures are
unable to share. On November 2nd, 1950, Mr. Albert Pierrepoint was called to testify as a witness before the Royal
Commission on Capital Punishment. He was asked how many
people he had hanged in his career as an executioner, and
answered: 'Some hundreds.'[3]

> *Q*. Have you had any awkward moments?—*A*. No, I have
> only seen one in all my career.
> *Q*. What happened?—*A*. He was rough. It was unfortunate;
> he was not an Englishman, he was a spy, and he kicked up
> rough.
> *Q*. He went for you?—*A*. Not only for me, he went for
> everybody.[4]

The acting Under-Sheriff for the County of London, Mr. H.
N. Gedge, was also examined by the Commission on the un-
pleasant character who had kicked up rough, and confirmed
Mr. Pierrepoint's view:

> Yes. He was a foreigner, and I personally have noticed that
> English people take their punishment better than foreigners.

. . . He just dived at the Executioner with his head, and then he just fought with everything he had. We managed to get the strap on his arms but—again it was unfortunate—it was a new strap and . . . he managed to get his arms free again. . . .[5]

There you are. Hanging is quite all right for Englishmen; they actually seem to like it; it is only the foreigners who cause trouble. The outsider appreciates neither the clean fun, nor the solemn ritualistic aspect of the procedure, nor the venerable tradition behind it. The Lord Chief Justice, asked by the same Royal Commissioners whether he was in favour of retaining the black cap, answered:

I think so. It is traditional, and I do not see any reason for interfering with a tradition which has existed over hundreds of years, unless there is some good reason for doing it. . . . The reason why the judge wears a black cap when passing sentence of death, I believe, is simply that the covering of the head, in ancient times, was regarded as a sign of mourning, and that is why it is done.[6]

Mr. Pierrepoint expressed equally strong views about the traditional aspects of the process:

Q. I imagine that people must talk to you about your duties? —*A*. Yes, but I refuse to speak about it. It is something I think should be secret. . . . It is sacred to me, really.[7]

One could hardly imagine a greater contrast in rank and dignity between two servants of the public; a fact which makes the similarity of their views on certain points the more remarkable. Thus, Lord Goddard was asked his views on the suggestion that women ought no longer to be hanged; he answered: 'I do not understand that point of view at all.'[8] Mr. Pierrepoint was asked whether there was anything particularly unpleasant in the execution of a woman. Mr. Pierrepoint said there wasn't.

Q. Do you find your duties very trying, or have you got accustomed to them?—*A.* I am accustomed to it now.
Q. You do not turn a hair?—*A.* No.[9]

Lord Goddard was not asked how many people he had sentenced to hang, nor whether he turned a hair; but he was asked whether he thought that fewer people ought to be sentenced to death, or that fewer ought to be reprieved. He answered that too many were reprieved.[10] He was asked whether he thought it proper that a man, certified insane, should be hanged. He said he thought it was perfectly proper.

Q. Even though he was insane, and presumably . . . not in a fit state to make his peace with God?—*A.* He could make his peace with God, I think, quite well.[11]
Q. Another suggestion that has been made is that, whenever the jury makes a recommendation to mercy, the Home Secretary should have to carry it out?—*A.* That, I think, would be most disastrous.[12]

I have no personal animosity against Lord Chief Justice Rayner Goddard; but as the highest judge in the realm, he is the symbol of authority, and his opinions, which I shall have frequent occasion to quote, carry immense weight in the debate about hanging. The views which he holds are not accidental; they are a very consistent expression of the attitude shared by all who favour the continuation of capital punishment. Their arguments, and the philosophy behind their arguments, have remained unchanged over the last two hundred years, as the pages which follow will show. They can only be properly understood in the light of past history.

The scaffold and the executioner are memories of the past in all Western European democracies except France. The death-penalty has also been abolished in several North American States, in virtually the whole of Central and South America, and in a number of Asiatic and Australian states; making altogether thirty-six countries, the major portion of the civilised world.

The British are a proverbially disciplined and law-abiding people—more so than the average of abolitionist nations, which include hot-tempered Latin Americans and Germans who had been exposed to the brutalising influence of the Nazi régime. Yet the defenders of capital punishment claim that this nation, unlike others, cannot afford to dispense with the services of the hangman as protector and avenger of society. They say that the example of other nations proves nothing, because conditions in this country are 'different'; foreigners may be deterred from crime by the threat of long-term imprisonment, the British criminal can only be deterred by the gallows. This paradoxical belief is so deeply rooted in the pro-hanging party that they do not even see it as a paradox. Many of them hate the idea of hanging and admit that the practice is repellent and evil, yet they believe it to be a necessary evil. This belief in the irreplaceable deterrent value of the death-penalty has been proved to be a superstition by the long and patient inquiries of the Parliamentary Select Committee of 1930 and the Royal Commission on Capital Punishment of 1948; yet it pops up again and again. Like all superstitions, it has the nature of a Jack-in-the-box; however often you hit it over the head with facts and statistics, it will solemnly pop up again, because the hidden spring inside it is the unconscious and irrational power of traditional beliefs. Hence all arguments are wasted unless we go back to the origins of that tradition, and unearth the elements in the past which exert such a strong influence on our present beliefs.

Let us go back, then, from Pentonville to the Tyburn tree. It will be an excursion into a strangely neglected and little-known chapter of English history, which is very curious indeed —a forensic wonderland where the March Hare wears a wig and Malice wades through gore.

2. The 'Bloody Code'

It will be convenient to proceed in two steps: to describe the unique method of dealing with crime which prevailed in this country around A.D. 1800, and then go even further back to explain how that situation came about.

At the beginning of the nineteenth century the criminal law of this country was commonly known as the Bloody Code. It was unique in the world inasmuch as it listed between 220 and 230 offences to be punished by death, from the stealing of turnips to associating with gipsies, to damaging a fishpond, to writing threatening letters, to impersonating out-pensioners at Greenwich Hospital, to being found armed or disguised in a forest, park or rabbit warren, to cutting down a tree, to poaching, forging, picking pockets, shoplifting, and so on, through 220-odd items. The exact number of capital offences was not even known to the best legal authorities.[13] Besides, each statute was so broadly framed that 'the actual scope of the death-penalty was often as much as three or four times as extensive as the number of capital provisions would seem to indicate'.[14]

We are not talking of the Dark Ages, but of the beginning of the nineteenth century, up to Queen Victoria's reign, when everywhere in the civilised world offences against property were being removed from the list of capital crimes. In 1810, Sir Samuel Romilly said in the House of Lords that 'there was no country on the face of the earth in which there had been so many different offences according to law to be punished with death as in England'.[15] Twenty years later Sir Robert Peel complained to the House of Commons: 'It is impossible to conceal from ourselves that capital punishments are more frequent and the criminal law more severe on the whole in this country than in any country in the world.'[16] And the greatest nineteenth-century authority at law, Sir James Stephens, talked of 'the clumsiest, most reckless, and most cruel legislation that ever disgraced a civilised country'.[17]

This state of affairs was the more puzzling as in some other respects British civilisation was ahead of the rest of the world. Foreign visitors were impressed by the exemplary fairness of British courts—and horrified by the savage penalties they inflicted. They were amazed to find the highways dotted with gibbets, creaking and groaning with the bodies of criminals. The gallows and the gibbet were such common objects in the English countryside that in early guide-books they were used as landmarks for the traveller; for instance:

By the Gallows and Three Windmills enter the suburbs of York. . . . You pass through Hare Street . . . and at 13'4 part for Epping Forest, with the gallows to the left. . . . You pass Penmeris Hall, and at 250'4 Hilldraught Mill, both on the left, and ascend a small hill with a gibbet on the right. . . . You leave Frampton, Wilberton and Sherbeck, all on the right, and by a gibbet on the left, over a stone bridge.[18]

Between London and East Grinstead alone, three gallows stood at different points on the highway, in addition to several gibbets where the dead criminal's body was suspended in chains 'till his corpse rot'. Sometimes a criminal was 'hung in chains' alive, and died only after several days. Sometimes the corpse was drenched in tar to make it last longer. Sometimes the skeleton was left hanging after decay of the body was completed. The last gibbeting took place in 1832 in Saffron Lane, near Leicester, when the body of James Cook, a book-binder, was suspended thirty-three feet high, his head shaved and tarred, but had to be taken down after a fortnight to stop the merrymaking of the Sunday crowds.[19]

'Hanging days' were, during the eighteenth and up to half-way through the nineteenth century, the equivalent of national bank holidays, only more frequent. We read, for instance, that in George III's reign, working hours for the poor 'were inordinately long, and there were very few holidays except just at Easter, Whitsuntide and Christmas, and on the eight "Hanging Days" at Tyburn'.[20]

According to Lord Templewood, there were about one hundred public executions a year in London and Middlesex alone:

'This constant round of spectacles had much the same effect on industrial production as mid-week races and football matches at the present day. It was, for example, common in London for coachmakers, tailors, shoemakers, and other craftsmen who were engaged to complete orders within a given time, to remind their customers: "That will be a hanging-day, and the men will not be at work".'[21] Yet we must remember that in 1800 the total population of England and Wales was only just over eight million (as opposed to forty-five million today).

The cherished symbol of the hanging tradition was the Tyburn Tree. The scenes that took place at the public executions were more than a national disgrace, they were outbursts of a collective madness, a kind of medieval St. Vitus's dance. Its distant echoes are still discernible when the notice of a hanging is posted at the prison gates. The crowds assembled to watch at Tyburn (the present Marble Arch) sometimes numbered a hundred thousand and more. An early chronicler gave this description of the scene:

> All the Way, from *Newgate* to *Tyburn*, is one continued Fair⸗ for Whores and Rogues of the meaner Sort. Here the most abandon'd Rakehells may light on Women as shameless: Here Trollops, all in Rags, may pick up Sweethearts of the same Politeness. . . . Nothing is more entertaining to them, than the dead Carcasses of Dogs and Cats, or, for want of them, Rags, and all Trompery that is capable of imbibing Dirt. These, well trempled in Filth, and, if possible, of the worst sort, are, by the Ringleaders, flung as high and as far as a strong Arm can carry them, and commonly directed where the Throng is the thickest.[22]

In the provincial towns, it was the same. A clergyman from Shrewsbury testified before the Select Committee of 1856 on the first public execution he had witnessed, the hanging of Josiah Misters in 1841:

> The town was converted for the day into a fair. The country people flocked in their holiday dresses, and the whole town was a scene of drunkenness and debauchery of every kind. . . . A very large number of children were present: children and females constituted the larger proportion of the attendance.[23]

The nineteenth century marched on, and some European countries had already abolished capital punishment altogether, others let it fall into abeyance; yet in England public hangings, although they were now transferred to places near the prison gates, remained a kind of officially sanctioned Witches' Sabbath. As late as 1864, this is how *The Times* described the crowd assembled to watch Mueller's hanging:

. . . sharpers, thieves, gamblers, betting men, the outsiders
of the boxing ring, bricklayers, labourers, dock workmen,
with rakings of cheap singing halls and billiard rooms, the
fast young men of London. . . . Before the slight slow vibra-
tions of the body had well ended, robbery and violence, loud
laughing, oaths, fighting, obscene conduct and still more
filthy language reigned round the gallows far and near.
Such too the scene remained with little change or respite till
the old hangman (Calcraft) slunk again along the drop
amid hisses and sneering inquiries of what he had had to
drink that morning. After failing once to cut the rope he
made a second attempt more successfully, and the body of
Mueller disappeared from view.[24]

Stampedes and fights of all against all were frequent occur-
rences; in 1807 the crowd of forty thousand became so crazed
at the execution of Holloway and Haggerty that nearly a
hundred dead and dying were lying in the street when the
show was over.[25]

Not only the lower classes were affected by the national
perversion. For distinguished onlookers grandstands were
erected as at contemporary football games; balconies and
windows in the vicinity were let at fabulous prices; ladies of
the aristocracy, wearing black Venetian masks, queued to pay
last visits to the condemned man in his cell; fobs and dandies
travelled all over the country to see a good hanging. The
Governor of Newgate Prison habitually entertained onlookers
of distinction, after an execution, for breakfast:

And if there were no more than six or seven of them hanged,
his guests would return grumbling and disappointed to
breakfast, complaining that 'there were hardly any fellows
hanged this morning'. His good-looking daughter, who did
the honours at table, admitted, however, that few did much
justice to the fare. The first call of the inexperienced was for
brandy, and the only person with a good appetite for the
broiled kidneys, a celebrated dish of hers, was the chaplain.
After breakfast was over the whole party adjourned to see
the 'cutting down'.[26]

Yet this was the age of romantic sensibility, when women swooned at the slightest provocation, and bearded men shed happy tears in each other's arms.

The victims were hanged singly or in batches of twelve, sixteen and up to twenty. Frequently the prisoners were drunk, and the executioner too:

> This day Will Summers and Tipping were executed here for housebreaking. At the tree, the hangman was intoxicated with liquor, and supposing that there were three for execution, was going to put one of the ropes round the parson's neck, as he stood in the cart, and was with much difficulty prevented by the gaoler from so doing.

Until fairly recent times, the executioner was usually a reprieved criminal, 'such as John Price, who was ultimately hanged himself, being, it is said, actually arrested in the process of performing his duty'.[27]

Whether drunk or not, public hysteria frequently caused the hangman to lose his nerve and bungle his job. The volumes of the *Newgate Calendar* abound in examples of people who had to be hanged twice, and even three times. In some cases the victim was revived by bleeding at his heels and then hanged again; in others the hangman and his assistants had to add their weight by hanging on to the victim's legs; in others his body was mangled or his head partly or entirely torn off. On several occasions the Royal reprieve arrived when the victim was already suspended, and he or she was then cut down. In one case, that of 'half-hanged Smith', 'he had hung near fifteen minutes . . . and being conveyed to a house in the neighbourhood, he soon recovered in consequence of bleeding and other proper applications'.[28]

These horrors continued through the nineteenth century. The whole process was carried out in such uncertain, haphazard and barbaric ways that not only were victims found to be alive fifteen minutes and more after the onset of strangling, but there are also authenticated cases of people reviving in the dissecting hall. Others were resuscitated by their friends after cutting down, by immersing the victim in hot water, bleeding, massaging the limbs, etc.[29]

It is unavoidable, in discussing capital punishment, to go into these ghoulish technicalities in order to make people realise what exactly we are talking about. For these are not entirely matters of the distant past. Official hypocrisy, taking advantage of the fact that executions are no longer public, pretends that modernised hanging is a nice and smooth affair which is always carried out 'expeditiously and without a hitch', as prison governors were instructed to say. But the hanging of the Nuremberg war criminals in 1946 was as terribly bungled, and the hanging of Mrs. Thompson in 1923 was a butchery as revolting, as any reported in the *Newgate Calendar*. Her executioner attempted suicide a short time later, and the prison chaplain stated that 'the impulse to rush in and save her by force was almost too strong'. Yet Government spokesmen tell us that all executions are smooth and nice, and Government spokesmen are honourable men.

Even more degrading, if possible, than the execution itself were the scenes which took place immediately after it. Mothers took their children up to the scaffold to have the hand of the corpse applied to them, for this was considered to have a curative effect; chips of the gibbet were carried off as a remedy for toothache. Then the body-snatchers went into action:

As soon as the poor creatures were half dead I was much surprised before such a number of peace officers to see the populace fall to hauling and pulling the carcasses with so much earnestness as to occasion several warm encounters and broken heads. These, I was told, were the friends of the persons executed, or such as, for the sake of tumult, chose to appear so, and some persons sent by private surgeons to obtain bodies for dissection.[30]

The spirit of the whole thing, and its elevating moral effect, were summed up in the famous *Ballad of Sam Hall*. I owe the version that follows to the courtesy of Mr. Monty Carew of the

'Players' Theatre', which revived this memorial of the Tyburn
Tree in the nineteen-thirties. Here it is:

THE BALLAD OF SAM HALL

(Anonymous, around 1800)

Oh my name it is Sam Hall, Samuel Hall,
Oh my name it is Sam Hall, Samuel Hall,
Oh my name it is Sam Hall and I hate you one and all;
You're a gang of muckers all—Damn your eyes!

Oh they say I killed a man, so they said,
Oh they say I killed a man, so they said,
For I hit him on the head with a bloody great lump of lead.
Oh I left him there for Dead—Damn 'is eyes!

Oh they put me into quod, into quod,
Oh they put me into quod, into quod,
Oh they put me into quod all for killing of that sod,
They did—so 'elp me God—Damn their eyes!

Oh the parson 'e did come, 'e did come,
Oh the parson 'e did come, 'e did come,
Oh the parson 'e did come and 'e looked so bloody glum,
And he talked of Kingdom Come—Damn 'is eyes!

So hup the steps I go, very slow,
So hup the steps I go, very slow,
So hup the steps I go and you muckers down below
Are standing in a row—Damn your eyes!

I sees Molly in the crowd, in the crowd,
I sees Molly in the crowd, in the crowd,
I sees Molly in the crowd, so I hollered out aloud
'Now ain't you bleedin' proud—Damn your eyes!'

And now I 'ears the bell, 'ears the bell,
And now I 'ears the bell, 'ears the bell.
And it is my funeral knell, and I'll meet you all in Hell
And I 'opes you frizzle well—Damn your eyes!

There was little discrimination of sex or age. Women convicted of high or petty treason (i.e. murdering a husband)

were not drawn and quartered, only burnt alive. Children
were not liable to the death-penalty if under seven years, and
fully liable over fourteen; between seven and fourteen they
could be and were hanged if there was 'strong evidence of
malice' because malice was held 'to supply age'.[31] Here are a
few cases:

In 1748, William York, a boy of ten, was sentenced to death
for murder. Chief Justice Willis postponed the execution to
find out whether it was proper to hang the child. All the judges
concurred that it was. Their ruling deserves to be quoted
because it epitomises the judges' blind belief, throughout the
centuries, in the unique and irreplaceable deterrent effect of
the death-penalty. The judges ruled that the child—

> is certainly a proper subject for capital punishment, and
> ought to suffer; for it would be a very dangerous consequence
> to have it thought that children may commit such atrocious
> crimes with impunity. There are many crimes of the most
> heinous nature . . . which children are very capable of com-
> mitting; and which they may in some circumstances be
> under strong temptation to commit; and therefore, though
> the taking away the life of a boy of ten years old may savour
> of cruelty, yet as the example of this boy's punishment may
> be *a means of deterring other children from the like offences*; and as
> the sparing of this boy, merely on account of his age, will
> probably have a quite contrary tendency, in justice to the
> publick, the law ought to take its course.[32] (Italics mine.)

In 1800 another boy of ten was sentenced to death for
secreting notes at the Chelmsford Post Office. The judge, in a
letter to Lord Auckland, explained as follows the reasons why
he had refused commutation of the sentence:

> All the circumstances attending the transaction manifested
> art and contrivance beyond his years, and I therefore refused
> the application of his Counsel to respite the Judgment on
> the ground of his tender years, being satisfied that he knew
> perfectly what he was doing. But still, he is an absolute
> Child, now only between ten and eleven, and wearing a bib,

or what your old Nurse (my friend) will know better by the name of a Pinafore. . . . To pacify the feelings of a most crowded court, who all expressed their horror of such a Child being hanged, after stating the necessity of the prosecution and *the infinite danger of its going abroad into the world that a Child might commit such a crime with impunity,* when it was clear that he knew what he was doing, I hinted something slightly of its still being in the Power of the Crown to interpose in every case that was open to Clemency.[33] (Italics mine.)

That was in 1800. Let us compare this with Lord Goddard's summing up to the jury in the case of Craig, sixteen, and Bentley, nineteen. It will be remembered that Craig, at sixteen, could not read and that Bentley was a Grade 4 mental deficient; and that both had been nurtured on gangster films and horror comics to which they were addicted:

Now let us put out of our minds in this case any question of films, or comics, or literature of that kind. These things are prayed in aid nowadays when young prisoners are in the dock, and they have very little to do with the case. These two young men—boys or whatever you like to call them— are both of an age which makes them responsible to the law. They are over fourteen, and it is surely idle to pretend these days that a boy of sixteen doesn't know the wickedness of taking out a revolver of that description and a pocketful of ammunition, and firing when he is on an unlawful expedition. . . .[34]

The Lord Chief Justice remained equally true to tradition when, in the 1948 debate, he successfully opposed raising the age limit for liability to suffer capital punishment from eighteen years to twenty-one years. According to British law, a person under twenty-one is not considered sufficiently responsible to sign a legal contract or to make a will; but he is sufficiently responsible to be hanged without signing a will.

Sentences of death were passed on children as late as 1833— when a boy of nine was sentenced to hang for pushing a stick through a cracked shop-window and pulling out printer's colour to the value of tuppence, but was respited owing to public protest.[35] Samuel Rogers relates in his *Table Talk* that he saw 'a cartload of young girls, in dresses of various colours, on their way to be executed at Tyburn'. And Greville describes the trial of several young boys who were sentenced to death 'to their excessive amazement' and broke into tears. He laconically remarks: 'Never did I see boys cry so.'

In 1801, Andrew Brenning, aged thirteen, was publicly hanged for breaking into a house and stealing a spoon. In 1808 a girl aged *seven* was publicly hanged at Lynn.[36] In 1831, a boy of nine was publicly hanged at Chelmsford for having set fire to a house, and another aged thirteen at Maidstone.[37] Three years later the Lord Chancellor, Lord Eldon, in opposing any mitigation of the law, had the temerity to state that 'he had been His Majesty's adviser for twenty-five years and so far as his knowledge extended, mercy had never been refused in any instance where it ought not to have been withheld'.[38]

Similar statements about mercy 'never being refused' where there is a 'scintilla of doubt' were made in the 1948 debate on capital punishment, and on later occasions after Bentley, Evans, Rowland, etc., had been hanged.

Let me repeat: we are not talking about the Dark Ages, but about the Period of Enlightenment, when all over Europe criminal legislation was rapidly being humanised. Influenced by the teachings of Beccaria, Montesquieu and Voltaire, capital punishment was abolished in Austria for the first time as far back as 1781 by Joseph II.[39] His brother, the Grand Duke of Tuscany, followed suit in 1786[40] and promulgated a penal code which proclaimed the readaptation of offenders to normal life as the main object of all punishment. Catharine the Great of Russia issued her famous 'Instruction' in 1767[41] which abolished capital punishment, and declared that: 'It is Moderation which rules a People and not Excess of Severity.'*

In Sweden, after the criminal reform of 1779, on the average only 10 people were executed per year.[42] In Prussia, under

---

* Though the new penal code which the 'Instruction' ordered to be drawn up was not promulgated, the 'Instruction' itself revolutionised Russian penology and was typical of the spirit of the time.

Frederick II, between 1775 and 1778, altogether 46 people were executed and among these only 2 for offences against property (robbery in the street).[43] During the same period (1775 to 1778) 149 people were hanged in London and Middlesex alone;[44] no statistics are available for the whole country, but the total must have amounted to a multiple of that figure. Detailed statistics are available for 1785,[45] in which year there were 97 executions in London and Middlesex, out of which only one for murder and the remaining 96 for offences against property. The murder rate in England was in fact *lower* than in most European countries.

This shocking contrast between England and the Continent was mainly due to the fact that hanging was regarded by the Bloody Code as a cure-all for every offence, from stealing a handkerchief upward. Yet these comparisons refer to the eighteenth century only. During the first third of the nineteenth, in the period between the Napoleonic Wars and the beginning of Victoria's reign, the contrast is even more staggering. The oldest democracy in Europe, which had never suffered the brutalising effects of foreign invasion, became distinguished, in Sir James Stephen's words, by 'the most reckless and most cruel legislation that ever disgraced a civilised country'.

How did this fantastic situation come about? The answer can only be traced in its outlines, but it is of the greatest relevance to the present situation.

3. Historic Origins of the Bloody Code

The situation round 1800 was not a heritage of the dark past, but the result of a deliberate turning-back of the clock. Three main causes seem to have been at work to make English criminal law during the eighteenth century develop in a direction opposite to that of the rest of the world:

(a) England's lead in the Industrial Revolution;

(b) the Englishman's dislike of authority, which prevented the creation of an effective police force;

(c) the peculiarity of English Common Law, which led to the emergence of a class of men with the authority of oracles,

opposed to any departure from precedent and to any con-
cession to the moving times.

Medieval Common Law imposed the death-penalty only on
a few grave offences, such as murder, treason, arson and rape.
Under the Tudors and Stuarts the law became more rigorous,
but at the beginning of the eighteenth century there were as
yet no more than fifty capital offences. At the beginning of the
nineteenth, there were nearly five times as many. The development of the Bloody Code was simultaneous with, and largely
caused by, the Industrial Revolution, which transformed the
nation as thoroughly as if it had been put through a cement-
mixing machine. It gave England the lead in the western
world, but at the same time produced social evils whose
distant echoes are still felt in our day.

'The terrible pace at which the world now jolts and clanks
along was set in our island where, first, invention was har-
nessed to organised capital. For fifty years that great change
was left uncontrolled by the community which it was trans-
forming.'[46] Towns were growing like hideous, squalid mushrooms, without any machinery of administration, local
government and public security. The ancient order of society
was disintegrating, but nobody had any experience or any
clear idea how to cope with the resulting social chaos, and
particularly with the new town proletariat of wage-earners,
uprooted from their rural existence, transformed into a race of
shiftless slum-dwellers. The spreading of extreme poverty with
its concomitants of prostitution, child labour, drunkenness and
lawlessness, coincided with an unprecedented accumulation of
wealth as an additional incentive to crime. All foreign visitors
agreed that never before had the world seen such riches and
splendour as displayed in London residences and shops—nor
so many pickpockets, burglars and highwaymen. 'One is
forced to travel even at noon as if one was going to battle,'
Horace Walpole wrote in 1752. It was this general feeling of
insecurity, often verging on panic, which led to the enactment,
by the dozen, of capital statutes, making any offence from
poaching and stealing from the value of one shilling upward
punishable by death. And each statute branched out like a

tree to cover any similar or related offences.

This process went on for over a hundred years, and was only brought to an end when Robert Peel, in 1829, created the modern police force. Had that been done a century earlier, the whole shame and terror could have been avoided. The reason why it was not done was, paradoxically, the Englishman's love of freedom, and his dislike of regimentation: the fear that a regular police force, once established, would be used to curtail his individual and political freedom.

Faced by the choice between the cop and the hangman, England chose the hangman. He was a familiar figure from the past; the cop was a new-fangled innovation of foreign countries, and a much too dangerous experiment. As all other curiosities in this chapter, I mention this not for curiosity's sake, but because it is directly relevant to the controversy of our day. The last-ditch stand of the defenders of capital punishment is made precisely on the same issue which started the whole disaster: to wit, that if hanging were abolished, the police would have to carry arms to cope with the emboldened criminal. We shall see later on that in some of the countries which abolished capital punishment, the police carried arms both before abolition and afterwards, in others carried no arms before abolition or after; and that there is no reason to believe that there would be any necessity for change in this country. But the point that interests us here is, once more, the powerful unconscious influence of tradition: up to this day, the idea of allowing cops to wear a revolver is more abhorrent to the Englishman's sensibilities than the continuance of hanging.

The panicky character of the emergency legislation of the eighteenth century is strikingly illustrated by the so-called 'Waltham Black Act'. It set the example and the pace of the whole development. In 1722, the Hampshire landowners were worried by a band of poachers who went around with their faces blackened to make recognition more difficult. They were following yet another and even more ancient tradition: that of the Roberdsmen, the followers of Robert, or Robin, Hood. The gentlemen of Hampshire appealed to Parliament, not knowing that they were going to make British history; and Parliament enacted a statute 'for the more effectual punishing wicked and evil disposed Persons going armed in Disguise, and doing Injuries and Violence to the Persons and Properties of His Majesty's Subjects, and for the more speedy bringing of Offenders to Justice'.

The Roberdsmen vanished from Hampshire, but the Waltham Black Act came to stay. It was enacted to meet a local and temporary emergency for a limited period of three years; and it stayed for 101 years, till 1823; and all the time it was ramifying. For it was so vaguely and generally worded that the judges could apply it to an unlimited range of offenders and offences, each time creating a precedent on which further convictions could be based. Altogether, the Waltham Black Act, by budding and ramification, created over three hundred and fifty new capital crimes. These referred to: persons either armed and having their faces blackened; or armed and otherwise disguised; or being merely otherwise disguised; or being *neither blackened nor disguised*; or principals in the second degree; or accessaries after the act. The offences included: offences against red or fallow deer, thefts of hares, connies and fish, destroying the heads of fishponds, cutting down 'a tree planted in any avenue, garden, orchard or plantation for ornament, shelter or profit', offences against cattle, setting anything on fire, shooting at any person, sending a letter demanding money if unsigned or signed by a fictitious name, and so on and so forth through 350-odd items.

A similar fate of growth by ramification befell the statute relating to 'Larceny in dwelling houses and shops'. It originally referred only to burglary, but eventually covered any theft over twelvepence without the previously essential element of breaking in. One of the earliest reformers, Eden, wrote in 1771 that except for members of the legal profession 'there are not ten subjects in England' who knew on what niceties or counts of the Larceny Law they could be hanged. Yet it was not repealed until 1833.

These barbarous laws were passed by Parliament 'without debate, enquiry, examination, evidence, or any general interest'.[47] Buxton describes a member of the House of Commons who, while writing a letter in the Committee Room:

—at one corner observed a gentleman seated at a table, and seemingly asleep, to whom a clerk was reading a piece of parchment, which looked like an act of parliament. Sir William was continually interrupted by a kind of chorus, with which every paragraph concluded: 'Shall suffer death without benefit of clergy.' At length Sir William said, 'What may this heinous offence be which you are visiting with so terrible a penalty?'—'Why, Sir,' replied the legislator, 'we country gentlemen have suffered much by depredations in our turnips,—we have at length determined to put a period to this practice; and my good friend the minister has been so obliging as to allow me to make it death without benefit of clergy.'[48]

I have tried to trace the origins of this madness which cast the shadow of the gallows over every hamlet, forest and borough of the land. But madness and panic last, as a rule, only a short time. This was the age when Beccaria's, Voltaire's and Montesquieu's teachings fell everywhere on fertile ground, except in England; and in England itself there were Jeremy Bentham, the Mills, Eden and Howard, Romilly, Selborne and other enlightened men, conscious of the national shame, who fought it with the power of the word and the pen. What, then, was the cause, and which were the forces that kept the madness going and resisted all attempts to stop it, all measures of reform, until the mid-nineteenth century? The answer is simple: the judges of England.

4. The Oracles

In the fifteenth and sixteenth centuries, most European countries adopted written codes based on the Roman Law, in replacement of their old customary 'common law' or 'folk-law'. Two hundred years later, a second wave of codification swept over Europe in the wake of the *Code Napoléon*. England alone has adhered to this day to common law, defined by Blackstone as 'not set down in any written statute or ordinance, but depending on immemorial usage for support'.[49] The validity and application of these usages are to be determined by the judges—'the depositories of the law, the living oracles, who must decide in all cases of doubt, and who are bound by oath to decide according to the law of the land'.[50] Their judgments are preserved as records, and 'it is an established rule to abide by former precedents. . . . The extraordinary deference paid to precedents is the source of the most striking peculiarities of the English Common Law.'[51]

The benefits of the Common Law as a bulwark of the Britons' political and personal freedom were enormous, and are an essential part of English history. One of the minor advantages derived from the refusal to accept Roman Law and/or Canon Law was that England alone never introduced torture as a method for extracting confessions—drawing and quartering, and pressing to death, were aggravated forms of execution, not methods of making the prisoner confess.* Continental law was *inquisitorial*, English law *accusatory*; it admitted of no pressure being exercised on the accused. Hence the superiority of English judicial procedure in giving the accused a fair trial, acknowledged all over the Continent.

But these benefits were heavily paid for. Dislike of regimentation by the police was a major cause for the prevalence of the hangman; dislike of law by code and statute left English legislation at the mercy of the wigged oracles, who, since precedent must be their only guidance, by the very nature of their calling had their minds riveted on the past. They not only administered the law; they made it. 'In earlier times unquestionably the judges regarded the Common Law as supreme and unchangeable by any authority other than themselves . . . . Today judges . . . observe Bacon's monition that their office is . . . to declare the law and not to make it. But in practice the judges undoubtedly legislate, if only by the extension of old rules to new sets of circumstances or even by laying down a new rule where there is no precedent.'[52]

It was the judges who interpreted the Waltham Black Act in such a way that it finally branched into over 350 capital

* This is not strictly true of pressing to death (*Peine forte et dure*), but the point is technical and unimportant.

offences; under whose guidance Parliament enacted more and more capital statutes which they could interpet and expand; and who fought tooth and nail against the repeal of any of them. The word of the Law Lords and the King's Bench carried, and still carries, decisive weight in influencing Government and Parliament, the leaders of the Church and public opinion; and it was, and is to this day, always thrown in against any attempt at making the law more humane—and thereby more effective. These are rather sweeping statements; let us proceed with the evidence. It will be seen to be directly relevant to the situation in our day.

In 1813, when Romilly's Bill for the abolition of the death-penalty for shoplifting was for the third time defeated by the House of Lords (see below), the later Chief Justice Common Pleas, Lord Wynford, stated the judges' attitude in an unusually frank manner. The text of his speech was *Nolumus leges Angliae mutari*—'We do not wish the laws of England to be changed'. The shoplifting act which reformers wished to abolish, he said, had been passed in Cromwell's day, 'in the best period of our history, and there was no reason for hazarding an experiment'. He would vote for the bill if it could be shown that a single individual had suffered under the existing law, but the humanity of judges was proverbial.[53] This, at a time when children from the age of seven upward were being publicly strangled.

The motto 'We do not wish the laws of England to be changed' referred, however, only to mitigations, not to aggravations, of the law. There is no known example of a protest coming from the judges against adding new capital offences to the statute, and a considerable number of death statutes were moved by themselves. It was a one-way process, which made every aggravation of the law irreversible.

Needless to say, there always existed humane judges who, in individual cases where the harshness of the law was too obvious, concurred with the jury, and often with the prosecution, in letting the poor wretch off. But as a body, the judges of England have, as far as historical evidence goes, at every crucial juncture exerted their influence in favour of maximum severity as against any humanitarian reform.

5. *The Revolt of Public Opinion*

The decisive struggle for the repeal of the absurd and
shameful Bloody Code took place between 1808, when
Romilly brought in his first Reform Bill, and Queen Victoria's
ascent to the throne in 1837. At the beginning of this legal
Thirty Years' War, the number of capital statutes was 220-odd;
at its end, they were reduced to fifteen.

During its first phase, the movement for reform was led by
Samuel Romilly, with little direct success; he committed
suicide in 1818. If Romilly was St. George, the dragon had
two heads: Chief Justice Lord Ellenborough and Lord Chancellor Lord Eldon. Supported by their learned brethren of the
King's Bench, by part of the Bishop's Bench and by some
noble fossils in the House of Lords, they opposed every reform
of the statutes on the same grounds on which capital punishment has always been defended and is being defended today:
that it is the only effective deterrent, that no alternative
punishment is equally effective, that mitigation of the law is a
dangerous experiment which would lead to an increase in
crime, and that public opinion won't stand for it.

The stubborn determination of the diehards and hang-hards
may be gathered from a single example: Romilly's Bill to
abolish the death-penalty for shoplifting to the value of five
shillings and over, was passed by the Commons and defeated
by the Lords no less than six times: in 1810, 1811, 1813, 1816,
1818 and 1820. It was only passed, long after Romilly's death,
in 1832. In the first House of Lords Debate on the bill, on May
30th, 1810, Chief Justice Lord Ellenborough made two
speeches which, later on, became almost as famous as Nelson's
'Kiss me, Hardy':

I trust your lordships will pause before you assent to an
experiment pregnant with danger to the security of property, and before you repeal a statute which has so long been
held necessary for public security. I am convinced with the
rest of the Judges, public expediency requires there should
be no remission of the terror denounced against this description of offenders. Such will be the consequence of the repeal

of this statute that I am certain depredations to an unlimited
extent would immediately be committed. . . .

My Lords, if we suffer this Bill to pass, we shall not know
where to stand; we shall not know whether we are upon our
heads or our feet. . . .

Repeal this law and see the contrast—no man can trust
himself for an hour out of doors without the most alarming
apprehensions, that, on his return, every vestige of his
property will be swept off by the hardened robber.[54]

A century and a half later, in the 1948 House of Lords
debate on the suspension of capital punishment for a trial
period of five years, their Lordships, one after the other,
unblushingly conjured up the same bogey. E.g., Viscount
Simon:

> We have no right . . . to risk an experiment which may put
> in jeopardy innocent human lives. . . . women who at this
> hour fear, as they never feared before, the knock at the door
> after it is dark.[55]

Romilly committed suicide, a defeated man, in November
1818. He was sixty-one when he died, one of the greatest
Englishmen of his time, whose name has been unjustly forgotten. In 1820 his famous Bill for the abolition of the death-
penalty for shoplifting was introduced for the sixth time—and
had again to be withdrawn when the law officers declared that
they would oppose it. Twelve years later, in 1832, Chief
Justice Lord Tenterden, still valiantly stood out against the
abolition of the death-penalty for sheep- and horse-stealing on
the familiar grounds that 'we have at present in this country
no substitute for the punishment of death'.[56]

The resistance began to break down only when Peel came
to the Home Office and created the modern police force in
1829. Ten years later, capital offences were at long last reduced
to the number of fifteen; and in 1861 to four (murder, treason,
arson in dockyards and piracy). This where the matter rests
until this day.

But let me add a footnote to the 1948 debate. After Lord

Goddard had praised Ellenborough, the Lord Chancellor, Lord Jowitt, seconded him with the following reflections:

> I think he [Lord Goddard] showed in that speech that Judges are not the inhuman creatures they are sometimes supposed to be . . . . When I think of some of the great Judges since Ellenborough's time, *I think, for instance, of Lord Romilly*—and who has done more to restrict and limit the death penalty than Romilly?—and of many other names which will occur to any educated person. . . .[57] (My italics.)

The italics are mine; the confusion is the learned judge's. Romilly was never a judge, but a ferocious enemy of the judges. He was not a Lord,* he was not 'since Ellenborough's time'; he died before Ellenborough. Translated into political terms, the passage would read as follows:

'It is untrue that the Conservative party was opposed to nationalisation. When I think of some of the great Tories, Sir Nye Bevan, for instance, who favoured nationalisation, and of many other names which will occur to any educated person . . .' etc.

It is worth noting that during the whole House of Lords debate, nobody remarked on Lord Jowitt's mistake. We shall meet with more examples of the amazing ignorance of social history among the learned oracles; it is a characteristic feature of their mentally inbred world.

6. 'Hanging is not Enough'

The attitude of the judges as a body to aggravated forms of execution was equally consistent. Sir Edward Coke (1552–1634) was perhaps the greatest English lawyer of all times. By his famous dictum that no royal proclamation can change the law, by his defence of the Common Law against the King, the Church and the Admiralty, he did more than any other man to establish the independence and fairness of British legal pro-

---

* Samuel Romilly's second son became a peer in 1866, but since he had nothing to do with reforming the criminal law and only became a judge twenty years after the events under discussion, he could not have been meant by Lord Jowitt.

cedure. But at the same time, Coke's name remains forever associated with the 'Godly butchery' of drawing, hanging and quartering, whose continuance he defended by a series of quotations from the Bible, as follows:

> For first after a traitor hath had his just trial and is convicted and attainted, he shall have his judgment to be drawn to the place of execution from his prison as being not worthy any more to tread upon the face of the earth whereof he was made: also for that he hath been retrograde to nature, therefore is he drawn backward at a horse-tail. And whereas God hath made the head of man the highest and most supreme part, as being his chief grace and ornament . . . he must be drawn with his head declining downward, and lying so near the ground as may be, being thought unfit to take the benefit of the common air. For which cause also he shall be strangled, being hanged up by the neck between heaven and earth, as deemed unworthy of both, or either; as likewise, that the eyes of men may behold, and their hearts condemn him. Then he is to be cut down alive, and to have his privy parts cut off and burnt before his face as being unworthily begotten, and unfit to leave any generation after him. . . .[58]

He also explained that this form of execution proved 'the admirable clemency and moderation of the King' because it did not foresee any additional torture—apart from disembowelling the traitor alive.

This barbarity continued, in somewhat mitigated from, well into the *nineteenth* century. It was again Romilly who put an end to it. But when he introduced his first 'Bill to Alter the Punishment of High Treason' he was accused by the law officers of the Crown of breaking down the bulwarks of the Constitution, and the great Coke's eulogy on drawing and quartering was quoted on that occasion. The Bill was rejected on Colonel Frankland's motion, who denounced it as yet another of 'these mischievous attempts to unsettle the public opinion with respect to the enormity of these atrocious offences'.[59] The Attorney-General said in the debate that he would not vote for such a punishment if it were newly invented, but since it had the sanction of centuries, he was against changing it. Romilly notes in his memoirs: 'so . . . the Bill is lost and the ministers have the glory of having preserved the British law, by which it is ordained that the hearts and the bowels of a man . . . shall be torn out of his body while he is yet alive.'[60]

A year later (1814) he reintroduced his Bill. This time, Lord Ellenborough and Eldon felt that the tide was against them, but they succeeded in introducing an amendment to the Bill whereby it remained part of the sentence that the body of the criminal should be cut into quarters. Since this was now to be done only after the criminal had expired, Romilly agreed to what one might call a reasonable compromise with the up-holders of tradition, and the Bill was passed.

I have mentioned before that in the case of women convicted of treason, drawing and quartering was considered to be offensive to the modesty of the spectators and therefore replaced by burning them alive. This form of execution was repealed only in 1790, against the strenuous opposition of the Lord Chancellor of the day, Lord Loughborough, who defended the stake on the grounds of its excellent deterrent value:

> because although the punishment, as a spectacle, is rather attended with circumstances of horror, likely to make a stronger impression on the beholders than mere hanging, the effect was much the same, as in fact no degree of personal pain was sustained, the criminal being always strangled before the flames were suffered to approach the body.[61]

This was palpably untrue since there are several cases on record where the hangman, having his hands scorched, did not complete strangulation. I mention this not for the sake of macabre detail, but because the defence of a savage method of execution on the grounds that 'it doesn't really hurt' is another *leitmotif* down to our day, when prison governors are instructed to state that the hanging was 'quick and expeditious without a hitch' and 'should be confined to as few words as possible'. Blackstone, the greatest legal authority after Coke, put up the same defence for drawing and quartering: 'There are but few instances, and those accidental or by negligence, of persons being disembowelled till previously deprived of sensation.'[62]

The *pillory* was only abolished in 1816. A year previously, Ellenborough had opposed its repeal on the grounds that there was no equally effective alternative punishment for it: it was as old as 1269 and 'particularly suited to perjury and fraud'.*

As for *transportation* (to Australia) the judges' attitude was particularly interesting. Whenever transportation for life was suggested as an alternative to capital punishment, they found it much too mild. Thus Ellenborough said in 1810 that life-long transportation was viewed by some prisoners as 'a summer's airing by emigration to a warmer climate'; and Lord Wynford, in 1832, said that it had 'no longer any terrors attached to it. It was rather an encouragement to crime . . . than a disuasive from it'.[64] But when public opinion demanded that transportation should be abandoned, Earl Grey (former Chief Justice Common Pleas) informed the House of Lords that: 'All the judges concerned in the administration of the criminal law except one . . . agreed that the punishment of transportation cannot be safely abandoned.'[65] The same contradictory arguments were used in the Lords debate of 1948 against life-imprisonment as an alternative to hanging: a life-sentence was considered either too cruel or too mild, or presumably both.

The last non-capital punishment particularly favoured by the oracles is *flogging*. In 1938 a 'Departmental Committee on Corporal Punishment' (the Atkins Committee) was appointed, which reported:

We are not satisfied that corporal punishment has that exceptionally effective influence as a deterrent which is

---

* In spite of its tradition of seven hundred years, the pillory was not a very reliable form of punishment: 'Some prisoners died from the brutality of the crowd; on the other hand the case was quoted in debate of one Dr. Shebbeare, who excited some sympathy, and had an umbrella held over his head by the Sheriff to shelter him from the elements, while a servant supplied him with refreshments. The judges were accordingly in some doubt as to whether, in imposing the punishment, they were sentencing a man to death or to an agreeable afternoon's relaxation.'[63]

usually claimed for it by those who advocate it as a penalty
for adult offenders.

They also expressly reported that the judges of the King's
Bench Division were not only in favour of the retention of
corporal punishment, but moreover wished to extend it.

As usual when such Committees are appointed to appease
public opinion, the report was put on ice, and nothing
happened for ten years. In 1948, the clause in the Criminal
Justice Bill abolishing corporal punishment was passed in the
House of Commons without a division. But when it came
before the House of Lords the Lord Chief Justice proposed to
abolish only the cat-o'-nine-tails, and to retain whipping. The
Lords obliged. They had listened with great respect to the Lord
Chief Justice's oration on the psychologically beneficial effect
of the whipping of convicts 'birched by a chief warder who
knows his business'.[66] It is indeed the most effective method to
prevent the reformation of a prisoner by utterly degrading him;
and if all goes well, it may cause a prison riot.

7. *The Judges and the Rights of the Accused*

Prisoners on a capital charge were not allowed counsel until
1836. In that year the Prisoners' Counsel Bill was introduced
and twice defeated before it was passed. Mr. G. Gardiner,
Q.C., comments:

Considering that at one sessions two-thirds of the prisoners
were under age, some under ten years, it is difficult, as one
looks back, to see how it was expected that these felons, some
barely out of the nursery, were expected to conduct their
own defence. The reform had nevertheless been opposed in
his time by that great criminal judge Sir Michael Foster,
and by Coke himself on the curious ground that 'evidence
ought to be so clear that it cannot be contradicted'. Lord
Denman C.J., who finally supported the Bill, expressed the
opinion that the result of it would be that counsel would be
compelled to take a case, which would be unjust to gentlemen who had entered an expensive profession. Sir Eardley

Wilmot took a distressingly unconfident view of judicial ability; he was perfectly certain that the Bill would be impracticable if the judge had to sift the chaff from the corn, and 'unmystify the speeches of Counsel'. No judge in the country 'possessed physical and mental power equal to the task'.[67]

The Bill was finally passed,

but the judges . . . were able to some extent to prune the measure. At the suggestion of the Chief Justice, King's Bench (Lord Denman) and the Lord Chief Baron of the Exchequer (Lord Abinger) the clause granting the prisoner a right to see the depositions was struck out.[68]

A person charged with a capital offence was not allowed to give evidence on his own behalf on the witness stand until the Criminal Evidence Act came into force in 1898. It had taken fifteen years for this act to pass. Several of the Law Lords fought the measure, and Lord Chief Justice Collins described it as a 'great public mischief' because the opportunity given to the judge to put direct question to the prisoner 'must sap the prisoner's confidence in the absolute impartiality of the judge'. As Mr. Gardiner points out, the argument was the exact reverse of the objection made against allowing the prisoner to be defended by counsel—namely, that counsel was unnecessary because the judge was *not* an impartial arbiter but 'the prisoner's best friend'.

The judges were equally determined in their opposition to the establishment of a Court of Criminal Appeal—which they succeeded in postponing by a modest *seventy years*. During this time the question had come before Parliament no less than *twenty-eight times*.

Before the Court of Criminal Appeal was established in 1907, there existed no body to which prisoners wrongfully sentenced to death could appeal; their only hope was the Royal pardon. The 1866 Royal Commission had considered the question, but the four judges who gave evidence, Lords Cranworth, Bramwell, Martin and Wensleydale, unanimously opposed it, on the grounds that it would 'worry prosecutors', that 'a Court of Appeal is not what one may call a natural thing', and because 'people in England are never convicted, except, in my judgment, upon the very clearest evidence'.[69]

Forty years later, in the 1907 debate, the Lord Chief Justice, Lord Alverstone, still opposed the dangerous innovation to the end because of his 'distinct conviction that the proposed change will undermine altogether the responsibility of juries', and because it would be 'tried for the first time in criminal law and in my judgment it is fraught with the greatest danger to innocent persons'. He emphasised, as Lord Chief Justices traditionally do on such occasions, that 'the views I have expressed are entertained by all my brethren in the King's Bench'. The Lord Chancellor, Lord Halsbury, duly sided with the Lord Chief Justice, as Eldon had sided with Ellenborough in 1810–18, and Jowitt was to side with Goddard in 1948, angrily exclaiming:

> It must be remembered that you are here dealing with experts who have had long experience of what they are talking about . . . I cannot understand why the legislature of this country in the most serious matter of the administration of the criminal law should be affected one way or the other because irresponsible persons think it proper to assume that they have knowledge superior to His Majesty's judges.[70]

The experts then went on to prophesy that the court would have to deal with no less than five thousand appeals every year and would cost the taxpayer 'astronomical sums'. They were wrong, as usual. The highest number of appeals in a single year was 710 (in 1910); and the astronomical expense amounted to £13,000 per year.[71]

8. The Doctrine of Maximum Severity

Of course, there were always kind and understanding judges on the lower rungs of the hierarchy. There were exceptions even at the top, such as Lord Brougham (Lord Chancellor 1830–4), and Lord Denman (Chief Justice 1832–50), who sided with the reformers. But the core of resistance against reform, around which the reactionary forces rallied, was the authority of the oracles. Robed with the august symbols of tradition, they lent to the public strangling of ten-year-olds a halo of respectability, and led this gentle nation through two centuries of gore.

The reasons for this development have already been mentioned: the unique character of British Common Law guaranteed the nation personal freedom, and exemplary fair treatment in its courts, at the price of a preposterously savage system of penalties. It led to the emergence of a powerful new class, the medicine-men of the Law, who monopolised the position of a 'fourth member of the legislature'. Guided by precedent only, under the hypnotic effect of exclusive preoccupation with the past, they were bound to develop a professional deformity, epitomised in the motto *Nolumus leges Angliae mutari*.

When Lord Goddard told the Royal Commissioners that in his opinion fewer people ought to be reprieved, and that it would be 'most disastrous' if the jury's recommendation to mercy should have to be carried out by the Home Secretary, he was not guided by personal motives of cruelty. He was faced with a dilemma which isn early as old as capital punishment, and gave the same answer which its defenders were logically compelled to give every time it arose. The dilemma is this: whenever social progress outpaces the Law, so that its penalties appear disproportionately severe to the public conscience, juries become reluctant to convict, and reprieves, instead of being an exceptional act of mercy, become virtually the rule, so that only a small proportion of the sentences are actually carried out and the threat accordingly loses its deterrent effect. We shall meet with this dilemma again in the next chapter. There are only two ways out of it: either to bring the law up to date and, by reducing its severity, make 'the punishment fit the crime'—or to increase both the terror of the threat, and the rigour of its application.

The first solution was formulated as early as 1746 by the Italian humanist and reformer, Cesare Beccaria, and became the guiding principle of legal reform in Europe during the Age of Enlightenment. Beccaria taught that the only aim of punishment was the protection of society, which could not be achieved by terror, because in the same proportion as punishments become more cruel 'human minds harden, adjusting themselves, like fluids, to the level of objects round them'. Terror has its own law of diminishing returns; in a century of savage punishments, people are no more frightened by the gallows than under a milder régime they are frightened of prison. Besides, legal barbarity begets common barbarity, 'the same spirit of ferocity that guides the hand of the legislature having guided also that of the patricide and assassin'.

Beccaria realised that 'severity breeds impunity', because men are reluctant to inflict on their fellow-beings the excessive punishments prescribed by inhuman laws. Accordingly, excessive penalties are less effective in preventing crime than moderate penalties, provided that these are inflicted promptly and with certainty. A disproportionately severe law, therefore, is not only morally wrong but also defeats its own utilitarian purpose; whereas a moderate law, graded according to the offence, if administered swiftly, smoothly and with the certitude of inevitability, is both more humane and more effective.

One may call this the principle of the 'minimum effective punishment'. I have already mentioned the influence which Beccaria's teaching gained all over Europe, from Russia to France, from Sweden to Italy. There was perhaps no single humanist since Erasmus of Rotterdam, who, without being attached to a definite political or religious movement, had such a deep effect on European thought.

One would have imagined that England, with its great democratic and liberal tradition, should have been the country most receptive to the new trend. Yet through more than a century, England swam against the current, and is doing it still. I have mentioned some of the reasons: the upheaval of the Industrial Revolution, and the reluctance to be regimented by police authority. But the main reason was the monopoly of the 'fourth legislature' in legal matters. Elsewhere, no such monopoly existed: the laws were codified, the judges doled them out for better or worse, but they had no power to *make* them. Penal legislation on the Continent reflected the social currents of the time; England alone let herself be guided by an exclusive class of alleged technical experts who, like the medieval alchemists, lived in a mysterious world of secret formulae, their minds riveted to the past, impervious to changing conditions, ignorant of the vital developments outside their closed world.

It was not by chance that they were opposed to every proposed reform of the law, threatening Parliament that 'every vestige of our property will be swept off by the hardened robber'. They knew by instinct and conviction that to give way on any point, meant to admit that the law was not fixed for all time but subject to change— and then their whole rigid and artificial universe would collapse. The change of social conditions leads to recurrent crises in criminal law which can only be solved either by mitigating its rigours, or by ever-increasing terror, adding capital statute to capital statute; they opted for the second alternative, with the results that we have seen.

So far we have discussed the influence of the 'fourth legislature' as a body. Taken as individuals, the great judges who made English history display the same common trend of rigid inhumanity. The heroes of common law—the Cromwells, Nelsons and Marlboroughs among the oracles—are Coke, Blackstone, Paley, Ellenborough and Stephen.

The first of them, Sir Edward Coke, who was called 'The Common Law Become Flesh', pointed the way by his classic answer to the classic dilemma: 'that for as much as many do offend in the hope of pardon, that pardons be very rarely granted.'[72] This solution of the deterrence problem remained the guide of the hang-hards through four centuries; it has been quoted on endless occasions by learned judges, and echoed by Lord Goddard's testimony before the Royal Commission that 'fewer should be reprieved'.

The next landmark was Sir William Blackstone (1723–80). His 'Commentaries' are used to this day as textbooks for law students. He was a contemporary of Beccaria, Montesquieu and Jeremy Bentham; yet he approved of drawing and quartering, the burning of women, and held that hanging the corpse of the criminal in chains on the gibbet was 'a comfortable sight to the relations and friends of the deceased'.

Archdeacon William Paley (1743–1805) was not a judge,

merely a Justice of the Peace, but his treatise 'On Crimes and Punishments' exercised a powerful influence on the trend of English criminal legislation during a long period. Paley taught that the main consideration in assessing the degree of punish-debt should not be the magnitude of the crime, but the facility with which it can be committed, and the difficulty of its detection. Consequently, he unreservedly supported capital punishment for petty thieving simply because 'the property being more exposed requires the terror of capital punishment to protect it'.[73] He also believed in the absolute incorrigibility of all criminals, in the futility of trying to reform them, and that some of them ought to be thrown into dens of wild beasts to perish 'in a manner dreadful to the imagination yet concealed from the view'. This was the man whose influence reigned supreme among the oracles for the next fifty years. The history of English criminal law is a wonderland filled with the braying of learned asses.

Incidentally, the title of Paley's treatise 'On Crimes and Punishments' is identical with Beccaria's *Dei Delitti e delle Pene* which was translated into English seven years earlier. Whether Paley chose the same title out of spite or ignorance, cannot be ascertained.

About Ellenborough no more need be said. The last and greatest nineteenth-century oracle was Sir James Stephen (1829–94) whose *General View of the Criminal Law of England* was the first systematic attempt since Blackstone to explain the principles of law and justice in a coherent form. He criticised the 'barbarous system' of the past, as the quotation on page 176 above shows; yet as far as his own time was concerned, Stephen conformed to the tradition. In 1883, a full sixty years after the death-penalty for forgery was abolished, Stephen demanded that if a man is 'determined to live by deceiving and impoverishing others' or 'if he is a habitual receiver of stolen goods', he should be put to death; and he continued:

'These views, it is said, are opposed to the doctrine that human life is sacred. I have never been able to understand what the doctrine means or how its truth is alleged to be proved.'[74]

That last sober phrase sums up the attitude of this chain of Abominable Snowmen, from Coke to Stephen and beyond. The terror of the French Revolution preserves in retrospect the grandeur of a tragic but essential chapter of history. The terror of the Bloody Code was wanton and purposeless, alien to the character of the nation, imposed on it, not by fanatical Jacobins, but by a conspiracy of wigged fossils. They quoted the Bible to defend drawing and quartering, and they quoted each other's quotations, and became more and more estranged from reality. Solicitors and counsel, prison chaplains and gaolers know criminals as individuals, and know that they are human. The judges only meet the accused in court, as a case, not as a human being. All the great oracles had a blind belief in the gallows as the only deterrent from crime, though the only criminals they had occasion to see were those who had obviously not been deterred. They were like physicians who would justify their favourite cure by the example of patients who have not been cured by it. Yet they must go on believing in their magic deterrent, for if they renounced that belief, they would stand condemned for those they have condemned, before their own conscience.

From Coke to Stephen and beyond, they all show the same curious trend of inhumanity because, though posing as experts, they knew little of human nature and the motives of crime.* Victims of their professional deformity, ignorant of the forces of heredity and social environment, hostile to any social and psychological explanation, the criminal was for them nothing but a bundle of depravity, who cannot be redeemed and must

---

* Thus, for instance, Sir Travers Humphreys (better known as Mr. Justice Humphreys) writes in his memoirs, *A Book of Trials* (1953):

'John George Haigh belonged to what is perhaps the largest class of murderers, that is, murderers for gain.'

According to Home Office statistics, during the years 1900 to 1949, 1,210 persons were convicted for murder in England and Wales. Out of these, 161 were committed for gain, 837 were *crimes passionels* and 213 were miscellaneous, or committed during a quarrel of a non-sexual nature. If we divide the last figure into halves, we get 268 murders for gain, out of a total of 1,210, or approximately 22 per cent. These statistics (see R. C. Report, p. 330), were available to the illustrious judge when he published his memoirs.

be destroyed. Like all who believe in terror as the only protection of society, and have no faith in humanity, they were frightened men. Their grotesque outcries against any relaxation of the terror statutes were caused by an irrational but genuine fear. From the psychiatrist's point of view, the horrors of the Bloody Code, the hanging of children, the saturnalia of the public executions, were symptoms of a condition known as anxiety hysteria. But psychiatrists, as we shall see later on, are considered by the oracles as their hereditary enemies, not only because they might see through the accused, but also, perhaps, through the judge.

In his *Lives of the Chief Justices*, Lord Campbell quotes a judge at Stafford Assizes who, having sentenced to death a prisoner for passing on a forged one pound note, exhorted him as follows to prepare for his journey to another world:

> And I trust that, through the merits and mediation of our blessed Redeemer, you may there experience that mercy which a due regard to the credit of the paper currency of the country forbids you to hope for here.[75]

The words convey a complete mental picture of the early nineteenth-century oracle: the nasal voice half-choked with phlegm, the august hrrumph, the corkscrew-braided tea doily warming the bald pate and making its wearer forget the ailing prostate; add it together, and you have the awe-inspiring majesty of the Capital Law.

English law is based on tradition and precedent. I hope that this—necessarily sketchy—excursion into the past may have dispelled some of the unconscious preconceptions which cloud the issue, and will help the reader to consider the problem of capital punishment against its historical background, with an unprejudiced mind.

II. The Hangman's Protection

or

Capital Punishment as a Deterrent

I

THE arguments in defence of capital punishment have remained essentially the same since Lord Ellenborough's days. In the most recent Parliamentary debates to date— February 10th and July 22nd, 1955—the present Home Secretary, Major Lloyd George, again patiently trotted out the three customary reasons why the Government opposed abolition: that the death-penalty carried a unique deterrent value; that no satisfactory alternative punishment could be designed; and that public opinion was in favour of it.

At present I am only concerned with the first and main argument. To give it a fair hearing, we must set all humanitarian considerations and charitable feelings aside, and examine the effectiveness of the gallows as a deterrent to potential murderers from a coldly practical, purely utilitarian point of view. This is, of course, a somewhat artificial view, for in reality 'effectiveness' can never be the only consideration; even if it were proved that death preceded by torture, or on the wheel, were more effective, we would refuse to act accordingly. However, it will be seen that the theory of hanging as the best deterrent can be refuted on its own purely utilitarian grounds, without calling ethics and charity to aid.

A deterrent must logically refer to a 'deterree', if the reader will forgive me for adding a verbal barbarity to the barbarous subject. So the first question is: who are the hypothetical deterrees, who will be prevented from committing murder by the threat of hanging, but not by the threat of long-term imprisonment? The fear of death is no doubt a powerful deterrent; but just how much more powerful is it than the fear of a life sentence?

The gallows obviously failed as a deterrent in all cases where a murder has actually been committed. It is certainly not a deterrent to murderers who commit suicide—and one-third of all murderers do.[1] It is not a deterrent to the insane and mentally deranged; nor to those who have killed in a quarrel, in drunkenness, in a sudden surge of passion—and this type of murder amounts to 80 to 90 per cent of all murders that are committed.[2] It is not a deterrent to the type of person who commits murder because he desires to be hanged; and these cases are not infrequent. It is not a deterrent to the person who firmly believes in his own perfect method—by poison, acid bath, and so on—which, he thinks, will never be found out. Thus the range of hypothetical deterrees who can only be kept under control by the threat of death and nothing short of death, is narrowed down to the professional criminal class. But both the abolitionists and their opponents agree that 'murder is not a crime of the criminal classes';[3] it is a crime of amateurs, not of professionals. None of the points I have mentioned so far is controversial; they are agreed on by both sides, and will be discussed at greater length in Chapter VIII, pp. 278 ff., 'Murderers as a Class'.

Who, then, are the deterrees for whose sake this country must preserve capital punishment? What type of criminal, to repeat the question in its precise form, can only be ruled by the threat of hanging, and nothing short of hanging? It is at this point that the issue between abolitionists and their opponents is really joined. The opponents' argument may be summed up as follows. As things stand, the professional criminal rarely commits murder; but if the threat of the gallows were abolished he would take to murder, and the crime-rate would go up.

This, of course, is an unproved assumption; a hypothesis whose truth could only be tested either (a) by experiment, or (b) by drawing on analogies from past experiences in Britain and abroad. The House of Commons in 1948 voted for the experiment. It said: let us suspend executions for five years, and see what happens. The House of Lords rejected it, after it was informed by the Lord Chief Justice that the twenty Judges of the King's Bench were unanimous in opposing the measure.[4] His main argument against the five-year suspension was that the experiment would be too dangerous; his second argument, that if the dangerous experiment were tried, abolition would come to stay. He used both arguments in the same speech.[5] So much for the experimental method.

2

Now for the second method: by analogy, or precedent. Perhaps the oddest thing about this whole controversy is that the Judges, who live on bread and precedent, never quote a precedent in support of their thesis that abolition leads to an increase in crime. After all, the burden of proof for this assumption lies on them; and since there is a gold-mine of precedent at their disposal of what happened after the abolition of capital punishment for some two hundred and twenty different categories of crime, why do they never, never treat us to a single case? Why do we never hear: you want to repeal the capital statute for murder; look what happened after the repeal of statute 14 Geo. 2, c. 6, s. 1 (1741) (burglary), 7 Will. 4 & 1 Vic.; c. 89, s. 2 (arson), 9 Geo. 4, c. 31, s. 16 (rape), 8 Geo. 1, c. 22 (1921) (forgery)? Why is it that the reformers, these reckless destroyers of the bulwarks of tradition, always rely on history for support, whereas on this particular issue the keepers of tradition act as if the past did not exist?

If the death-penalty were a more effective deterrent than lesser penalties, then its abolition for a given category of crime should be followed by a noticeable increase in the volume of that crime, precisely as the hanging party says. But the facts tell a different story. After the great reform, the crime-rate did not rise; it fell—as everybody except the oracles had expected. And yet the era of reform coincided with one of the most difficult periods in English social history. As if History herself had wanted to make the task of the abolitionists more difficult, the repeal of the death-penalty for offences against property during the 1830s was immediately followed by the 'hungry forties'. The great experiment of mitigating the rigour of the law could not have been carried out under more unfavourable circumstances. Yet half-way through the experiment, when the number of capital offences had been reduced to fifteen, His Majesty's Commissioners on Criminal Law, 1836, summed up their report as follows:

> It has not, in effect, been found that the repeal of Capital Punishment with regard to any particular class of offences has been attended with an increase of the offenders. On the contrary, the evidence and statements to be found in our appendix go far to demonstrate that . . . the absolute number of the offenders has diminished.[6]

And at the conclusion of this most dangerous experiment in the history of English criminal law, Sir Joseph Pease was able to state in the House of Commons that 'the continual mitigation of law and of sentences has been accomplished with property quite as secure, and human life quite as sacred'.[7]

'Deterrence' is an ugly and abstract word. It means, according to the *Oxford Dictionary*, 'discouragement by fear'. If the arguments in favour of the gallows as the supreme deterrent were true, then public executions would have the maximum discouraging effect on the criminal. Yet these public exhibitions were known to be the occasion when pickpockets gathered their richest harvest among the crowd—at a time when picking pockets was punishable by death. A contemporary author[8] explains why: 'The thieves selected the moment when the strangled man was swinging above them as the happiest opportunity, because they knew that everybody's eyes were on that person and all were looking up.'

Public executions not only failed to diminish the volume of crime; they often caused an immediate rise in their wake. The hanging of a criminal served, less as a warning, than as an incitement to imitate him. Fauntleroy confessed that the idea of committing forgery came to him while he watched a forger being hanged. A juryman, who found Dr. Dodd guilty of forgery, committed soon afterwards the same crime and was hanged from the same gallows. Cumming was hanged in Edinburgh in 1854 for sexual assault, which immediately led to a wave of similar assaults in the region. In 1855, Heywood was hanged in Liverpool for cutting the throat of a woman; three weeks later, Ferguson was arrested in the same town for the same crime. The list could be continued indefinitely. The evidence was so overwhelming that the Select Committee of the House of Lords was appointed in 1856; it recommended that public executions should be abolished because they did not deter from crime. The Lords would not believe it, and did nothing. Ten years later, the Royal Commission of 1866 inquired into the same question, and came to the same result as the Select Committee. One of the most striking pieces of evidence before the Commissioners was a statement by the prison chaplain in Bristol, the Reverend W. Roberts, that out of 167 persons awaiting execution in that prison, 164 had previously witnessed at least one execution.[9] What would the British Medical Association say of the value of a patent medicine for the prevention of polio, if it were found in 167 polio cases that 164 had been treated with that medicine?

Two years after the Royal Commission's reports, Parliament decided that executions should henceforth be private. However, if watching with one's own eyes the agony of a person being strangled on the gallows does not deter, it seems logical to assume that an unseen execution would deter even less. One may further argue that if the penalty of hanging does not frighten even a pickpocket, it would not frighten a potential murderer, who acts either in momentary passion, or for incomparably higher stakes. Yet these were not the conclusions reached by the lawgivers. They assumed that while watching an execution from a few yards' distance did not act as a deterrent, reading a Home Office communiqué about it did.

The results of the abolition of the death-penalty for crimes against property provide a powerful argument for abolishing it altogether. But in itself, the argument is not conclusive. The fact that abolition of the death-penalty did not increase the volume of cattle-stealing strongly suggests, but does not prove, that abolition of the death-penalty would not increase the volume of murder. That proof can only be initiated by analogy with other crimes; it must be completed by actual precedents for the crime of murder itself.

3

Fortunately, these precedents are available through the experience of the thirty-six states which have abolished capital punishment in the course of the last hundred years. They are listed below.[10] The dates in brackets indicate the year in which the death-penalty was abolished or abandoned.*

Europe: Austria (1919; reinstated by Hitler; abolished for the second time in 1950), Belgium (1863), Denmark (1933; in abeyance since 1892), Finland (1826), Iceland (1944), Italy (1890, restored by Mussolini in 1931; abolished again in 1944), Luxembourg (1822), The Netherlands (1870), Norway (1905, in abeyance since 1875), Portugal (1867), Sweden (1921, in abeyance since 1910), Switzerland (1874 and 1942, see appendix), Turkey (1950), Western Germany (1949).

Latin America: The Argentine (1922), Brazil (1891), Colombia (1910), Costa Rica (1880), Dominica (1924), Equador (1895), Mexico (Mexico City and seven states, 1929 and after), Nicaragua (1893), Panama (1903), Peru ('end of nineteenth century'), Uruguay (1807), Venezuela (1873).

U.S.A.: Michigan (1874), Rhode Island (1852), Wisconsin (1853), Maine (1876), Minnesota (1911), North Dakota (1915).

Other Countries: Queensland (1913), Israel (1948), Nepal (1931), Travancore (1944).

The evidence has been studied by criminologists and Departments of Justice all over the world, and summarised

* Several countries behind the Iron Curtain have also abolished capital punishment for non-political offences, but these have not been included in the list.

with previously unequalled thoroughness by the British Parliamentary Select Committee of 1929–30 and the Royal Commission on Capital Punishment of 1948–53. The report and evidence of the first fills some eight hundred closely printed pages; the report of the second, plus its Minutes of Evidence, nearly fourteen hundred pages of quarto and folio. The conclusion of the Select Committee is summed up as follows:

> Our prolonged examination of the situation in foreign countries has increasingly confirmed us in the assurance that capital punishment may be abolished in this country without endangering life or property, or impairing the security of Society.[11]

The conclusions of the Royal Commission were essentially the same, although more cautiously expressed. Their terms of reference prevented them from considering the question whether capital punishment should be abolished or not; they were only allowed to make recommendations concerning changes in the existing capital law. Moreover, their report was unanimous,* whereas the Select Committee report of 1930, as the previous Royal Commission report of 1866, was a majority report. The Commission's final conclusion regarding the expected consequences of abolition (which they managed to smuggle in, though the terms of reference excluded this question) was formulated thus:

> There is no clear evidence of any lasting increase [in the murder-rate following abolition] and there are many offenders on whom the deterrent effect is limited and may often be negligible. It is therefore important to view the question in a just perspective and not to base a penal policy in relation to murder on exaggerated estimates of the uniquely deterrent force of the death-penalty.[12]

They reached this conclusion by taking two types of evidence into account: on the one hand, the crime statistics of

---

* Except for some minority reservations on subjects which are irrelevant to the issue under discussion.

foreign countries; on the other, the opinion of the British
Police Force, the prison services and the judges. It is to this
second or local, evidence that the expression 'exaggerated
estimates' refers; and in their conclusions the Commissioners
make some allowances for it. But in the text of their report, as
distinct from their cautious 'conclusions', they make their
findings unmistakably clear. They dismiss the police's and the
judges' contention that abolition would entice burglars to wear
firearms: 'We received no evidence that the abolition of capital
punishment in other countries had in fact led to the consequences apprehended by our witnesses in this country.'[13]
Their opinion on the general effect of abolition on the crime-
rate in foreign countries is equally unambiguous. They
analysed the staggeringly extensive material which they had
assembled under three headings:

(a) by comparing the homicide statistics of a given country
before and after abolition of the death-penalty;
(b) by comparing the homicide statistics of neighbouring
countries of a similar social structure, some of which have
abolished the death-penalty and some not, over the same
period of time;
(c) by analysing the possible influence of the number of
executions in a given country in a particular year on the
homicide rate in the immediately following period.

Concerning (a), they state: 'The general conclusion which
we have reached is that there is no clear evidence in any of the
figures we have examined that the abolition of capital punishment has led to an increase in the homicide rate, or that its
reintroduction has led to a fall.'[14]

Concerning (b), their findings are mainly based on comparisons between the homicide curves in closely related states in
the U.S.A.; and between New Zealand and the Australian
states:

If we take any of these groups we find that the fluctuations in
the homicide rate of each of its component members exhibit
a striking similarity. We agree with Professor Sellin that the

only conclusion which can be drawn from the figures is that there is no clear evidence of any influence of the death-penalty on the homicide rates of these States, and that, 'whether the death-penalty is used or not, and whether executions are frequent or not, both death-penalty States and abolition States show rates which suggest that these rates are conditioned by other factors than the death-penalty'.[15]

Concerning (c), they state: '. . . about the possible relation between the number of executions in particular years and the incidence of murder in succeeding years . . . we are satisfied that no such relationship can be established.'[16]

4

Once more the mountains laboured and a mouse was born. The mountainous statistical survey of the Royal Commission of 1948 merely confirmed the findings of the Select Committee of 1930, which confirmed the findings of all abolitionist countries in the course of the last century for crimes against property: to wit, that abolition has not caused an increase in murder nor stopped the fall of the murder-rate in any European country; and that in the non-European countries, the U.S.A., Australia and New Zealand, the ups and downs of the murder-rate show a striking similarity in states of similar social structure whether the death-penalty is used or not.

The defenders of capital punishment are well aware that the statistical evidence is unanswerable. They do not contest it; they ignore it. When pressed in debate, they invariably fall back on one of two answers: (a) 'statistics lie' or 'do not prove anything'; (b) that the experience of foreign countries has no bearing on conditions in Britain.

That 'statistics don't prove anything' is, of course, nonsense; if it were true, all insurance companies, physicists and engineers would have to go out of business, and the Chancellor of the Exchequer could never present a Budget. Statistics are indispensable in every human activity; and like every tool they can be put to careless and dishonest use. Statistics cannot prove or disprove that smoking 'causes' lung cancer; it can prove that the average Englishman is taller than the average Italian. In the first example, the observational range is too small in relation to the number of causative factors involved.* In the second example, the statistician merely states a fact which can be interpreted in various ways; by race, nourishment, climate, and so on.

In discussing the statistics of abolitionist Europe, we have to distinguish with great care between fact and interpretation. The facts are beyond dispute: throughout the twentieth century, abolition was in no European country followed by an increase in the murder-rate, and was in nearly all countries followed by a decrease. These facts can be interpreted in the following manners:

(1) Abolition causes a fall in the murder-rate.

(2) Abolition causes an increase in the murder-rate, but this increase is too small to stop the general downward trend of the murder-rate, which is due to different causes.

(3) Abolition does not perceptibly influence the murder-rate one way or another.

All three interpretations are possible, although the examples of post-war Germany and post-war Italy seem to contradict the second hypothesis; but that, of course, is not conclusive. It is at this point that the comparisons between similar states with different legislation comes in. They prove that 'both death-penalty states and abolition states show rates which suggest that they are conditioned by other factors than the death-penalty. . . . The general picture is the same—a rise in the rates of the early twenties and a downward trend since then.'[17]

This eliminates interpretations (1) and (2) and leaves us with (3): that the death-penalty cannot be proved to influence the murder-rate one way or another.

Let me make the point clearer by a familiar example. If the medical profession wants to test the efficiency of a new serum there are, by and large, two methods of doing this. The first is

---

* Thus it is possible that people of a certain temperament and constitution are more liable than others both to become heavy smokers and to develop lung cancer, without any causal relationship between the two.

to administer the serum to a number of patients and see how the results compare with the use of older medicines. The substitution of prison sentences in lieu of capital punishment was an experiment of this kind. It showed that it was followed nearly everywhere in Europe by a fall in the fever chart of crime. This in itself did not prove that the new treatment was the direct *cause* of the improvement, because perhaps the epidemic was on the wane anyway; but it did prove that the new treatment could at least not be sufficiently harmful to impede the fall on the fever chart, whatever the cause of that fall. The second method is used as a check on the first. The new serum is administered to patients in one hospital ward, and the rate of recovery is then compared to that in a second or 'control' ward, where treatment is continued on the old lines. If the rate of recovery remains substantially the same in both wards, the B.M.A. will conclude that the new treatment is just as good or bad as the old one, as far as its deterrent effect on the disease goes. The choice will then be decided by other considerations. If the new treatment is less painful or repellent, then only the oldest fogeys of the profession will, just for the hell of it, stick to their ancient method.

To sum up: the experience of the civilised world proves as conclusively as the most rigorously sifted evidence can ever prove, that the gallows is no more effective than other, non-lethal, deterrents.

But statistics don't bleed; let us always remember the individual sample falling through the trap.

5

So much for the contention that 'statistics don't prove anything'. The second stock answer of the hang-hards runs: 'Foreign experience doesn't prove anything, because foreigners are different'. It was said in defence of death for shoplifting when all the rest of Europe had abandoned it; it is repeated today with the same unction. The grain of truth in it is that no nation is like any other nation; thus the example of, say, Switzerland *alone* would be of little value because Switzerland is a more 'peaceful' country than England. But the whole point of the statistical approach is that, over a large number of samples, individual differences cancel out, and the general trend common to all is revealed.

Now the evidence concerning abolition embraces thirty-six countries with vastly different populations, and in different periods of development; agricultural and industrial nations, old and new civilisations, countries rich and countries poor, Latin, Anglo-Saxon and Germanic races, hot-tempered and placid people, countries which became abolitionist after a long period of peace and security, and others, like Germany and Italy, which have only just emerged from war, demoralised by defeat, brutalised by years of totalitarian terror. The convincingness of the proof rests precisely in the fact that, however different the countries and conditions, abolition was nowhere followed by an increase in the crime-rate, or any other noticeable ill-effect.

6

The general reader who is new to this controversy would naturally assume that the opponents of abolition have their own arguments, figures and evidence on the same reasoned and factual level as the abolitionists, and that it would require a good deal of expert knowledge to decide which party is right. This is not the case. The defenders of capital punishment have produced no evidence of their own; nor contested the correctness of the documentary material assembled by Royal Commissions, Select Committees, etc.; nor even tried to put a different interpretation on it. They simply ignore it, as they ignore the experience gained from mitigations of the law in this country's own past. When challenged, they invariably and uniformly trot out the same answers: there is no alternative to capital punishment; statistics don't prove anything; other nations can afford to abolish hanging, but not Britain, because 'the type of the British convict is absolutely different in his attitude towards things from any other nation in the world'.[18] Other nations can afford to abolish hanging but not Britain, because the criminal Englishman (or Welshman or Scotsman) is different from any other criminal in the world; for foreigners prison may be a sufficient deterrent, the English criminal needs the gallows. He lives in crowded cities, whereas foreigners tend their rural sheep. Incidentally, the Royal Commission has shown that the British crime-rate is the same in urban and rural areas,[19] and thereby exploded another old myth. But then, English rural areas are different from other rural areas; and so on. What indeed is the use of piling argument upon argument?

Since the Select Committee's report, the Royal Commission has vastly extended the scope of the former's inquiry, and arrived at the same results. The answer of the hang-hards remained the same. It seems hardly believeable that in a nation-wide controversy which has now been going on for some twenty-five years, one side should produce, with ant-like diligence, facts, figures and historic precedent, mobilise the whole array of psychiatry and social science, borne out by impartial Royal Commissions—and the other side should content themselves with evasion and stonewalling. The legend about the hangman as the protector of society has been refuted and exposed to ridicule on every single past occasion, and yet it popped up again on the next.

This is perhaps the saddest aspect in this whole heart- and neck-breaking business. For it shows that an officially sponsored lie has a thousand lives and takes a thousand lives. It resembles one of the monster squids of deep-sea lore; it spurts ink into your face, while its tentacles strangle the victim in the interest of public welfare.

Part Two

THE LAW

III. Reflections on the Hanging of a Pig

or

What is Criminal Responsibility?

IN Mangin's *L'Homme et la Bête*[1] there is an engraving, entitled: 'Infliction of the Death Penalty on a Sow.' The sow,
dressed in human clothes, legs pinioned, is held down on the
scaffold by the executioner, who is fixing the noose round its
throat. Facing the sow is the town clerk, reading the sentence
from a scroll; at the foot of the scaffold is a jostling crowd,
much of the same kind as the crowds which used to assemble
around the Tyburn Tree. Mothers are lifting up their children
to give them a better view; and a stern worthy is pointing his
finger at the screaming sow, obviously explaining: 'She is only
getting what she deserves.'

Animals guilty of killing a human being were, in the Middle
Ages, and in isolated cases up to the nineteenth century, tried
by lawful procedure, defended by counsel, sometimes acquitted, more often sentenced to be hanged, burned, or buried
alive. The sow on the engraving had killed a baby, and was
hanged in 1386 at Falaise; a horse which had killed a man was
hanged at Dijon in 1389; another sow, with a litter of six,
was sentenced for the murder of a child at Savigny in 1457, but
the baby pigs were reprieved 'in lack of positive proof of
complicity'.

A further capital crime for animals beside homicide (with or
without malice aforethought) was sexual intercourse with a
human being. In such cases both partners in crime, man and
animal, were burned alive together, according to the Lex

Carolina. The last recorded case was the burning of Jacques Ferron in 1750 at Vanvres for sodomy with a she-ass; but the animal was acquitted after the Parish Priest and several leading citizens had testified that she was 'the victim of violence and had not participated in the crime of her own free will'.[2] Capital punishment of animals fell gradually into abeyance in the eighteenth century; the last recorded case is the trial and execution of a dog for having participated in a robbery and murder, in Délémont, Switzerland, 1906.[3]

Why do we find the hanging of an animal even more revolting and disgusting than the hanging of a human being? The question deserves some reflection.

Take the word 'disgusting' first. Most of us, who are not vegetarians, have no strong feelings of disgust about the painless slaughtering of cattle and the shooting of game; the idea of executing an animal is disgusting because it appears to us as a purposeless and 'artificial' way of ending its life, made even more gruesome by a grotesque ceremony. But hanging a man or a woman is an equally unappetising and artificial ceremony. Both the murderer and the soldier have a motive to kill, which makes their act more or less spontaneous; in the execution chamber this redeeming aspect of spontaneity is absent, and only the ghastly ceremonial aspect of breaking a neck remains. However, aesthetic revulsion is only a minor point. The real question is why we find capital punishment of animals *intellectually* more revolting than capital punishment of humans.

Let us look at the problem from the point of view of the protection of society. We know that hanging pigs won't deter other pigs from attacking babies left carelessly lying around; properly penning up the pigs is a quite sufficient protection of society. But this answer won't hold good either, because experience proves that executing the human criminal is also no more effective as a deterrent than penning him up; thus once the belief in deterrence falls, hanging a man is just as pointlessly cruel as hanging a horse. Why, then, are we more horrified by the idea of strangling a horse? Because it is a helpless creature? A woman pinioned or strapped to a chair and hoisted to the rope is just as helpless.

We must try another approach. Let us put it this way: 'The

poor, dumb creature did not know what it was doing, it is not responsible for its acts; and hence the proceedings of the court are an absurd farce.' Now at last we seem to be getting somewhere. But are we really? For if you have ever seen the guilty look in your dog's eye after he stole a chop or chewed up your slippers, you know that the jury would have no choice but to find him criminally responsible according to the M'Naghten rule: *that he knew the nature of his act, and knew that it was wrong.*

A pig, of course, is less intelligent than a dog, and may be said to be lacking, comparatively, in moral sense. But feeble-mindedness and lack of moral sense do not abolish criminal responsibility, nor are they sufficient grounds for pleading 'guilty but insane'. Straffen was mentally defective, yet he was sentenced to death, after Mr. Justice Cassels instructed the jury to bear in mind only the M'Naghten Rules and '*not* that he is feeble-minded, *not* that he has a lack of moral sense'. [4] Thus the Prosecution would have not particular difficulty in proving that the sow, according to her dim lights, knew what she was doing, and knew that she was doing something that was not permitted, for as soon as the keeper appeared on the scene she ran away guiltily instead of approaching him as usual in the expectancy of food. We can go even further than that and still remain on solid legal ground: every animal capable of being tamed and domesticated would be found criminally responsible in our Courts—for the simple reason that the process of taming itself is based on establishing in the animal's mind distinctions between what is permitted and what is not. Similarly, discipline in mental homes can only be maintained because all lunatics, except those in the padded cell, are able to distinguish between 'right' and 'wrong' with reference to the regulations in their wards. As Lord Bramwell remarked some eighty years ago: 'The present law lays down such a definition of madness that nobody is hardly ever really mad enough to be within it.' [5] It is true that if a feeble-minded creature is hauled up in court, the court may, according to Section 8 of the Mental Deficiency Acts, send him to an institution, or place him under guardianship instead of passing judgment—*except if the offence is punishable by death*; in which case judgment must be passed on the creature. [6]

Hence counsel for the defence of the animal must try another line. Stupidity and lack of moral sense won't get his client off. Nor a plea of 'diminished responsibility'; because a creature can have its responsibility diminished in Scotland, but can't have it diminished in England and Wales.

The last hope is to get the charge reduced from murder to manslaughter. In the case of the horse who kicked its master to death, 'provocation' might perhaps do the trick, for the horse had been nervous and irritable ever since it was shocked by a blunderbuss in the battle of Cherbourg, and witnesses testified that its nasty master had fired off a firecracker in front of its nose to tease it. So the fool had only to blame himself if the horse went off its head. But that won't do either; firstly because provocation is not a mitigating circumstance if committed by mere word or gesture.* And secondly, because the provocation must be such as to satisfy the jury (a) that it deprived the accused of his self-control, and (b) that *it would also have deprived any other reasonable man (or horse) of self-control.* Thus a creature 'who is mentally deficient or mentally abnormal or is "not of good mental balance" or who is "unusually excitable or pugnacious" is not entitled to rely on provocation which would not have led an ordinary person to act as he did'.[7] This nicety of the law referring to provocation is usually called 'the test of the reasonable man'.[8] It states expressly that when the jury has to decide whether the provocation was sufficient to deprive a reasonable man of his self-control, they ought *not to* 'take into account different degrees of mental ability'.[9] That means that the jury, in assessing the effect of provocation must not consider the living individual before them but an abstract ideal being. This fantastic ruling was approved by the Court of Criminal Appeal (in 1940), and again by the House of Lords (in 1942).[10] Accordingly, the firecracker let off in front of the shell-shocked horse, which made the creature go off its head, does not justify a plea of provocation because a reasonable horse wouldn't have gone off its head; nor calling a refugee from a Nazi concentration camp a filthy Jew, because

* Except 'in circumstances of a most extreme and exceptional character'.[8] There has been no recent case in which mere words or gesture have been accepted as sufficient provocation.

a reasonable person wouldn't turn a hair.

As a last resort, Counsel might try to argue that the poor horse did not act with 'malice aforethought'; if he could prove that, the charge would be reduced from murder to manslaughter. But how could he prove that? For in the phrase 'malice aforethought' 'neither of the two words is used in its ordinary sense. . . . It is now only an arbitrary symbol. For the malice may have in it nothing really malicious; and need never be really aforethought, except in the sense that every desire must necessarily come before—though perhaps only an instant before—the act which is desired. The word "aforethought" in the definition has thus become either false or else superfluous.'[11]

And yet this meaningless phrase is still the basic criterion of murder. 'The statement of the modern law most commonly cited as authoritative is that given in 1877 by Sir James Stephen in his *Digest of the Criminal Law*: "Malice aforethought means any one or more of the following states of mind preceding *or coexisting* with the act . . . by which death is caused, and *it may exist where the act is unpremeditated*." '[12]

The short and long of the matter is: if animals were still prosecuted in our courts, the jury, according to the law as it stands, would have no choice but to bring in a verdict of guilty against the pig, the horse and the cow, and to add a strong recommendation for mercy. Only the dog with rabies would get off, for that dog alone would qualify as 'M'Naghten mad'.

The absurdity of the law when applied strictly and literally has been known to the legal profession for a long time. In 1874, a Select Committee of the House of Commons reported: 'If there is any case in which the law should speak plainly, without sophism or evasion, it is where life is at stake; and it is on this very occasion that the law is most evasive and most sophistical.'[13] Seventy-five years have passed since, yet in spite of countless attempts to reform it, the law is substantially the same today as it was a hundred years ago. The most glaring example of its 'evasive and sophistical' nature are the famous M'Naghten Rules—which for reasons which will presently become apparent, deserve a chapter to themselves.

IV. The Case of the Mace-bearer

I NOW propose to describe an individual murder story in some detail. It is a case that was tried in 1950 and given little publicity at the time or since. It was one of the cases in which the accused drew a red on the roulette: the jury returned a verdict of guilty but insane, though they knew perfectly well that he was not insane either according to Saint M'Naghten or in any accepted sense of insanity. It is a humdrum story about ordinary people which demonstrates the absurdity of the murder law in a neater way than more dramatic cases.

Donald Martin* was at the time a respectable and respected citizen of the age of fifty. He was Town Hall Superintendent and Mace-bearer at the Borough of Notting Hill, and lived on a flat in the Town Hall called 'caretaker's premises'. On official occasions he walked behind the Mayor, carrying the mace in solemn procession. His wife Violet, also middle-aged, was working for the National Savings Association in the same Town Hall. They had one child, a pretty girl called Sally, aged seventeen.

On Wednesday, September 27th, 1950, Mr. and Mrs. Martin had lunch at an A.B.C. in Baker Street and, returning to caretaker's premises, had an argument. Martin tried to persuade Violet to give up her job so that she could spend more time in looking after their flat, and also that she should consult the Marriage Advice Bureau. Violet refused, whereupon Donald hit her on the head—the first time in his life that

---

* The facts of the case are as stated; the names of the participants have been altered to avoid distress to their families. 'Notting Hill Town Hall', which does not exist, stands for the existing Town Hall of a London borough.

he had hit her—then, leaving her lying on the floor, went to the kitchen, took his razor out of its case, replaced the case neatly at right angles to his brush and comb on the shelf, went back to Violet, cut her throat, and when satisfied that she was dead, telephoned the police. When the police arrived, he was sitting at the top of the staircase waiting for them, perfectly composed. He remained equally composed while waiting for his trial and never revealed any real remorse for what he had done.

Donald was the third in a family of eleven children, of which ten survived. His father was a workman in the painting and decorating trade. His mother was a simple woman, who had led a very hard life. There was no hereditary mental disease in the family, and all of its members got on reasonably well in life. It is true that the father was said to have been a violent-tempered man who once broke the nose of one of his daughters with a blow, but such incidents, alas, are not very exceptional in hard-up, working-class families of that size.

Donald was a normal child, average in school, who got on well with his schoolmates and took an active part in all sports; he particularly excelled in boxing. According to his mother, he was always well behaved, never quarrelsome or violent; the only complaint about him was that he had been excessively 'tidy and particular'. Out of school hours he earned money for the family by polishing boots and selling newspapers. At fourteen, on leaving school, he held a job as a grocer's errand boy for twelve months, then another as a milkman for eighteen months. He subsequently worked in a rubber factory for a year, but did not like indoor work, and became a baker's roundsman.

At the age of nineteen, he enlisted in the Royal Tank Corps. He served altogether eighteen years in England, India and Egypt, reaching the rank of Sergeant and Acting Company Quartermaster-Sergeant. When he left the Army at the age of thirty-seven, his character was described as exemplary; he was awarded the long-service and good-conduct medal and granted a service pension. He then got employment at Notting Hill Town Hall, at first as a porter, and, during the next twelve years, gradually worked his way up to be Town Hall Superintendent and Mace-bearer.

A more decent and ordinary career could hardly be imagined. Yet Donald Martin bore a cross, part real, part imaginary, under whose weight he finally collapsed. He was, so to speak, a common-or-garden martyr of that commonplace Calvary: a marriage between incompatible partners.

He met Violet when he was twenty-two, while stationed with his Company in Dorset. She was at that time a laundry-maid. A year later he became engaged to her; another two years later they were married; another fortnight later, during their honeymoon, she infected him with syphilis.

He did not realise this at the time. He only found out about it eight years later, when he was stationed in India, and a medical examination revealed a syphilitic infection of the central nervous system. The date of the infection was then traced back to the appearance of a small genital ulcer a fortnight after his marriage, which he had noticed at the time but ignored as harmless. He received treatment in military hospitals in England, India and Egypt, over a period of more than two years, and was then reported cured.

The medical examination which led to the discovery of the disease was caused by an incident at the Army Barracks in Poona. This happened in the eighth year of their marriage, and one year after Violet had given birth to their daughter Sally. They were living in married quarters. Donald suspected that Violet, who had been sexually cold towards him from the beginning of their marriage, was committing adultery with a Company Sergeant. There was a quarrel, after which he stole a revolver from the Armoury, intending to shoot Violet, the baby and himself. Before he could do so, however, an officer and N.C.O. came to arrest him for taking the revolver and ammunition without authority. He was court-martialled, but pleaded that he could not remember what he was doing. He was sent for observation into hospital; where, in the course of a medical examination, he was discovered to be suffering from syphilitic meningo-encephalitis.

Yet the idea of shooting Violet, the baby and himself had already occurred to Donald prior to this discovery. What had been going on during those first eight years of their married life to drive him to this point? We only have a few glimpses of the idyll between Donald and Violet. One of them is provided by Donald's repeated complaints about her sexual coldness towards him, and by his description 'how she would merely lie on her side and go on reading a book whilst he had sexual intercourse with her'. But in the law of murder this mortal offence to the male's pride is not known as a provocation to a reasonable man.

Nothing could be more commonplace than the fact that during twenty-four years of their married life Donald loved Violet desperately and Violet treated Donald like dirt. He was not a lovable man. He was narrow-minded, vain, pedantic and egocentric, obsessed with tidiness, and respectable appearances; a hypochondriac, constantly afraid of microbes and infections. Yet he forgave her the honeymoon present she had given him, and forgave her all that she did to him during the sixteen years that followed his first impulse to do away with her and himself and their child; in return, she kept adding provocation to provocation, of a kind not mentioned in the law books.

He kept himself under control. Only twice during all these years did he lose his temper: the first time when he was twenty-nine and had a fight with a soldier who taunted him; the second time, three years later, on the occasion when he got hold of the revolver. His Army record describes him as an excellent N.C.O., a good driver and mechanic, and a man who could confidently be recommended for any position of trust.

He was thirty-seven when he left the Army and started work at the Town Hall. The next ten years or so, the life of Donald and Violet was outwardly uneventful. He had an excellent work record. After being appointed Town Hall caretaker, he was responsible for porters and domestic staff and managed them well, though occasionally he was inclined to employ Army Sergeant methods. During the war he was superintendent of the local A.R.P. office, and an active member of the Civil Defence Club, to which Violet often accompanied him for dances and whist drives. He took great pride in his functions as a Mace-bearer. He did not betray the inner strain under which he lived and which he held in check by a rigid, meticulous, indeed fanatical, observance of his civic duties—as a man with a broken spine carries his head held stiffly up by a metal harness.

Perhaps the only odd thing about him was the exaggerated seriousness, verging on obsession, with which he took his duties. Having once been reprimanded for forgetting to hoist the flag for Princess Elizabeth's birthday, he wrote a letter to Buckingham Palace, asking for a complete list of royal birthdays. When the time came to ask for an increase in salary, he sent an inquiry to a number of other caretakers at town halls regarding their salaries; then wrote a letter of seven closely covered foolscap pages to the Town Clerk, enumerating in detail all the important duties which he was called on to perform.

Since his main pride and obsession in life were order, discipline and tidiness, Violet, with the psychological insight that hatred provides, tormented him by being slatternly about their flat, never cooking a hot meal except once a week on Sunday, and turning caretaker's premises into a place of lewdness and abomination.

For by now the daughter, Sally, had become an attractive girl with an alarmingly developed temperament. At the age of seventeen, Sally had a 'steady' named Horace, and besides him several sailor friends in the Merchant Navy. On one occasion, three sailors on three different ships simultaneously applied for special leave to visit their fiancée, Sally Martin.

Horace, the civilian steady, was always hanging around caretaker's premises, and 'carrying on' with Sally, with the consent and encouragement of Violet. This, of course, was a constant agony to Martin, the disciplinarian and prig; but he also had some additional reasons for loathing his daughter's young man. Horace had pimples on the back of his neck and Martin, who lived in horror of germs and infection, caught the pimples, so he thought, by washing out the sink after Horace had been there. On another occasion, he found a packet of contraceptives in Horace's pocket.

During the last year, the squalid cross became too heavy to bear. Donald believed that Violet and Sally were in alliance against him. At times they would 'send him to Coventry' for several days on end. On one occasion they both left and were gone for a fortnight, leaving Donald to fend for himself in the flat. On several other occasions Violet left to stay with a sister, and threatened never to come back again. She knew that what he cherished most in life was his job at the Town Hall, and that if she left him he would lose it. She told him repeatedly that to sleep with him was repellent and distasteful to her, and encouraged him to have relations with other women. He tried this at the final stages, but it did not help.

Downstairs in the Town Hall he was still the strict and self-important Company Sergeant of Poona; upstairs at care-taker's premises he was virtually reduced to the state of an untouchable. In the Civil Defence Club he appeared, impec-cably dressed, a paragon of respectability; in his sordid home he felt that he was drowning in dirt, pimples, contraceptives and fornications, real and imagined. He clutched at every straw. He implored Violet to give up her job because he thought that if she did so she would have more time to look after the flat, and all would be well. He sought advice from a doctor, who talked of sending him on to a psychiatrist, and then all would be well. He sought advice from the Marriage Advice Bureau, and implored Violet to go there, because they would talk to her sensibly and all would be well.

About six weeks before the end, Violet again left him. She went to stay with her sister in Dorchester, and said she would never come back. Whilst she was away, Donald cleaned, painted and decorated the flat. Then he followed her to Dorchester and persuaded Violet to come back and 'give it another chance'. Donald's mother, aged seventy-four, was invited to an egg-and-bacon tea to welcome Violet on her return, and the old woman felt that a real reconciliation had taken place. Then Sally, who had also been away, came back too, and then Horace, and the contraceptives, and the pimples.

He became so miserable that he could hardly eat. Some time before the end he developed a duodenal ulcer. He was operated on and put on a gastric diet—which he could not keep because Violet refused to cook for him. He then became suspicious, and later convinced, that Violet was having sexual relations with their daughter's young man.

The incidents of the last three days are as drab and commonplace as the rest.

On Monday, September 25th, Donald is reported to have asked Sally to help him with Hoovering the flat, which she refused. There were a few words.

On Tuesday, September 26th, Donald called on a Mrs. Tiplady, Sanitary Inspector at Notting Hill Town Hall, and asked her to inspect his flat in her official capacity, to confirm that his wife was neglecting it. Mrs. Tiplady obliged and wrote a report.

On Wednesday, September 27th, he again called to see Mrs. Tiplady, excitedly waving a *Daily Mail*, in which a sensational article on the neglect of the homes of married women who went out to work had appeared. Then he called at Violet's office, asking her to give up her job. Then they had lunch at the A.B.C., Baker Street, and they had an argument. Then they went on to the flat and he asked her again to give up her job and to consult the Marriage Advice Bureau. She refused, threatened to leave him again and spoke to him, as he described it, 'in a manner she had never done before'. Considering the time they had spent together, it must have been quite some manner to speak in. Then he hit her for the first time in his life; and then a quarter-century of repressed hatred burst to the surface, and he fetched his razor and cut her throat. She must have resisted, because there were cuts on her hands and arms.

While awaiting his trial, he slept well and ate well, and said he felt much happier now that he was in prison. In his statements he was frank and co-operative and unhesitatingly volunteered information which was prejudicial to him. He only made one misleading statement, at an early interview, when he denied having ever been unfaithful to Violet. His only complaint about conditions in prison was that he could not keep his clothes as tidy as he would like to and as he always had done. He did not seem to be aware that he had committed a crime and seemed to have no sense of guilt. He said to one of his visitors that a girl with whom he used to go out before he met Violet, and whom he had not seen for many years, had written to him on reading about the case: this had led to an amorous correspondence and her visiting him in prison. He hoped that if acquitted he could marry her.

When Donald Martin was tried for murder at the Old Bailey, the defence plea was guilty but insane. What else could Counsel plead? Not provocation, for Violet did not physically attack him, and her refusal to go the the Marriage Advice Bureau would hardly have caused a 'reasonable man' to lose control of himself. Nor the absence of malice aforethought, since after knocking her down he went to the bathroom, extracted the razor, and put down the case with care and pre-meditation before he murdered her. There could also be no doubt that when he committed his act he knew what he was doing, and that what he was doing was wrong. There exists no paragraph in criminal law which Counsel could plead to reduce the charge from murder to manslaughter. There exists no paragraph in criminal law which would have enabled the judge and jury to spare the life of Donald Martin. Yet judge and jury, and even Counsel for the Crown, felt that it was not really necessary to hang Martin, either to avenge society or to protect society against other Mace-bearers who contract syphilis on their honeymoons. And because they all felt this strongly, charity and common sense prevailed; and the jury with a sigh of relief sent Mace-bearer Martin to be detained at the King's pleasure among the lunatics in Broadmoor.

V. Free Will and Determinism

or

The Philosophy of Hanging

I

LET us return once more to the seemingly pointless question why we find the hanging of an animal so much more repellent than the hanging of a human being.

We saw that before the law as it stands, neither the horse which killed its master, nor the dog who stole the Sunday joint would have a chance of getting off, because they knew what they were doing and that what they were doing was wrong. Of course, the dog couldn't plead, except by wagging its tail and showing balefully the whites of its eyes; but some criminals behave as equally dumb creatures in the dock, and there is always counsel to plead for them. Yet, although we know that a well-trained dog knows its duty, and consequently knows right from wrong, and would be found 'criminally responsible', we feel that man is nevertheless *more* responsible, or responsible in a different and higher sense, than an animal. We are ready to grant the dog or the chimpanzee the excuse that they were obeying an 'irresistible impulse' and could not control themselves, whereas we assume more or less consciously that man *can* control himself, and that, when he commits a crime, he does it out of his own choice, independently from causative compulsion, out of his own free will.

We say: the dog couldn't help doing what he did, but the human criminal could have resisted the criminal impulse if he had 'tried harder', 'made a greater effort', 'kept himself under better control'. 'Harder', 'greater', 'better'—than what? Than the effort or resistance which he actually did put up. Our belief that he *ought* and *could* have put up a greater effort than he actually did, implies the assumption that the same person faced with the same situation has the choice of reacting to it in two different ways. In other words, that *the same cause may lead to two or more different effects*. This assumption goes against the very foundations on which modern science is built. Yet it is this assumption which underlies the concept of 'criminal responsibility', and which is implied in the whole body of the Law.

The issue of free will *versus* determinism is hardly mentioned at all in the century-old controversy on capital punishment. Yet it is really the heart of the matter. It is shunned because it is the oldest and most awe-inspiring problem of philosophy, and probably an insoluble one. Yet I will try to show that our inability to solve the problem is the strongest argument against capital punishment.

The dilemma is not one of abstract philosophy; it permeates all our actions in daily life. On the one hand I know that everything that happens is determined by the laws of nature, and, since I am part of the natural world, my conduct is *determined* by heredity and environment. But at the same time, contradicting this knowledge, I feel that I am *free* to choose whether at this moment I shall go on writing this text, or call it a day and have a drink at the local. My scientific education tells me that the outcome is predetermined by my past, and that what I experience as my 'free choice' is an illusion. It tells me, moreover, that the satisfaction that I shall feel tomorrow for having resisted temptation is equally illusory; if a man is compelled by the laws of nature to do what he does, we can no more praise or blame him for it than we can blame a watch for being fast or slow. From the scientific point of view a man's actions appear indeed as strictly determined by the genes which transmit his heredity, by the functions of his glands and liver, by his upbringing and past experiences which mould his habits and thoughts, his convictions and philosophy, as the functioning of a watch is determined by its springs, wheels and bearings, or as an 'electronic brain' is determined by the circuits, amplifiers, resistances, rules of action and memory-stores which have been built or 'fed' into the machine. If I feel a glow of satisfaction after a certain act, it is because I have been conditioned to experience just this type of emotion after this kind of act. If I feel guilt or remorse, it is because this type of reaction too has been hammered into me.

The function of education, then, according to the deterministic view, is to set up in the individual such habits and reaction-patterns that in a situation of conflict he will 'automatically' tend towards the socially useful solution, because his expectation of outer reward or inner satisfaction will be one of the factors which determine his conduct; whereas the built-in expectation of punishment or remorse will act as an automatic deterrent. The function of the law from this strictly deterministic point of view is reduced to deterrence, plus reform through corrective reconditioning. Praise and blame, punishment as vengeance or retribution, have no logical place in a scientific world-view which treats man as part of the natural universe, and his character and actions as subject to its laws. He reacts in any given situation as he must, for he could only act otherwise if either his character or the situation or both were different. If Mace-bearer Martin had not killed Violet, he would not have been Martin and Violet would not have been Violet. To say that Donald ought not to have killed Violet means simply that Donald ought not have been Donald. There was an old saying in Vienna: 'If my granny had four wheels, she would be called an omnibus.'

In a consistently deterministic system of law, the definitions used in our courts would be regarded as pure nonsense. 'Criminal responsibility' would be nonsense because 'responsibility' implies a freely chosen course of action, whereas free choice is illusion and all action determined by the past. 'I could not help it' would be a complete defence, for none of us can help being what we are and behaving as we do. Such a purely pragmatic concept of law has been advocated by various schools; it has a strong appeal to the scientifically minded and to all adherents of materialistic philosophy. It was, for instance, the basis of the Marxist theory of law up to and including the first years of the Russian Revolution. But developments in Russia are a vivid example of the difficulties which a strictly deterministic concept of the law must of necessity meet, for in no other country is the vindictive, retributive element of punishment more vehemently emphasised than under the Soviet régime. Its materialistic philosophy denies that man has a free choice in his actions, yet he is called a traitor, a 'cannibal' or a 'hyena' if he makes the Wrong choice.

This paradox is not confined to the law; it has its roots in the common everyday experiences of every human being. For we all feel that, regardless of what we have learnt about causality and determinism, it nevertheless 'depends on me' what I shall do within the next five minutes; or at least that it depends on me within certain limits. Henry Sidgwick[1] has formulated the dilemma in a very neat form:

Is my voluntary action at any moment completely determined by (1) my character as it has been partly inherited, partly formed by my past actions and feelings, and (2) my circumstances, and the external influences acting on me at the moment? Or not?

Detached reasoning will compel most of us to answer the question with a reluctant 'yes'. But our intimate, direct experience cries out a passionate 'no'. For, to quote William James, our 'whole feeling of realtiy, the whole sting and excitement of our voluntary life depends on our sense that in it things are *really being decided* from one moment to another, and that it is not the dull rattling off of a chain that was forged innumerable years ago'.[2] This 'sting and excitement' may of course be an illusion. But the point is, that even if it is an illusion, it is a useful and *necessary* illusion for the functioning of both the individual and society.

Let us assume that, by rational conviction, I adhere to a strictly determinist philosophy. I shall nevertheless feel satisfaction or remorse after a given choice of action, even though the choice was predetermined and the satisfaction or remorse are merely the results of my early training. Even on these premisses, the experience of satisfaction and remorse are for me real mental events, and essential determinants of my future actions. Yet though the origin of these emotions is causally traceable, their message is a denial of causality, because the glow of my satisfaction and the sting of my remorse both derive from the implied conviction that I *could have acted in another manner* than I did. In other words, my conscience can only express itself in the emotional language of praise or blame, even if I know that logically there is nothing to praise or blame because I am not a free agent but a clock. In fact all education, whether guided by religious or purely pragmatic principles, always aims at setting up this kind of emotional orchestra in the mind which sounds its horns and trumpets in a permanent Judgment Day, *as if* the actions of the self were free. Thus the individual, though all his actions may be causally determined and though he may be intellectually convinced that this is so, cannot function without the emotionally implied belief in his own freedom.

Now let us take the opposite case: the person who rejects determinism and is convinced of the reality of free will. For him it is, of course, much simpler to harmonise emotion and intellectual belief, conscience and conviction. His conviction may be erroneous, and each time he believes that he is making a free choice he may in fact be acting under compulsion. But in this case his disbelief in determinism is one of the factors which determine his behaviour; he can only execute the prearranged pattern by denying that it is prearranged; destiny can only have its way by making him disbelieve in it. Thus in both cases: where a person intellectually believes in freedom and where he does not, the result is the same: unconsciously and emotionally he acts on the assumption that he is free.

The same paradox applies to society as a whole. The aim of the historian, the psychologist, the social scientist, is to explain social behaviour by the interplay of cause and effect, by unravelling the conscious and unconscious forces behind the act; and their approach must always be detached and ethically neutral. Their aim is to trace and measure, not to judge. Nevertheless, moral judgments seep into all our reactions and determine social behaviour; praise and blame, approval and disapproval, whether scientifically justified or not, are as essential to the functioning of society as they are to the functioning of the individual. Man cannot live deprived of the illusion that he is master of his fate; nor deprived of moral indignation when he sees a little brute blowing up a frog with a bicycle pump, or a big brute gassing people by the million. Fatalism and ethical neutrality may be the only correct philosophy, yet they are denials of the brave and pathetic endeavour of the human species.

Here, then, is the dilemma. According to science, man is no more free in the choice of his actions than a robot machine—an extremely subtle and complex type of machine, yet a machine. But he cannot help believing that he is free; moreover, he can only function by believing this. Every human institution reflects this dilemma; and the law, which is meant to regulate human behaviour, reflects it in the most concentrated manner, like a distorting mirror. Hence the paradoxical nature of that part of the law which deals with the supreme problem of the taking of life.

Its absurdity derives from the notion of 'criminal responsibility'. A man can only be held responsible for his act on the assumption that he was not compelled to commit it, but chose to do so of his own free will. The accused is considered innocent until proved guilty, and the burden of proof rests on the prosecution. But he is considered responsible, i.e. having a free will, *unless proved insane*; and the burden of proof rests in this case, and in this case alone, on the defence. It is not even necessary to labour the point that the archaic humbug of the Rules makes this proof impossible even in the case of the feeble-minded and persecution maniacs. If the Rules were amended and improved, the basic paradox would remain, that *the accused is considered to possess a free will unless the defence proves the contrary, namely, that he is subject to the universal laws of nature.*

This paradox is not confined to capital law. But in all other branches of the law there is a comfortable way out of it. The judge trying a burglar need not bother about the insoluble question whether burglars have a free will or not. He can by-pass the problem, and judge each individual case on its merits, by the rule-of-thumb of his experience and common sense, because in all cases, *except capital offences*, the sentence is left to the discretion of the court. Consequently, it does not matter in non-capital cases that the notion of criminal responsibility is absurd, because this problem does not affect the outcome; hence the defence will hardly ever bother to raise the question of insanity. But in a murder trial the penalty is not left to the discretion of the court; in this case alone, in the whole criminal law, the penalty is rigidly fixed by statute. When a man is tried for his life, and in no other case, the abstract postulate of the freedom of the will assumes practical significance: it becomes the noose which breaks his neck.

2

However, we have seen before that the belief in freedom, even if illusory, has a necessary and useful function in society. Does it not follow, then, that the law is justified in adopting this useful belief and basing its notion of criminal responsibility on it? The answer is that free will may or may not exist; but the *kind* of free will which is implied in the law is self-contradictory and unacceptable to any scientist, philosopher or theologian with tuppenny worth of logic in his brain.

The word 'freedom' can only be defined in the negative: it always means freedom *from* restraint of one kind or another. The physicist says that the molecules of a gas have more 'degrees of freedom' than the molecules in a liquid, which again have more than those in a solid. Similar distinctions can be made between degrees of personal and political freedom, freedom from censorship, and so forth. Modern physics has come to grant to the components of certain types of atoms freedom in the sense that they are not restrained by the causal laws which govern the behaviour of larger bodies. Whether a radioactive atom will or will not split at a certain time is apparently not determined by any of the known forces which operate in our familiar, macroscopic world. But this freedom is not absolute. If the behaviour of radioactive atoms were subject to no law at all, the world would not be a cosmos but a chaos. In fact, though they enjoy freedom in the sense described, the total number of atoms which will split in a given quantity of a radioactive substance is rigidly determined at any given time. So much so, that the geologist measures the age of rocks and fossils, of meteors and of the earth itself, by the amount of radioactive decay that he finds in them. The break-down of the classical type of causal determinism in modern physics merely leads to its replacement by a different type of statistical determinism.

Here again freedom means freedom from one kind of restraint—but not absolute freedom which would mean randomness and chaos. So when we talk of the 'freedom of the will', we must at once ask 'freedom from what?' *The freedom implied in criminal law means freedom from heredity and environment;* it means, in Sidgwick's formulation, that the subject's volun-tary action is *not* determined by his character and circum-stances; 'what free will requires is that our volition should be uncaused'.[3] But a world in which every man at any moment performs uncaused and unaccountable acts, and yet is punished for some, glorified for others; a world in which free will reigns absolute, would be a logical absurdity, a tale told by an idiot. It is even more frightening than the determinists' robot man in a clockwork universe: that, at least, is a tale told by an engineer.

Once we deny that man's actions are determined by the physical order of events, we must either substitute a different kind of order or renounce reason. The denial of natural causation creates a void which can only be filled by the assumption of an extra-natural, or supernatural, kind of causation. To put it bluntly: *the concept of criminal responsibility implies the existence of a super-natural order; it is not a legal, but a theological, concept.*

Let me substantiate this somewhat abstract argument in a more concrete manner. When we say: 'a man is guilty', this can always be translated as meaning: 'there was insufficient effort'. If only he had tried harder, made a greater effort, in action or restraint, he would not have become guilty.

A person can only become guilty in two ways: by inadequate positive effort or inadequate negative effort, i.e. restraint, Positive effort is required in all situations where the person drifts towards passivity through indolence, fatigue, lack of vital endowment. The student fails at an examination because he has not 'concentrated hard enough'; a people becomes enslaved because it failed to 'stand up' against tyranny; a man loses his job because he did not 'pull his weight'; the mountaineer freezes to death because he did not make enough effort to stay awake. In every case the subject is found guilty, and moreover *feels* guilty on the assumption—unproved and unprovable —that he *could* have made a greater effort than he did, that there was *a reserve of psychic energy which he did not use.*

The more common type of guilt results from a failure of effort to *inhibit* a culpable impulse, the effort to resist provocation and temptation. It makes no difference whether the subject is prone to crime because his instinctual cravings are overdeveloped or perverted; or whether his restraining mechanisms are defective. Broadly speaking, the sadist and sexual delinquent belong to the former, the psychopath, the morally defective, the drug addict and the alcoholic to the latter type. But whether the offence was caused by too much steam or by defective brakes, the law assumes, and the repentant sinner also assumes, that there was in him an untapped reserve of effort, a hidden store of brake-lining, which he failed to find or to use.

Let me compare these assumptions regarding 'effort of the will' with our assumptions regarding 'efforts of the body'. We know that an engine can only produce a limited number of horse-powers and that any person, even an athlete or weight-lifter, can only produce a limited and well-defined amount of energy. A man can hold his breath for so many seconds and not longer; he can cling with his fingers to a ledge over a precipice so long and not longer. And if the law of Ruritania decreed that a man is guilty unless he can carry a hundred-weight on his back, we would call it a very foolish and barbaric law indeed. A person in danger of life will sometimes perform physical feats which in normal circumstances would be above his capacities, and may seem miraculous. But we know that this is caused by over-stimulation of his supra-renal glands under the effect of rage or fear, and that the adrenalin thus released into his bloodstream feeds additional energy in the form of glucose to his muscles. The same effect can be achieved by injecting the adrenalin, or some other drug, directly into his veins. It is a quite un-mysterious physiological process; and the additional effort thus induced has its strict limits.

We have methods of measuring the physical resources of a man; if these are found to be below a certain standard, he will be unfit for Army service and certain manual jobs, but we do not blame or punish him for it. But we do blame, punish or hang a man because his psychic energy does not reach the required standard. We do not expect the colour-blind to 'pull himself together' and achieve normal sight, but we do assume that a homosexual could turn to the opposite sex if he only tried a little harder.

The interrelation of mind and body is an exceedingly complex problem; it is even doubtful whether we are justified in making a distinction between the two. Yet we apply different and well-nigh opposite standards to efforts of the will and efforts of the body. We recognise that a person's physical powers are limited, but we assume that his will-power is not subject to quantitative limitation. We know that a man cannot lift a mountain, but we assume that he can 'make', or manufacture, 'moral' effort *ad lib.*, as if he were endowed with an unlimited quantity of spiritual adrenalin. Moreover, the question whether he will or will not draw on this additional source of moral energy is not determined by the mould and pressure of the past—otherwise we would be back in the determinist clockwork universe. Hence, to say that the accused *ought* to have made a greater effort to restrain himself means to say that a man with a given self in a given set of circumstances is free to react in more ways than one; and that means that the decision which way he will react lies outside the circumstances and outside the self. It implies the existence of a factor 'X', beyond time and causation, beyond the order of nature. It is, as I said before, a matter not for the lawyer but for the theologian.

When the Lord Chief Justice said about the maniac Ley that since he passed the M'Naghten test 'he could make his peace with God quite well' he was voicing the views of the law quite correctly. By assuming that man's actions are not determined by his heredity and upbringing, the law grants him a free will; and since this freedom cannot mean arbitrary, random choices, it is assumed that it somehow expresses the design of God. Why this design includes brutes who strangle little children is a headache for the theologian, not for the judge. Quite so. But to decide by the M'Naghten Rule, or by any other rule, that in one case the criminal obeyed the command of his endocrine glands and should therefore be spared, whilst in another case he used his metaphysical freedom to execute a higher design and must therefore be hanged, seems a rather arbitrary procedure.

The dilemma between freedom and predestination is the essence of the human predicament. The law rightly evades the horns of the dilemma by giving the court discretion regarding each individual sentence. The only exception which excludes the possiblity of reasonable compromise is the capital sentence; which therefore is logically untenable and ethically wrong.*

---

* I have taken pains to state the case for both free will and determinism as objectively as possible. But once a writer ventures into this field it would be unfair for him to withhold his own personal beliefs. I shall state them as shortly as possible in this private footnote, for they are not meant to persuade, and do not affect the argument. I think that free will is a fantastic notion, but also that man is a fantastic creature. I believe in the unprovable existence of a factor x: an order of reality beyond physical causation, about whose nature only a negative statement is possible: namely, that in its domain the present is *not* determined by the past. If it were so determined, we would once more revert to the conception of the machine-universe. But a present *not* determined by the past is both a necessary and sufficient condition for the experience of relative freedom—not the freedom of anarchy and arbitrariness, but of an order based on the time-negating concept of the *creatio continua*. Continuous creation, a concept of theological origin, postulates that the world was not created once and for all by an act resembling the winding of a clock, but is continually being created—as, in the view of one school of modern physics, matter is constantly being created in interstellar space. If that be so, the experience of freedom, the possibility of making a choice which is *influenced but not strictly determined* by heredity and environment would be the subjective reflection of an objective process negating time and injecting moral responsibility into the amoral edifice of nature.

VI. Lord Goddard and the Sermon on the Mount

or

The Philosophy of Hanging Continued

I

A FTER this metaphysical excursion, let us return to earth and Mr. Albert Pierrepoint. All punishment is supposed to serve three main purposes: retribution; protection of the society by deterrence; and reformation of the offender. Let us examine how the free-will controversy affects each of these three points.

We shall take deterrence first, for it is generally agreed that this is the main object of capital punishment. This in itself indicates that the modern trend is towards the determinist view: for the threat of the death-penalty is meant to act as a causative factor—which can only be effective on the assumption that environmental influences determine at least in part the criminal's actions. If the will were completely free, the threat would be pointless.

But this point is of merely academic interest in showing that unconscious determinist assumptions guide even the defenders of capital punishment. Apart from that, the question whether we side with the determinist's depressing robot-universe or his opponent's mystical world of freedom and moral responsibility,. has no bearing whatsoever on the deterrence issue. The facts, which prove that capital punishment is a more objectionable but not a more effective deterrent than its alternatives, are equally valid for the determinist and the mystic.

For the remaining two issues, however, retribution and

reform, the free-will controversy is relevant. It will be simpler to treat the two issues together.

In our day, even among the upholders of capital punishment, the majority denies that they are guided by motives of vengeance against the criminal. In spite of these denials, retribution is a powerful unconscious motive which infiltrates and confuses the other issues. The popular argument, 'he deserves to be hanged', 'you are only concerned with the murderer not with the victim', etc., has a strong and lasting emotional appeal.

From the determinist point of view, vengeance against a human being is as absurd as punishing a machine. But even if I sometimes have the foolish desire to hit my old car on the bonnet for breaking down, it would be more logical to hit the garage mechanic, or the foreman, or the chairman of the firm who made it. If, guided by vengeance, we punish the criminal, then we ought also to punish the alcoholic father, the over-indulgent mother who made him into what he is, and his parents' parents, and so forth, along the long chain of causation back to the snake in Paradise. For they all, including teachers, bosses and society at large, were accessaries to the crime, aiding and abetting the act long before it was committed. Disapproval, punishment, vengeance, have no place in the determinist's vocabularly; the only legitimate target of his resentment must be the universe as a whole, and the laws of nature that govern it.

If, on the other hand, we accept freedom of the will with its inevitable religious consequences, then vengeance appears not as a sin against logic but a sin against the spirit. For if the murderer is not merely a robot with a faulty switch, but the executor of a mysterious design, then we move in a realm beyond the reach of human justice. If you believe that man is a recipient, for good or evil, of some influence beyond natural causation, then you have no right to break the vessel because you dislike the wine. If it is part of a higher design that children should be murdered or killed by epidemics, then the murderer can no more be the object of vengeance than the polio virus, for both are part of the same incomprehensible pattern. Every religion and every metaphysical system has to face the problem of evil: the fact that evil has been included in the design. No satisfactory answer has yet been found, or is likely ever to be found. The law assumes that man is free and responsible in his actions; it dumps the problem why God granted man the freedom to choose evil on the theologian, to the latter's embarrassment. During the Middle Ages, freedom of the will was one of the principal problems of theology, and every sect had a different answer to it. Some held that divine omnipotence amounted to 'determinism by predestination', where the human automatons acted as foreseen and intended by God. Others taught that God allowed man sufficient rope to hang himself or climb on it to Paradise; this, however, was again held to contradict the notion of God's omnipresence. But if there is no final answer to the challenge, vengeance as an answer is the most futile, and a negation of the very essence of Christianity.

'Blood for blood, life for life' was the law of Israel during the Bronze Age, appropriate to the conditions of the time, and is still the law of the primitive nomads of the desert. It was repudiated in the Sermon on the Mount, and it was repudiated by Israel itself, which abolished capital punishment when it regained sovereign statehood. Orthodox talion justice survives in our time only in the vendetta codes of Sicilian bandits and organised gangsters.

The early Church's repudiation of the blood law was not accidental; it came from the core of the Christian teaching which makes punishment justifiable only in so far as its purpose is to reform the offender, and which states that no human being is evil beyond redemption. In ancient Mosaic law, the death-penalty was statutory not only for murder, but for sabbath-breaking, slave-trading, blasphemy, the cursing of parents, adultery, and a number of other offences; in fact the situation before the Christian repeal may be compared, *mutatis mutandum*, with conditions in Ellenborough's day. The bishops of 1810 who supported the Bloody Code used arguments not unlike the Pharisees' against Jesus, and the bloodthirsty shepherds were still going strong in the Lords' debate of 1948. Dickens knew them well when he wrote:

Though every other man who wields a pen should turn himself into a commentator on the Scriptures—not all their united efforts could persuade me that executions are a Christian law. . . . If any text appeared to justify the claim, I would reject that limited appeal, and rest upon the character of the Redeemer and the great scheme of His religion.[1]

So strongly did the early Church feel about abolition that the Emperor Julian had to disqualify Christians from holding certain administrative offices, because: 'their law forbade them to use the sword against offenders worthy of capital punishment.'

Perhaps the clearest formulation of the problem was given by St. Augustine, himself a reformed profligate and sinner, a saint with an endearing sense of humour—*vide* his famous 'Give me chastity, but not yet'. When some Donatists, a heretic African sect, had confessed to a heinous murder of Christians, Augustine pleaded with his friend Marcellinus not to inflict the death-penalty on the murderers:

We do not wish to have the sufferings of the servants of God avenged by the infliction of precisely similar injuries in the way of retaliation. Not, of course, that we object to the removal from these wicked men of the liberty to perpetrate further crimes, but our desire is rather that justice be satisfied without the taking of their lives or the maiming of their bodies in any particular; and that, by such coercive measures as may be in accordance with the laws, they be drawn away from their insane frenzy to the quietness of men in their sound judgment, or compelled to give up mischievous violence and betake themselves to some useful labour.[2]

The passage sounds curiously modern, almost as if it had been written by a member of the Howard League for Penal Reform. St. Augustine's opponents argued, as they argue today, that the times were too turbulent for such a daring experiment—he lived from A.D. 354 to 430, and in Africa to boot.

To sum up, vengeance as a motive for capital punishment is absurd from the determinist and indefensible from the free will point of view. Yet though easy to dismiss in reasoned argument on both moral and logical grounds, the desire for vengeance has deep, unconscious roots and is roused when we feel strong indignation or revulsion—whether the reasoning mind approves or not. This psychological fact is largely ignored in abolitionist propaganda—yet it has to be accepted as a fact. The admission that even confirmed abolitionists are not proof against occasional vindictive impulses does not mean that such impulses should be legally sanctioned by society, any more than we sanction some other unpalatable instincts of our biological inheritance. Deep inside every civilised being there lurks a tiny Stone Age man, dangling a club to rob and rape, and screaming an eye for an eye. But we would rather not have that little fur-clad figure dictate the law of the land.

2

The problem of free will affects the criminal law in yet another, indirect but important, way. The gradual humanisation of the penal system—juvenile courts, probation, parole, 'open prisons', and so on—is due to our growing insight into the social roots of crime, into the influence of heredity and environment on the offender, into the causal determinants of human behaviour. Yet at the same time, the principle of criminal responsibility, which implies freedom of the will, cannot easily be dispensed with. The only possible course in this dilemma is, as we saw, to muddle along as best one can; and by and large the courts in this country muddle along quite well by tending to show leniency where there is reasonable hope of reform, by taking mitigating circumstances into account, and by trying 'to make the punishment fit the crime'. The only exception is the law concerning capital charges which, by its rigidity, makes compromise impossible, and prevents the court from taking circumstances into account which, in all other cases, would count as mitigating factors in assessing the sentence. Thus, it is up to the court to send a mentally defective person to an institution instead of passing sentence on him— in all except capital cases. If a mentally defective person 'is charged with murder and the jury are satisfied that he committed the act, they have no option but to convict him of murder and the judge is obliged to pronounce the sentence of death'.[3] The same applies to mercy killers and surviving partners in a suicide pact. They are, thank God, eventually reprieved; but before that is possible, the Judge must put on the black cap and pronounce the terrible words.

The Royal Commission's report stresses the inhumanity of the capital law over and again. It underlines the terrible anomaly that the *only* hope for a person who is proven to be epileptic, feeble-minded, suffering from delusion, or otherwise mentally deranged, rests not with the law but with the person of the Home Secretary: 'This is the natural consequence of a law which has the basic defect of prescribing a single fixed automatic sentence for a crime that varies widely in character and culpability. . . . The rigidity of a law that gives the court no discretion to select the appropriate sentence can be corrected only by the Executive [i.e. the Home Secretary].'[4] And again: 'The outstanding defect of the law of murder is that it provides a single punishment for a crime widely varying in culpability.'[5]

The Commissioners contemplated various reforms to make the capital law more elastic, and enable the court to exercise common sense and humanity. But they were well aware that minor reforms did not go to the core of the problem and that 'a stage has been reached where there is little room for further limitation short of abolition'.[6] They only made one really radical proposal, whose adoption would, however, not lead to a reform of the existing law but to its negation: the proposal to let the jury decide at their own discretion whether a man found guilty should suffer the penalty subscribed by the law, or not: 'We have reached the conclusion that if capital punishment is to be retained and at the same time the defects of the existing law are to be eliminated, this is the only practicable way of achieving that object. . . .'[7] We recognise that the disadvantage of a system of "jury discretion" may be thought to outweigh its merits. If this view were to prevail, the conclusion would seem to be inescapable that in this country a stage has been reached where little more can be done effectively to limit the liability to suffer the death penalty, and that the real issue is now whether capital punishment should be retained or abolished.'8*

The reason why the law relating to capital punishment cannot be reformed is basically simple. It could only be reformed at the price of undermining the concept of criminal responsibility by such deterministic notions as 'irresistible impulse' or 'diminished responsibility'—that is, *by making determinism statutory*, as it were. This necessity does not arise in the case of other offences, because the sentence is elastic. Yet even by revolutionising the basic concepts of Common Law for the sole purpose of making capital law a little less barbaric, its self-contradictions would remain. Since the frontiers between 'responsible' and 'irresponsible' are fluid, problematical and bedevilled by metaphysical problems, any drawing of the line by legal definition would be arbitrary. And since it is impossible to define when a man acted freely and ought to die, or when he acted under compulsion and ought to live, the only solution is to bring capital law into line with the remaining body of the Common Law by eliminating the unique, fixed, all-or-nothing penalty which admits of no gradations.

Yet it is precisely this rigidity which makes capital punishment so precious to the reactionary wing of the legal profession, and why they want to preserve it at all costs. For the death-penalty is the symbol and bulwark of an antiquated conception of justice; and if it falls the whole conception falls. This point was made abundantly clear in the arguments which the Lord Chief Justice used against the proposed relaxation of the murder law by introducing such notions as 'diminished responsibility' or 'irresistible impulse'. They knew that these concepts

* The 1957 Homicide Act attempted, against the advice of the Royal Commission, to make a distinction between capital and non-capital murder. In the 1969 Parliamentary debates, a number of retentionists voted for abolition because they considered it as the lesser evil compared to a return to the 1957 law—which, among other absurdities, made murder by shooting a capital offence, murder by poisoning a non-capital one.

would serve as a Trojan horse which, once admitted within the
fortress of Common Law, would play havoc with it. Lord
Goddard told the Royal Commissioners:

> Once you begin to admit the doctrine of irresistible impulse,
> I do not know where it is going to end. I think that it is
> sometimes overlooked that if you once admit irresistible
> impulse as a defence, you are not going to admit it only with
> regard to murder, but you have got to admit it in every
> case. . . . Are you really going to say that this doctrine of
> irresistible impulse is to be readily admitted in the criminal
> law? There is the old case of the Judge who had the appeal
> made to him that the prisoner was suffering from the disease
> called kleptomania; he said: 'This is just the disease that I
> am here to cure.'[9]

He rejected on the same grounds the proposal that the
gravity of a provocation should be assessed according to the
character and temperament of the provoked person, in lieu of
the test of the 'reasonable man':

> If you leave it to the question whether this particular man
> was provoked—well, any man is going to give evidence and
> is going to get his friends to come and give evidence that he
> is a peculiarly excitable person and you are letting in consi-
> derations there which do not apply to any other branch of
> the law.[10]

True; though in other branches of the Law people are not
hanged, which after all is a consideration that should be 'let
in'. But imagine the havoc if witnesses were called to testify
that the individual in the dock *was* an irritable person, and *not*
a reasonable man! The argument boils down to this: if we stop
hanging murderers on the grounds that they acted under an
inner compulsion, then Judges would be encouraged to apply
similar considerations to other offenders who acted under
similar mental stress. If the hangman is no longer the correct
cure for the mentally defective, then the 'old judge' may no
longer be the correct cure for the kleptomaniac. There exist,

alas, modern judges, magistrates and juries who, disregarding Coke and M'Naghten, take social factors and emotional pressures into account when deciding the length of the sentence. But, fortunately, this danger does not exist in the case of a capital offender; the jury cannot alter the length of the drop, nor strangle him on parole, nor apply latitude in breaking his neck.

To sum up. The deficiencies of the capital law are irremediable because the death-penalty is based on a philosophical concept of criminal responsibility which does not admit the compromises with the determinist view practised in other courts. Regarding all other offences, the administration of the law is elastic; the death-penalty, by its nature, excludes gradings of culpability. This rigidity and finality, which is the very essence of the capital law, is at the same time the reason of its attractiveness and symbolic value for the anti-progressive forces in society.

VII. Doomed by Mistake

or

What is a Fair Trial?

> Timothy Evans was arrainged by a cop
> Timothy Evans took the fatal drop
> All the Queen's Counsel and Home Office men
> Couldn't put Evans together again
> (after Lewis Carroll)

INNOCENT men have been hanged in the past and will be hanged in the future unless either the death-penalty is abolished or the fallibility of human judgment is abolished and judges become supermen.

If (a) capital punishment were in itself a desirable thing, and if (b) the number of people innocently hanged were very small indeed, then the danger of an occasional miscarriage of justice would not represent a conclusive argument. The question, however, is not whether an occasional error is in itself an argument against hanging, but how often such errors occur, and whether they are *exceptional* phenomena or *inherent* in the system.

Let us go back to the last Royal Commission but one, the Commission appointed by Queen Victoria in 1864. The chief witness on the question of judicial error was Sir Fitzroy Kelly, the former Attorney-General and Solicitor-General, whose testimony was summed up in the Commission's report as follows:

After careful consideration and examination, he has come to the conclusion that it is not in any way reasonably to be

doubted that in many instances innocent men have been
capitally convicted, and in certain numbers of instances,
few of course, but yet formidable numbers, have been
actually executed . . . Well remembers that there were,
between the years 1802 and 1840, 22 cases of capital convictions, seven of which resulted in the execution of the
convicts, and in the rest of which the sentence was mitigated,
or a pardon granted. But in the whole of the 22 cases the
innocence of these persons was established, or, at least,
established satisfactorily to those who investigated the
matter, and in most of the cases to the satisfaction of the
advisers of the Crown.[1]

These were the cases where the innocence of the victims was
virtually proven; but, Kelly continued, 'There is presumptive
ground for believing that [other] innocent persons have
suffered death for want of having influential or wealthy friends
to procure an investigation of their case, or to make such
efforts as were successful in the instances of Kirwan, Dr.
Smethurst, and others.'[2] He added that the Sheriff of London,
Mr. Wilde, 'had given him the names and particulars of the
cases of five persons who in a single year were erroneously
convicted and sentenced to death'.[3]

That, one may say, was a long time ago, and justice has
improved since. But the annual number of executions has
remained substantially the same since the beginning of Queen
Victoria's reign (ten to fourteen executions per year), and the
law and court procedure has also remained substantially the
same.* It is not at all a reassurance to the public that in 1864
the possibility of judicial error was as pompously and categorically denied by the Law Lords and Home Secretaries as it is
today. In 1864, before Kelly gave the evidence just quoted,
Lord Wensleydale 'was not aware of a capital case in which he
thought the verdict illfounded'; in 1948, Sir Maxwell Fyfe
stated with the same assurance that 'there is no practical

* The only differences relevant to this chapter are that since 1896 the
accused man has been allowed to give evidence from the witness box (which
is often a doubtful blessing); and the establishment of the Court of Criminal
Appeal.

possibility' of justice miscarrying: 'the Honourable and Learned Member is moving in a realm of fantasy when he makes that suggestion'. A couple of years after Lord Wensleydale's statement, they hanged Mrs. Biggadyke for poisoning her husband—a crime to which a convict confessed on his death-bed. A couple of years after Sir Maxwell Fyfe's statement, we hanged Timothy Evans.*

Every country and every age has its famous cases of men convicted by judicial error. In all cases, once a man has been found guilty, proving his innocence is an extremely arduous process, which demands the dogged efforts of lawyers and friends over a great number of years. France had its Dreyfus case; in spite of the genius of Zola, it took twelve years to reverse the verdict. Austria had Hilsner, who was proved innocent after he had spent eighteen years in prison. In Hungary, Steven Tonka was hanged for the murder of his daughter in 1913 and proved innocent fourteen years later— when a farewell letter of the girl was found announcing her intention to commit suicide. In Holland, which has no capital punishment, Tuennisen and Klundert were convicted of murder in 1923 and found innocent six years later. But England, where the accused is supposed to have a fairer trial than anywhere else, again holds the record of famous cases.

Oscar Slater was sentenced to hang in May, 1909, but the sentence was commuted, forty-eight hours before his execution, to penal servitude for life. His trial was so grossly unfair that Sir Conan Doyle, after reading the verbatim report, decided that the man was innocent and started a campaign in his favour. In spite of Doyle's immense reputation, it took no less than nineteen years before the newly created Scottish Court of Criminal Appeal annulled the sentence. Had Slater been executed, who would have kept up an agitation for nineteen years to vindicate a man already dead?

This is the crux of the matter. Once a man is dead, the chances of proving that he was innocent are virtually nil. It is an axiom of the law that the burden of proof should lie with the prosecution; but when you try to vindicate a man, and a

* For an account of the Evans case see *Ten Rillington Place* by Ludovic Kennedy, London, 1961.

dead man to boot, it is up to the defence to establish positive proof of his innocence—and such proof is technically impossible, unless some extraordinary hazard intervenes. And since it needs a near-miracle for a judicial error to be detected, it is not unreasonable to assume that the number of undetected errors may be greater than we believe. If in a scrupulously clean hospital I find a fly in my soup, the inference is that there must be a host of them about.

To illustrate how exceptional the circumstances must be for proof of innocence to be possible, take the following example. In 1835, a man was found guilty of murder, sentenced to death and then transported for life to Australia. Nearly forty years later, he met the real murderer on that continent; even so, it took two Parliamentary debates and the eloquence of John Bright to obtain the Queen's pardon. The reader will say, 'Ah, but such cases are rare and exceptional'. He is making a common logical mistake. The exceptionality of the case does not mean that judicial errors are rare; it proves, on the contrary, that it needs exceptional luck to *detect* a judicial error. In spite of this, there is a long row of cases, stretching from Queen Victoria's days to ours, in which judicial error was either admitted, or all but technically proved. Biggadyke (1869) and Habron (1876) were proved innocent years after they were sentenced. Even the late Lord Birkenhead confessed to a lingering doubt about the justice of hanging Mrs. Thompson (1923); Marshall Hall was convinced of the innocence of several of his convicted clients; the cases of Podmore (1930), Rouse (1931), Thorne (1934), Hoolhouse (1938), Rowland (1946), Bentley (1952) belong to the same category; and in at least one case, Evans (1950), the Home Secretary responsible for his execution admitted later on that he was hanged though not guilty as charged.

No doubt judge and jury always try, according to their lights, to give a man a fair trial. If judicial errors nevertheless continue to occur with monotonous regularity, this cannot be due to accident; *the probability of error is inherent in the judicial procedure.* I shall now briefly examine some of the main sources of error and uncertainty in murder trials. They fall under the following headings: (*a*) fallibility of witnesses; (*b*) fallibility of experts; (c) coincidence; (d) to (h) fallibility of juries, judges, appeal judges and Home Secretaries; (i) carelessness of solicitors and counsel; (j) unworkability of the M'Naghten rules.

(a) Fallibility of Witnesses

Identification by witnesses is always more or less a gamble because no record is more notoriously unreliable than human memory. Sully, in *Mistaken Identity*,[4] quotes a series of classic experiments, such as:

Fifteen students were subjects in a testimony experiment. Asked the date of a local flood, three gave the right year, but six gave a particular wrong year; asked the number of classrooms opening off a corridor, two gave the right number, but nine a particular wrong number; asked the colour of a particular book used in the school, five agreed in truth, but nine agreed in error.[4]

Every psychological textbook is full of examples of the illusions, suggestibility and tendency to self-deception of human memory, and a history of crime would be written as a comedy of errors by mistaken witnesses if the results were not so tragic.

In 1896, a certain Adolf Beck was sentenced to seven years for robberies from women. In 1904 he was again convicted of similar offences. He was identified on the first occasion by ten, on the second by five women. Nine years after his first conviction the real culprit, Smith, was found; Beck, was discharged and paid five thousand pounds as compensation. If he had been convicted of a capital offence and executed, who would have bothered after nine years? Yet circumstantial evidence in murder cases depends on testimony of precisely this kind.

At this point a word must be said about identification in general. A suspect may be 'identified' by witnesses either in Court or from police photographs or at a parade. If in Court, the witness is solemnly asked: 'Do you see that person in this room?' Whereupon the witness will earnestly turn towards the figure standing between two policemen in the dock and say cheerfully: 'That's him. There he is.' As for identification parades, the police are instructed that the suspect should be 'placed among eight or more persons who are, as far as possible, of the same age, height, general appearance and position in life'. When the parade is held in a prison, the participants in the parade are prisoners—who on this occasion are presumed to occupy the same 'position in life' as the suspect, and are either dressed up in their civvies taken out from the moth balls, or fitted out from the prison stores. If the parade is held in a police station, the participants are collected in a more imaginative manner. A half-hour or so before the appointed time, plain-clothed policemen scan the streets for passers-by similar in 'age, height, appearance, position', etc., and ask them to volunteer for the parade.

In one case, the prisoner suddenly announced just before the parade that he usually wore spectacles, whereupon spectacles were obtained from the lost property room for all the persons paraded; but as none of the others were used to them, they all looked myopic and silly except, of course, the prisoner.[5]

From the psychological point of view, all identification parades are inconclusive to the point of being farcical. Most people have seen 'thought-readers' performing in a music-hall, who are able to find a needle hidden in the lapel of a gentleman in an audience of several hundred, by following unconscious hints, involuntary eye or muscle movements. A thought-reader, of course, is a trained man, but he has to find a needle in a haystack, whereas the witness only has to pick out a man, who *knows* that he is suspected, among half a dozen others who know that they are not. The gentleman with the pin has a self-conscious look—and so has the suspect at the identification parade who knows that the officials at the parade *expect* him to be picked out, and is under great nervous strain. It is an amusing parlour game; as evidence to hang a man it is less amusing.

(b) Expert Testimony

In 1931, a certain John Binney was convicted of writing blackmailing letters by the testimony of two handwriting experts. After Binney was sent to Dartmoor, blackmailing letters in the same handwriting continued to arrive, and he was released.

In these cases, expert opinion was unanimous. But in murder trials both sides call, as a rule, their own experts, and it is up to the jury to decide which side to believe.

In 1925, Norman Thorne was hanged for the murder of a girl friend. The defence claimed that the girl had committed suicide, and that Thorne had buried her body in a panic. Medical witnesses for the prosecution testified that there was no evidence of suicide and that death had occurred in a certain manner. Three medical witnesses for the defence testified that it was impossible for death to have taken place in the manner stated by the prosecution, and that in their view the girl had committed suicide. The jury of twelve laymen decided to believe the prosecution experts and disbelieve the defence experts, and Thorne was hanged.

The *Law Journal* commented that: 'Thorne's execution would leave a feeling of profound disquiet in the minds of many people.'

In 1953 Mrs. Merrifield was convicted and hanged for the poisoning of another woman by arsenic. The pathologist giving evidence for the prosecution said the victim had been poisoned. The pathologist for the defence said she had died a natural death. The case is the more remarkable because the pathologist for the defence whom the jury did not believe was Professor Webster, chief of the Forensic Laboratory in Birmingham for twenty years, who had been the *prosecution's* witness in every murder case of the Midlands Circuit for many years. We are left to infer that Professor Webster was a sufficiently reliable expert to secure a conviction, but not reliable enough to secure an acquittal even by 'reasonable doubt'. The summing up of the judge in that particular case will be described under (e).

(c) Coincidence

In 1876, William Habron was convicted of shooting a policeman in Manchester. The policeman had been responsible for the previous arrest and conviction of Habron on a minor charge and Habron had publicly stated his intention to get his own back on him. Habron's boots were covered with mud of the same type as the soil where the murder was committed; his hobnails exactly fitted the footmarks in the vicinity of the crime. Who would believe that all this was due to coincidence? Because of his youth, Habron was granted a reprieve, and three years later the notorious Charles Peace, before being hanged, confessed to the murder for which Habron stood convicted.

There is no need to go on with examples; everybody remembers coincidences in his life which are so extraordinary that no court would believe in them. Yet coincidence plays a great part in murder trials—for a simple reason. A guilty man will always try to explain away the evidence against him as due to sheer coincidence; and this makes the law apt to disbelieve in real coincidence when it occurs.

(d) The Juror's Dilemma

I have said before that no doubt every jury, before whom a man stands on trial for his life, intends to give him a fair trial. But good intention is not enough to guarantee the result. How is a jury of laymen to decide which of the conflicting medical or psychiatric evidence to believe, which to reject?

An eminent lawyer, Mr. Pritt, Q.C., testifying on behalf of the Howard League before the Select Committee of 1930, had this to say on the subject:

> I see every day, in civil cases, decisions arrived at, sometimes in favour of my clients and sometimes against my clients, and so far as I can exercise any judgment about them perhaps one-third of them are wrong. I have seen a certain number of criminal cases tried and I think some of those decisions have been wrong. . . . I regard it as impossible to believe that the only Court that never makes a mistake is the Court where a dozen men are placed together in a box, who may have never seen each other before, presided over by a Judge who may never have tried criminal cases before, sitting down there, and, to the best of their ability, trying to

sort out the evidence on one side and the other, and trying to arrive at the truth of a very difficult story about which, *ex hypothesi*, someone is not telling the truth.[6]

Whatever Mr. Pritt's political opinions, he is an outstanding lawyer and he summed up the point neatly. Sometimes the jury must listen to controversial evidence and to counsels' speeches during three or more days. They are men and women of average—and sometimes, inevitably, of less than average—intelligence, without legal training. A clergyman recently wrote to the London *Times* that in conversation with jurors, 'They have all emphasised the point that they found it well-nigh impossible to retain a clear impression of all that had been said to them in the course of the trial. They confess that, try hard as they did, they found it very hard to clear their minds of early prejudice and bias.'[7]

In such cases much depends on the judge's summing up. This may last several hours. Yet when the jury retire, they have no written record of the summing up, nor of counsels' speeches, nor of the evidence before them. In recent letters to *The Times* several writers suggested that a written report, at least of the summing up, be given to the jury, or that the speeches, examinations and cross-examinations should be recorded on a tape recorder and played back to them at request. It seems fantastic that this minimum condition for a considered verdict should not exist. We live in an age where crooners and Light Programme skits are being recorded for posterity, but where a man's life is at stake, we leave it to the dubious memory of twelve tired householders to recall who said what and why.

In the February, 1955, debate in the House of Commons, the former Home Secretary, Mr. Chuter Ede, made a profoundly shocking statement on the subject. He said (my italics):

I wonder what goes on inside the jury room. I was once foreman of a coroner's jury. I have sat at quarter sessions and wondered by what processes jurors have, on occasion, managed to evade the specific hints which have been dropped to them by the chairman in his summing up. But I had a little enlightenment as to what happened, because, *on at least two, and, I think three occasions*, I had a letter from a juror after I had announced my decision about a recommendation.

The juror said, 'You have let me down. I stood out for a long time against a verdict of guilty. Then the foreman said, "We have been here a long time and you are the only person standing out. If we make a strong recommendation of mercy, will you then fall into line, and . . . you can rest assured that the Home Secretary will grant a reprieve." ' I did not grant a reprieve when, after consulting the trial judge and asking him the grounds on the evidence for making a strong recommendation for mercy, the judge said, 'I really have not the remotest idea'. That is what happened.[8]

So long as a Home Secretary is in office, he will always say that miscarriages of justice are a one-in-a-million chance. But when repentance makes him lift a corner of the veil of official secrecy, one shudders at the discovery how much of one's notion of a 'fair trial' was built on illusion.

(e) The Summing Up

By and large the learned judge's summing up is the only compass available to a jury adrift in the fog. And that compass is liable to very odd deviations indeed.

Take the case of Reginald Woolmington, who in 1935 was sentenced to death at Bristol for the murder of his young wife. I am quoting another ex-Home Secretary, Lord Templewood:

The jury at Somerset Assizes a few weeks previously had failed to agree, and a new trial had been ordered. The original failure to agree should have been a sufficiently clear indication that the case was not proved 'beyond reasonable doubt'. At the second trial, however, *the judge directed the jury that it was incumbent on the accused to prove his plea* that the death of his wife was the result of an accident. . . . Can there not have been other cases in which the wrong direction of a judge has led to an innocent man's death?[9]

The jury complied with the judge's direction and found Woolmington guilty. The case went to the Court of Criminal Appeal, which sustained the judge's decision and confirmed the verdict. However, the Attorney-General (Lord Caldecote, then Sir Thomas Inskip) granted permission for the case to go to the House of Lords, who ordered the release of Woolmington on the obvious grounds that the burden of proof must always remain with the prosecution. The *Law Journal* commented at the time: 'It is interesting if unprofitable to speculate as to the number of murderers (to say nothing of innocent persons) lying mouldering in lime and ignominy . . . who would have been respectably alive and well if our Judges had known the law.'

As a rule, however, the views of the judge are conveyed to the jury in subtler ways, and frequently in unreproachable terms. In the case of Mrs. Merrifield, who was hanged for poisoning another woman, in spite of the fact that the foremost Home Office pathologist in the Midlands testified that she had died a natural death, the jury's possible qualms of conscience were put at rest by being addressed as follows by Mr. Justice Glyn Jones in his summing up:

Counsel for the defence has said to you more than once that the prosecution must exclude every chance and every possibility that the inferences they ask you to draw are mistaken. . . . That is not the law. You need only deal with such possibilities of error as you may think to be reasonably likely. If juries are to be deterred from doing their duty because the ingenuity of counsel can propound some hypothesis, however unlikely, on which the evidence of crime can be explained in a manner consistent with innocence, then few persons charged with crime would ever be convicted.[10]

The operative words are 'the ingenuity of counsel can propound some hypothesis, however unlikely'. Just how unlikely is a hypothesis confirmed by a Home Office expert who is habitually relied upon by the prosecution? Does this sort of thing agree with the public's idea that the chance of error is so small as to be practically negligible? Does it agree with the statement by the ex-Home Secretary, Sir John Anderson, that 'The risk, under the conditions as they exist in this country, of the capital penalty being executed on any one who was not in fact guilty of the crime of which he had been convicted is so small, indeed so infinitesimal, that that consideration can be dismissed'?[11]

In his work on *Courts and Judges in France, Germany and England*,[12] one of our outstanding writers on law, Sir. R C. K. Ensor, sums the matter up with refreshing frankness: 'It is very easy for a bad judge, especially in a jury case, to defeat justice by the crassest stupidity or partisanship, without perpetrating any technical misdirection of the jury or explicit twist of the law, of which an Appeal Court could take cognizance.'[13]

(f) The Court of Criminal Appeal

Sometimes, however, cases do go before the Criminal Appeal Court. Its existence is for the public mind an additional safeguard and reassurance that no mistakes can be made. Very few know even its composition. It is composed of the Lord Chief Justice and of two judges of the Queen's Bench Division —that is, the same judges who, when sitting singly, conduct the murder trials. Ensor comments: 'It is scarcely plausible that an assembly of this same class of judges should be much wiser than the individuals composing it; and in fact the Court of Criminal Appeal has laid itself open to very considerable criticism.'[14]

The Court of Criminal Appeal can neither re-try a case nor order a re-trial. Its own view of its function is: 'It is not sufficient to show merely that the case was a very weak one or that the members of the Court of Criminal Appeal feel some doubt as to the correctness of the verdict. If there was evidence to support the conviction, the appeal will be dismissed.'[15]

(g) Home Office Inquiries[16]

We now come to the last but one station in our pilgrim's progress to the gallows. After a man has been sentenced to death and whether or not his case has been taken to the Court of Criminal Appeal, the Home Secretary has the power to

order a further inquiry if he thinks that a miscarriage of justice
may have occurred. Such inquiries are held in private and are
not bound by the rules of evidence. Two such inquiries were
held in recent times, on the Rowland case* and on the case of
Timothy Evans. In both cases, the investigator appointed by
the Home Secretary reported that he was satisfied that no
miscarriage of justice had taken place.

It is a relief that there is no need to go into the inquiry and
reopen the sewers of the Christie-Evans case, since the Home
Secretary responsible for Evans's execution has since admitted
in the House of Commons[17] that Timothy Evans died as a
consequence of a miscarriage of justice. After Mr. Chuter Ede's
admission, the Home Office Inquiry Report retains only
academic interest. Mr. Reginald Paget, Q.C., in discussing the
report, commented:

> I have not been able to discover any case in which an inquiry
> of this sort has reported that justice did go wrong, and when
> I asked the Home Secretary whether historically a private
> inquiry had ever discovered a great miscarriage of justice,
> he, too, did not know of one.

The theory behind it all is, apparently, that any official
admission of error would undermine the public's confidence in
the fairness of British justice. It is not only an immoral but also
a mistaken theory: if the full truth were known, it would not
undermine faith in British justice, only faith in capital punishment. For the public have enough common sense to know it to
be inevitable that judges and jurors should sometimes be mistaken. But if the full truth about a series of doubtful cases were
known, public opinion would realise that the irrevocability of
the death-penalty turns human error into inhuman error. We
cannot avoid mistakes; but we can avoid the fatal consequences
of mistakes.

(h) The Home Secretary

The Home Secretary is the last person who stands between
the condemned man and God. He takes the decision whether a

---

* For an account of the Rowland case see *Hanged—And Innocent?* by
Paget, Silverman and Hollis, London 1953.

man should live or die, without being responsible either to the Cabinet or to Parliament. He is only responsible to God; but he has certain responsibilities towards the Police Force he represents; and to his political party; and to his future career. We have seen before what curious changes have occurred in several Home Secretaries' attitudes to capital punishment depending on whether they were in or out of office. As to particular cases, the effect of extraneous considerations became evident when mercy was refused to Derek Bentley in the teeth of public protests, charity and precedent. Precedent demanded that Bentley should be reprieved on at least five grounds: the jury's recommendation; his youth; his mental deficiency; that he was said to be under arrest and co-operating with the police when the murder was committed; and that even had he been an accomplice to murder, accomplices are never executed unless the principal is executed too.

Norman Thorne, found guilty against the medical evidence for the defence that the victim committed suicide, was not reprieved. Mrs. Woolmington, found guilty against the Home Office pathologist's evidence, was not reprieved. Rowland, Evans, Bentley, were not reprieved. Yet the former Home Secretary, Sir John Anderson, stated in the 1948 debate: 'Where there is a scintilla . . . of doubt—the Home Secretary has invariably advised commutation.'

Scintilla means 'spark' or 'atom'. Some atom; some spark.

(i) The Handicap of Poverty

Money makes a great deal of difference in life; we assume that it makes no difference when a man is tried for his life. This is one more mistaken assumption.

The fees paid to the defence under the Poor Prisoners' Defence Act are shockingly small. In a letter to *The Times* a solicitor, Mr. N. M. Jordan, mentioned the fact that for defending a destitute person subsequently found guilty of murder, counsel for the defence received five guineas, while the brief for the leading counsel for the prosecution was marked seventy-five guineas—both fees being paid out of public funds. The solicitors received for six appearances at the

Magistrate's Court proceedings altogether three guineas.[18] Where the plea is guilty but insane—and that is by the nature of things a most frequent plea for the defence—everything depends on obtaining the services of a highly qualified psychiatrist whose repute carries weight in court.

Let us look at the situation from the psychiatric expert's point of view. The psychiatrist I am quoting is Dr. J. A. Hobson, of the Middlesex Hospital, who gave evidence for Christie and in a number of other notable cases:

> Recently there was a man awaiting trial for murder who, for two months between the proceedings in the lower court and the assizes, *was not seen by his solicitor*. Though the circumstances of his offence were such as to suggest the likelihood of mental abnormality, no effort was made for him to be examined by a psychiatrist. A leading counsel was called in at the last minute. He at once appreciated the omission in the preparation of the case, and on the evening before the trial asked me, apologetically, to examine the man. I did my best, but my examination was too brief to be complete. There was no time to make necessary outside investigations, which I should have done if I had been called in earlier, and no time to write a report.
>
> I found Counsel at his club and we had a short conference at 11 p.m. Next morning I gave evidence at the Central Criminal Court and was subjected to hostile examination by the Judge. His summing-up was against us, but the Jury brought in a verdict of 'Guilty, but insane'. I am sure that the verdict was the right one. . . . I am equally sure that if Counsel had not called in a psychiatrist at the eleventh hour, this man would have been found 'Guilty' and might have been hanged.[19]

Dr. Hobson is a psychiatrist. Mr. Silverman is a lawyer and politician. He treats the consequences of the existing situation from a different angle:

> Rowland . . . was quite penniless. . . . In such cases legal aid is invariably granted at an early stage. Such aid covers

nominal fees to counsel and solicitor and the expenses of witnesses. No funds are made available for enquiries or investigations of any kind. There is no possibility of making available to the defence anything comparable to the complex, elaborate, nation-wide organization available to the prosecution for the preparation of their case: the detective force, the centres of forensic science and medicine, the expert witnesses.[20]

There is a stock answer to this, which may strike the reader as somewhat naïve and surprising. The answer is that the prosecution's business is not to secure a conviction or to 'make a case', but to put before the Court all the relevant facts both against and in favour of the accused. It is a beautiful theory but a somewhat abstract one.

According to theory the prosecution should put all relevant material unearthed by the police at the disposal of the defence, but this is not the practice. In a recent letter to *The Criminal Law Review*, Mr. A. E. Taylor reports:

In the course of the trial [R. *v.* Xinaris (1955)], leading counsel for the defence, having elicited from a witness for the prosecution that he had made a statement to the police, demanded that it should be produced for his inspection. Senior counsel refused.[21]

The judge, Mr. Justice Byrne, ruled that the defence was entitled to see the statement; and only at that point was a whole bundle of statements, which witnesses for the prosecution had made to the police, handed over to the defence. The fact that a specific ruling was required and that the ruling was found worthy to be reported in a technical journal, shows how completely abstract the notion is that the prosecution takes a paternal and objective interest in the man they are trying to convict. When Mr. Eddowes demanded in a letter to *The Times* that—

The names of all persons interviewed, and copies of all statements taken by the police, should be disclosed to the defence. At present it rests upon the shoulders of prosecuting counsel to decide which, if any, statements taken by the police and in his possession should be disclosed,—[22]

Miss Normanton, Q.C., answered that this was quite unnecessary and 'would lead to an enormous increase to the clerical costs of trials'.[23] All this gives the prosecution an immense and unfair advantage over the prisoner, and particularly so in cases where the defence has no funds for investigation of its own.

Everybody in trouble will try to get hold of the best physician, or the best lawyer, he can afford. It is a generally accepted state of affairs that one's prospects in the law court depend to no small extent on the convincingness and eloquence of one's lawyer. There are endless books about famous lawyers who saved their clients in seemingly hopeless situations. It is a terrifying thought that a poor man on trial for his life should have, other things being equal, a poorer chance than another. If there is even a slight risk that a man's financial means could influence his chances of suffering capital punishment, then a fair trial is only possible if we abolish either financial inequality, or abolish capital punishment. The impartiality of the immense machine behind the prosecution is abstract theory; the cases I have quoted are hard, everyday reality.

(j) The Laws of Probability

Miscarriage of justice can be understood in a narrower and a broader meaning. In its most limited sense we mean by it a man being found guilty of a murder which another committed: e.g., Evans and possibly Rowland; and cases where the victim may have died by natural death or suicide or accident (Thorne, Woolmington, Merrifield, etc.). I have already warned against the erroneous conclusion that because it requires an exceptional chance for such mistakes to come to light, therefore mistakes must be equally exceptional. There was, at the initial stages, nothing exceptional about the cases of Evans and Rowland. They were routine trials, based on identification by witnesses and circumstantial evidence which in both cases was fairly convincing. Both names would have been forgotten for ever but for the appearance of Christie and Ware on the scene.

When a man denies his guilt, he can only be convicted on evidence of this kind. Such evidence can never amount to certainty, only to near-certainty. The amount of doubt varies from case to case, but is never entirely absent, for it is inherent in the nature of evidence; we can reduce the amount of friction in a machine, but never completely eliminate it. In some cases, certainty amounts to nearly 100 per cent; in others, where experts contradict each other and the memory of witnesses seems more erratic and vague than usual, the balance of probabilities degenerates considerably. If I am a juror in a trial where the accused denies the act, I can never expect 100 per cent certainty; I can merely say to myself: 'I shall vote "not guilty" unless I am at least 95 per cent certain that he did it.'

Yet an average of 95 per cent certainty means, according to the laws of probability, that *every twentieth man* convicted on circumstantial evidence is the victim of a miscarriage of justice.*

To measure certitude in percentages is of course an arbitrary procedure, yet any insurance company would base its policy as confidently on predictions of this type as they base their car insurance premium on the average number of accidents per annum. And if Lloyds were to insure every man on trial for his life against miscarriage due to 'vagaries of memory, erroneous recognition, fallibility of experts and juries, faulty summing up, short-comings of legal aid, Appeal Court hazards, Home Secretaries' professional diseases, and other imperfections inherent and ingrained in the procedure commonly referred to as a "fair trial" '—the premium would probably be much higher.

All this applies to errors of justice in the strictly limited meaning. But no hard-and-fast line can be drawn between miscarriages of this type and others due to the outdated and

---

* Imagine a roulette table with nineteen white numbers and one black number. The nineteen white numbers represent the ninety-five per cent certainty, the black number the five per cent doubt. The chances then are that on an average one throw in twenty will draw a black.

self-contradictory nature of the law. The fact that mental deficiency, epilepsy, paranoia, do not in themselves justify a plea of insanity makes the question whether a mentally deranged murderer will be found criminally responsible or not, quite literally into a toss-up; it replaces the symbolic scales of justice by a game of dice. And if we remember the answers given by the Lord Chief Justice to the Royal Commission's questions regarding the propriety of executing human beings thus afflicted, we realise that it is time to close this indecent game down.

The death-penalty is the only punishment inflicted by the law that is irrevocable. An irrevocable penalty, even if it could be morally and logically justified, presupposes an in-fallible tribunal and an omniscient law. Only if these conditions were fulfilled could a murder trial be justifiably called a fair trial. Without them a fair-minded judge, plus a fair-minded jury, do not add up to a fair trial. Once this is realised the 'scintilla' of doubt will grow into an angry conflagration, and burn down the last, creaking Model T version of the Tyburn Tree.

Part Three

THE END OF THE NIGHTMARE
VIII. The Alternative to Hanging

1. The Nightmare

DOSTOIEVSKY says somewhere that if in the last moment before being executed, a man, however brave, were given the alternative of spending the rest of his days on the top of a bare rock with only enough space to sit on it, he would choose it with relief. There is indeed a Kafkaesque horror attached to an execution, which goes beyond the mere fear of death or pain or indignity. It is connected not with the brutality but with the macabre, cold-blooded politeness of the ceremony, in which the person whose neck is going to be broken is supposed to collaborate in a sensible manner, as if it were a matter of a minor surgical operation. It is symbolised in the ceremonial handshake with the executioner; it is present in the delinquent's knowledge that in the embarrassed stares of the officials he is already mirrored as a dead man with a blue face and ruptured vertebrae; and that what for him is the final, violent termination of life is for them merely an unpleasant duty, followed by a sigh of relief and a plate of bacon and eggs. The Romans deprived their victim of the dignity of death by throwing him to the beasts in the arena with a clown's mask attached to his face; we put a white cap over his head, and if the victim is a woman she is made to put on waterproof underwear on the morning of the execution.[1]

Officialdom wishes to make us believe that the operation itself is always quick and expeditious. This is not true. A confidential Home Office instruction to Prison Governors dated January 10th, 1925, runs in part as follows:

> Any reference to the manner in which an execution has been carried out should be confined to as few words as possible, e.g., 'it was carried out expeditiously and without a hitch'. No record should be taken as to the number of seconds and, if pressed for details of this kind, the Governor should say he cannot give them, and he did not time the proceedings, but 'a very short interval elapsed', or some general expression of opinion to the same effect.*

When the Home Secretary was subsequently asked in the House of Commons whether he would not publish the whole instruction, he answered:[2]

> It would be most undesirable and entirely contrary to established practice to make the terms of such instructions public . . . the less said at the inquest either by Governors or anyone else, the better . . . it is preferable to draw a veil over these cases.

The truth is that some prisoners struggle both in the condemned cell and under the noose, that some have to be carried tied to a chair, others dragged to the trap, limp, bowels open,

---

* This extract came to light during the trial of Major Blake, former Governor of Pentonville, for publishing official secrets in December 1926.[1a] For thirty years it had been quoted in the literature on the subject, and its authenticity was never challenged. But when, in March 1956, I quoted that infamous Instruction in an article in *The Observer*, Lord Mancroft, Under-Secretary, Home Office, accused me, in the House of Lords debate of March 8, of having omitted two vital phrases: 'After the words "without a hitch", the following sentence should be inserted: "If there has been any hitch or unusual event the fact must, of course, be stated, and a full explanation given." At the end of the extract, the following sentence should be added: "If there has been any undue delay it must be so stated and an explanation given." ' Subsequently the Home Office admitted that these two oddly worded phrases had never been published until Lord Mancroft produced them. They had evidently been added to the Instructions at a date which the Home Office refused to disclose. On March 15, in the House of Lords, Lord Mancroft apologised to the Editor of *The Observer* and myself.

arms pinioned to the back, like animals; and that still other things happen which should only happen in nightmare dreams. In the Commons debate of 1948, the then Mr. Beverley Baxter mentioned one case which the Home Office did not succeed in hushing up, the case of a sick woman of twenty-eight whose insides fell out before she vanished through the trap:

> After her execution two of the warders . . . came to my office, and their faces were not human. I can assure you, Sir, they were like people of another world. Edith Thompson had disintegrated as a human creature on her way to the gallows, and yet somehow they had to get her there. . . .[3]

Everybody who took part in that scene suffered some damage to their nervous system. The executioner, Ellis, attempted suicide a few weeks later. The Governor of Holloway, Dr. Morton, was described a few days later by a visiting magistrate: 'I think I have never seen a person look so changed in appearance by mental suffering as the Governor appeared to me to be.' The prison Chaplain, the Rev. Glanville Murray, said of the scene of the execution: 'When we were all gathered together there, it seemed utterly impossible to believe what we were there to do. . . . My God, the impulse to rush in and save her by force was almost too strong for me.' When it was over, the Deputy Governor of Holloway, Miss Cronin, who was 'not at all a sensitive or easily moved person', remarked of the hanged woman: 'I think if she had been spared she could have become a very good woman.'[4]

These nightmare scenes are not exceptional. But the horror of the operation remains even if there is no struggle or dementedness in the condemned cell. The preparations on the previous day when executioner and assistant discreetly take the measure and weight of the victim to determine the length of the drop; the dress rehearsal of dropping a stuffed sack of the same weight to make sure that the estimated length of rope will neither strangle the victim too slowly nor tear his head off; the jolly domino game in the condemned cell while the preparations go on and the hour draws nearer; the stratagems to make him sit with his back to the door through which the executioner will enter; the brisk, businesslike opening of that door, the pinioning of the hands behind the back and the walking or dragging him to the execution shed and on to the white chalk mark on the trap; the tying of his legs while two officers stand at his sides on planks thrown across the trap, to hold him up; the fixing of the white cap and the noose with its sliding brass ring—in a few years' time, when Lord Goddard and Mr. Pierrepoint have, with God's help, been defeated, all this will appear as unthinkable as drawing, quartering and pressing to death appear to us today.

As for the final surgical act itself, the Home Office states that 'as now carried out, execution by hanging can be regarded as speedy and certain'. The emphasis on 'now' refers to the improved technique of a drop of variable length, and of the sliding ring which is supposed to hold the knot of the noose in its place under the left jaw. Before this innovation, the agony of slow suffocation without loss of consciousness could last up to twenty minutes, not to mention various forms of mutilation and lacerations, jaws torn off by hitting the edge of the trap, gashes torn in the neck, heads partly or entirely torn off, and people being hanged twice or even three times in succession. All that, we are told, are matters of the past; the new method is infallible; it causes instantaneous loss of consciousness by 'a physical shock of extreme violence'.[5] As a result of the improved method, the first, second and third cervical vertebrae are fractured or dislocated; the spinal cord is crushed or lacerated or torn from the brain stem, and if the initial shock is not fatal, the process is completed by strangulation. There is no chance, we are told, 'of a later recovery of consciousness since breathing is no longer possible. The heart may continue to beat for up to 20 minutes, but this is a purely automatic function.'[6]

Let us hope that this is true, or at least true in the majority of cases; though one is entitled to a certain scepticism regarding the infallibility of the improved method from the medical point of view, particularly where the extremely complex neurological problem of consciousness, and the loss thereof, are concerned. The *Encyclopaedia Britannica*, 1955 edition, which was published after the Royal Commission's investigations, expresses this scepticism in an indirect way:

> *It is said* that the dislocation of the vertebrae causes imme-diate unconsciousness . . . the heart may continue to beat for up to 20 mins. but this is *thought to be* a purely automatic function.[7] (*Italics mine*.)

The fact is: we do not know for certain. A violent shock of this type is as a rule, but not always, followed by instantaneous unconsciousness. One classic example to the contrary is the so-called crowbar case, known to all neurologists and surgeons —a labourer whose brain was pierced from crown to jaw by a two-inch crowbar, and who walked, fully conscious, for medical help with the crowbar inside his brain.

A second reason for being sceptical about official assurances regarding the swift and painless character of the operation is that, like any other operation, the efficacy of breaking a neck depends entirely on the skill of the surgeon. On this point we can rely on the first-hand evidence of Pierrepoint. Questioned about the Scottish method of hanging which differs from the English, Pierrepoint said:

> The Scottish [method] is very good, but I think it is very, very old, antediluvian. It is about time it was altered in Scotland.
>
> *Q.* What is the difference?—*A.* The apparatus is very old . . .
>
> *Q.* So it is much less exact?—*A.* It is not perfect. It is all right if you understand the job and you can work these things out, but a stranger can soon make a blunder of it.

Pierrepoint was then questioned on the English method:

> *Q.* The knot, as you showed us this morning, must always be under the angle of the left jaw?—*A.* Yes.

Q. That is very important, is it?—*A*. Very important.

Q. Why is it very important?—*A*. If you had the same knot on the right-hand side it comes back behind the neck, and throws the neck forward, which would make a strangulation. If you put it on the left-hand side it finishes up in front and throws the chin back and breaks the spinal cord.[8]

In one case, at least, we have direct evidence of a bungled execution, quite recently, after introduction of the improved technique: in case 'L 1942' the report of the Coroner on a Pentonville Hanging contains the significant words 'noose slipped on jaw'.[9]

When the operation is over, the victim is buried within the prison walls. Unlike in America, the body is not handed over to the relatives, for a technical reason which sums up the obscene ignominy of the whole thing: in the words of the Royal Commission Report, 'hanging . . . leaves the body with the neck elongated'.[10]

If hanging is the modern form of the Godly butchery, the alternatives of the guillotine, of electrocution or the gas chamber are no better, and possibly worse, because the preliminaries take longer. Lethal injections can only be relied on if given intravenously—a procedure which necessitates the voluntary collaboration of the patient. The Royal Commission considered that the condemned man should be offered this 'as an alternative, pleasanter method of execution', but rejected it for a number of reasons. One of these was 'the vaccilation that might be evoked in a prisoner by having to make so crucial a decision . . . and the need to have the hangman waiting in the background in case his services should be required after all, gradually perhaps losing his skill from disuse'.[11]

Irony is a rare feature in Royal Commission reports.

2. *Murderers as a Class*

That it would be *unsafe* to let murderers live is an argument in which many well-meaning people believe, though they

loathe the idea of hanging and would rather do away with it.
But the public's idea of the murderer is modelled on exceptional and untypical cases (Heath, Haig, Crippen, Christie),
which receive the widest publicity and are part of the national
folklore. The murderer is either thought of as a homicidal
maniac, or a hardened criminal, or a monster planning the
'perfect murder'. But these popular figures who impress themselves on the public imagination are no more typical of
murderers as a class, than Lawrence of Arabia was of British
subalterns as a class.

The statistics at the Home Office show that during the fifty
years 1900–49 only in one out of twelve cases was the murderer
found so dangerous for public safety or his crime so 'unpardon-
able' that he was executed—that means only 8 per cent of the
total. In Scotland, the proportion was even lower: 4 per cent.
Every analysis of the motive and circumstances under which
the crime was committed shows the extreme rarity of the cold-
blooded type of murder. Half a century ago, Sir John Macdonell, Master of the Supreme Court, analysed the criminal
statistics from 1886 to 1905 and found the following result:
90 per cent of the murders were committed by men, and nearly
two-thirds of their victims were their wives, mistresses or
sweethearts. The peak day for murder is Saturday, and the
peak hours 8 p.m. to 2 a.m. Approximately 30 per cent
of the murders were caused by drink, quarrels and violent
rage, another 40 per cent by jealousy, intrigues and sexual
motives, and only 10 per cent by financial motives. Sir John
Macdonell concludes his survey in the following words (my
italics):

I hesitate to draw any conclusions from imperfect data
as to matters of great complexity, but I am inclined to
think that this crime is *not generally the crime of the so-called
criminal classes* but is in most cases rather an *incident in
miserable lives in which disputes, quarrels, angry words and blows
are common.*[12]

Half a century later, the Royal Commission examined the
statistics of the year 1900–49 and came to the conclusion that

they 'confirm Sir John Macdonell's statement that murder is not in general a crime of the so-called criminal classes'.[13]*

The evidence of the extreme rarity of the cases where a murderer found fit for release committed a second crime, is in itself sufficient to show that the risk run by the community through the substitution of life for death sentences, is almost entirely an imaginary one. It is certainly smaller than the joint risks of executing innocent people and of letting guilty people off because the jury is not certain enough to hang the man, but would send him to prison in the knowledge that the case can be reopened. We have seen that these are the inevitable consequences of an outdated law, and the chances are that there are more murderers at large for this reason in England than in countries where capital punishment was abolished.

* *Note to the Danube Edition.* The Home Office Report 'Murder—1957–68', published in December, 1969, once more confirmed these findings. The following extract from a pamphlet written shortly after publication of the Report conveys the gist of the matter:

'The Royal Commission for Capital Punishment 1949–53 concluded that murder is not a crime of the professional criminal but of amateurs with a disordered mind. And the disordered mind is almost entirely indifferent to the consequences of its actions and the type of penalty it may incur. According to Home Office statistics, one-half of all female murderers and one-third of all male murderers commit suicide after their deed, and one-half of those who do not commit suicide are found to be insane or of diminished responsibility. At a conservative estimate, therefore, about two-thirds of the "murder population" is demonstrably suffering from mental disorders, and the actual proportion is even higher, as in many cases the murderer objects to a defence of diminished responsibility. Moreover, well over half of male murders kill their own children, wife, girl friend or other relative; among female murderers the corresponding figure is still higher. The professional criminal who kills for gain is a rare exception among murderers as a class. (*Murder and Capital Punishment*, published by Christian Action Publications Ltd. for The National Campaign for the Abolition of Capital Punishment, London, December 1969.)

IX. The Monthly Sacrifice

We shall look upon crime as a disease. Evil will be treated in charity instead of anger. The change will be simple and sublime. The cross shall displace the scaffold. Reason is on our side, feeling is on our side, and experience is on our side.

VICTOR HUGO

IN 1938, a Gallup poll on the question whether the death-penalty should be maintained or not, showed 50 per cent 'ayes' in favour of hanging, and 50 per cent 'nays' and 'don't knows'. Nine years later, in a similar poll, the 'ayes' in favour of hanging had increased to 68 per cent. Another eight years later, in July, 1955, the *Daily Mirror* arranged a new poll which revealed a complete reversal of public opinion: 65 per cent voted against the death-penalty—about the same proportion which previously had voted for it.

Such wild fluctuations of public opinion are unusual in a country where the floating vote amounts only to a small fraction of the total, and General Elections are decided by narrow margins. There is, no doubt, a steady, gradual increase in the number of people who favour a more humane adminis- tration of the law; but this slowly mounting tide does not account for the violent gales which blow now in one direction, now in the other. When the vision of the gibbet appears on the nation's horizon, opinion swings and twists like the body suspended from it; eyes bulge and reason is strangled. If the last victim happens to arouse pity—a feeble-minded boy for instance, unhinged by the movies, or a mother of two children, half-crazed by gin and jealousy—up go the 'nays' of mercy like a flight of doves; if he is a cool customer like Christie, up go the 'ayes' like a swarm of vultures. Let us agree that this is not a dignified or desirable state of affairs.

The manner in which governments and politicians handle the problem of the death-penalty is no more dignified, though less excusable. In the two most recent Parliamentary debates on the subject—February 10th and July 22nd, 1955—the present Home Secretary, Major Lloyd George, who, in 1948, had voted for the abolition of hanging, defended it on the familiar grounds: its unique value as a deterrent, the difficulty of finding a satisfactory alternative punishment and, lastly, that public opinion is opposed to abolition. All this as as old as Methuselah and no more need be said on the first two points; but the third, alas, cannot be dismissed. It is true, of course, that governments only use public opinion as a shield when it is convenient to them. When public opinion demanded that Bentley be reprieved, the Government disregarded it. On a previous similar occasion, the then Home Secretary, Lord Brentford, explained that 'no Secretary of State worthy of his name could permit himself to be influenced in a matter of that kind by public clamour'. Mob mercy, he continued, was as bad as mob execution. There was no difference between a lynching mob and a mob petitioning for a royal reprieve.[1] Thus the argument proved to be beautifully reversible: Heads I win, tails you swing.

Public opinion is still the strongest passive support of the hang-hards. The main reasons for this are ignorance, prejudice and repressed cruelty.

The public's ignorance of the facts and arguments of the issue is of course artificially fostered by official spokesmen and other oracles. The bogies conjured up by Ellenborough have not lost their effect even after a century and a half. The public is made to believe that only the hangman can protect them against 'the hardened robber'; that it is quite impossible for an innocent to be hanged; that no mentally sick person is hanged; that all the burglars of the realm are impatiently waiting for Abolition D-Day to arm themselves with guns, and that the day of the hanging judges is past. They are also being given the impression that hanging is a normal thing outside England in the contemporary world, that only some small freak nations, like Switzerland or Norway, have engaged in freak experiments of penal reform, that all murderers are monsters, that sex-maniacs must either be hanged or turned loose, that thirteen reprieves per year would cost the tax-payer millions and that the dislocation of the cerebral vertebrae and rupture of the jugular vein is a humane and instantaneous procedure which is always carried out 'swiftly and without a hitch'.

The effect of this official smoke-screen is that the stark reality of the gallows is hidden in the background, and, at the same time, the public is led to believe that the whole subject is a highly controversial one in which the arguments of both sides are evenly balanced and can only be judged by experts. Once the smoke-screen is dispelled, people will realise that hanging is simply a stupid and cruel relic of the past, much more stupid and cruel than they ever imagined. About half a dozen books were written in the last few years crammed with facts in favour of the abolition of hanging. Why has nobody written a book in defence of it? I believe the reason is, as I have tried to show, that the strongest case against capital punishment is to be found in the arguments of its defenders. I would like to challenge them to produce quotations from abolitionists as silly or ignorant or dishonest as the collection of pro-hanging found in the arguments of its defenders. I would like to challenge them to produce quotations from abolitionists as silly or ignorant or dishonest as the collection of pro-hanging quotations in this book.

Ignorance can be cured, but not callousness. Those who feel strongly that this nation should continue to break people's necks or strangle them to glory, display a curious mixture of insensitivity and sentimental traditionalism which makes them impervious to reasoned argument. They believe that legal murder prevents illegal murder, as the Persians believed that whipping the sea will calm the storm. They will say that England cannot do without hanging, and when you point to the example of other countries which get along perfectly without it, they will say that foreigners are different. They will say that English justice makes hanging by legal error impossible, and when you quote names of people who were hanged in error, they will answer that you cannot expect any system to be perfect. They will say that hanging is the most humane method of execution, and if you quote cases of a man having to be carried to the drop 'strapped sitting in a chair' or women dragged to it in a free-for-all fight, they will answer that mentioning such matters is in bad taste. As a former Home Secretary said: 'The less said at the inquest, the better; it is preferable to draw a veil over these cases.'[3] What matters is that the victim is dead, not the manner in which he was made to die, and the nation is busy washing their hands.

Those who are determined that this barbarity should continue are to be found in all classes and professions, from retired Colonels to bus drivers; the boundary is not defined by income or education. George Bernard Shaw wrote that the treatment of the 'human vermin in the Commonwealth', including idiots and morons, ought to be 'kill, kill, kill, kill, kill them'. His arguments were essentially the same as the charwoman's 'What I always says is let 'em swing; that's what I always says'; which again are essentially the same as certain speeches I have quoted from the House of Lords. The division is not between rich and poor, highbrow and lowbrow, Christians and atheists: it is between those who have charity and those who have not. The Bishops who in 1810 voted death for a five-shilling theft had no more charity than the atheist Shaw.

In this age of mass production, charity has come to mean dropping sixpence into a box and having a paper-flower pinned on one's lapel. But originally it had a different and revolutionary meaning: 'Though I have all faith so that I could remove mountains, and have not charity, I am nothing. And though I bestow all my goods to feed the poor, and have not charity, it profiteth me nothing. And though I speak with the tongues of men and of angels, and have not charity, I am become as sounding brass or a tinkling cymbal.' Charity in this ancient meaning of the word is about the most difficult virtue to acquire: much more difficult than equity, mere kindness, or even self-sacrifice. For true charity presupposes a rare combination of gifts: humility-plus-imagination. Humility without imagination makes the pious bore; imagination without humility makes the brilliant cynic. But where the two appear together, they are an active healing force for the ailments of man and the wounds of society—and a burden on him who is blessed and cursed by possessing it. For his motto must then be: *homo sum: humani nihil a me alienum puto*—I am human and nothing human is alien to me.

This guilty recognition of an inner kinship may, however, be repressed from consciousness and turn with a vengeance into the opposite of charity. When Ruth Ellis had shot her lover in a frenzy of jealousy and resentment, women were in general less inclined to demand a reprieve than men. Many of them, involved in similarly unhappy circumstances, may have felt some unconscious envy at the thought that if they were denying themselves the luxury of murdering a faithless lover or husband, then those who indulge in it ought to pay the price. Their apparent moral indignation was a mixture of envy and vindictiveness. Sexually frustrated women will persecute their luckier sisters under the same cloak of moral righteousness.

There also exists a kind of pseudo-charity, expressed in sayings like 'you ask for sympathy for the murderer, but what about the poor victim?' The answer is that we sympathise with the victim but we do not wish to add a second crime to the first. We sympathise with the victim's family, but do not wish to cause additional suffering to the murderer's family.

There is a spoonful of sadism at the bottom of every human heart. Nearly a century ago, Charles Dickens wrote that 'around Capital Punishment there lingers a fascination, urging weak and bad people towards it and imparting an interest to details connected with it, and with malefactors awaiting it or suffering it, which even good and well-disposed people cannot withstand'. His contemporary, John Bright, knew that 'capital punishment, whilst pretending to support reverence for human life, does in fact, tend to destroy it'. And even earlier, Samuel Romilly said that cruel punishments have an inevitable tendency to produce cruelty in people. The image of the gallows appeals to their latent sadism as pornography appeals to their latent sexual appetites.

The point is not to deny the existence of the fur-clad little man in us, but to accept him as part of the human condition, and to keep him under control. Newspaper editors cannot be expected to stop making the most of hanging, so long as hanging exists. In countries from which the death-penalty has vanished, this dirty sensationalism has vanished too, and murder trials do not get more publicity in the Press than cases of burglary or fraud now get in this country. For the fascination of the murder trial, and its appeal to unconscious cruelty, lies in the fact that a man is fighting for his life like a gladiator in the arena, and in the thrilling uncertainty whether the outcome will be thumbs up or thumbs down. One only wonders why the bookmakers and tote do not come in.

A short time ago, there was a national outcry against horror comics, particularly from the judges who defend the real horror of hanging. Yet a horror comic is always less exciting, because it deals with fictitious events, than the matter-of-fact statement that a real person, whose photogrpahs we have seen, whose words we have read, has been officially strangled. The drawings of monsters and mad sextons enamoured of drowned blondes are less pernicious, because of their science-fiction remoteness, than the studiedly sober report about the traces of brandy found in the executed woman's stomach. Moral deterrent, public example, reverence for human life—what bloody hypocrisy! So long as there are bull fights there will be *affecionados*, and so long as there are gladiators there will be a circus audience. There is a poisoned spray coming from the Old Bailey which corrupts and depraves; it can only be stopped by abolishing its cause, the death-penalty itself. Two centuries ago, visitors to this country were puzzled to find the road to London dotted with grizzly gibbets. They are still puzzled by the contradiction between the Englishman's belief in the necessity of hanging and his proverbial virtues of tolerance to man, kindness to animals, fussing over plants and birds. They fail to understand the power of tradition, his reluctance to abandon any of his cherished prejudices. Tradition has a hypnotic effect which commands blind belief, an instinctive recoil from any new departure as a 'dangerous experiment', and unwillingness to listen to reasoned argument. This is why the principal defenders of hanging have always been the most tradition-bound bodies of the nation: the House of Lords, the Bishops Bench, the upper ranks of the gowned and wigged profession. Yet in spite of their power and influence over the public mind, chunk after chunk of sacred tradition has been wrenched from their hands: the pillory and the ducking chair, the stake and the gibbet, the cat-o'-nine-tails; and within the next few years the strangling cord will be wrested from them too.

For despite the inertia of man's imagination and its resistance to reason and fact, people are beginning to realise that the deliberate taking of life by the State is unjustifiable on religious or philosophic or scientific grounds; that hanging by mistake will go on as long as capital punishment will go on, because the risk is inherent in its nature; that the vast majority of murderers are either mentally sick and belong to the mental sick ward, or victims of circumstance, who can be reclaimed for human society; and that the substitution of the life sentence for the death-penalty exposes the peaceful citizen to no greater risk than that of being killed by lightning in a bus queue, and considerably less than the risk of being a passive accomplice in the execution of an innocent or a mentally deranged person, which the citizens of this country run on the average thirteen times a year.

It is not only a question of the thirteen individual lives which we offer annually as a sacrifice to the stupid moloch of prejudice. The gallows is not only a machine of death, but a symbol. It stands for everything that mankind must reject, if mankind is to survive.

References and Sources

Abbreviations

R.C.M.: Royal Commission on Capital Punishment, 1949–53, Minutes of Evidence.

R.C.R.: Royal Commission Report on Capital Punishment, 1949–53.

S.C.M.: Minutes of the Select Committee on Capital Punishment 1929–30.

S.C.R.: Report of the Select Committee on Capital Punishment 1929–30

The numbers refer to *paragraphs*.

Chapter I (Pages 171 to 207)

1. Charles Duff, *A New Handbook on Hanging* (London, 1954); 2. *The Observer*, July 1st, 1952; 3. R.C.M., 8402; 4. R.C.M., 8405–8410; 5. R.C.M., 8302; 6. R.C.M., 3212; 7. R.C.M., 8468; 8. R.C.M., 3123. 9. R.C.M., 8466–8467; 10. R.C.M., 3112; 11. R.C.M., 3252; 12. R.C.M., 3125; 13. Leon Radzinowicz, *A History of English Criminal Law and Its Administration from 1750*, vol. i (London, 1948), p. 4; 14. Ibid., 5; 15. Hansard 1810, vol. xv, column 366; 16. Hansard, April 1st, 1830, column 1179. Quoted from S.C.R. p. 8; 17. Quoted from Radzinowicz, op. cit., p. 24; 18. W. Andrews, *Bygone Punishments* (London, 1899, p. 39); 19. Ibid., p. 75; 20. B. Williams, *The Whig Supremacy, 1714–1760* (Oxford, 1945); 21. Viscount Templewood, *The Shadows of the Gallows* (London, 1951), p. 21; 22. B. Mandeville, *An Inquiry into the Cause of the Frequent Executions at Tyburn* (London, 1725), pp. 18–26. Quoted from G. Ryley Scott, *The History of Capital Punishment* (London, 1950), pp. 46–7; 23. Minutes of Evidence of the Select Com-

290   REFLECTIONS ON HANGING

mittee of the House of Lords, 1856, p. 3; 24. E. Cadogan, *The Roots of Evil* (London, 1937), p. 147; 25. G. Ryley Scott, op. cit., p. 55–7; 26. E. Cadogan, op. cit., pp. 147–8; 27. Ibid., p. 139; 28. G. Ryley Scott, op. cit., p. 137; 29. Ibid., pp. 200 ff.; 30. E. Cadogan, op. cit., p. 141; 31. Radzinowicz, op. cit., p. 12; 32. Ibid., pp. 12 f.; 33. Ibid., p. 13; 34. Quoted from R. T. Paget, Sydney Silverman and Christopher Hollis, *Hanged—and Innocent?* (London, 1953), p. 98; 35. Radzinowicz, op. cit., p. 14; 36. G. Gardiner and N. Curtis-Raleigh, 'The Judicial Attitude to Penal Reform', *The Law Quarterly Review* (April, 1949), p. 8; 37. Ibid., p. 8; 38. Ibid., p. 8; 39. Radzinowicz, op. cit., pp. 290 f.; 40. Ibid., pp. 291 f.; 41. Ibid., pp. 295 ff.; 42. Ibid., pp. 289 f.; 43. Ibid., pp. 287 f.; 44. Ibid., p. 147; 45. Ibid., p. 148; 46. Trevelyan, *British History in the Nineteenth Century and After* (London, 1943), p. xiv; 47. Sir Thomas Fowell Buxton in 1821, quoted by Radzinowicz, p. 36; 48. Quoted by Radzinowicz, op. cit., p. 36; 49. *Encyclopaedia Britannica* (1955 edition), article on 'Common Law', vol. vi, p. 122; 50. Ibid., p. 122; 51. *Encyclopaedia Britannica* (1955 edition), article on 'Common Law', vol. vi, p. 123; 52. Ibid., p. 123; 53. Gardiner and Curtis-Raleigh, op. cit., pp. 2 f.; 54. House of Lords Debate, May 30th, 1810; 55. Hansard, April 27th, 1948, column 411; and June 2nd, 1948, column 106; 56. Gardiner and Curtis-Raleigh, op. cit., p. 10; 57. Hansard, April 28th, 1948, columns 546–7; 58. Radzinowicz, op. cit., pp. 221 f.; 59. Ibid., p. 519; 60. Ibid., p. 519; 61. Gardiner and Curtis-Raleigh, op. cit., p. 15; 26. Ibid., p. 14; 63. Ibid., p. 6; 64. Ibid., pp. 10 f.; 65. Ibid., p. 11; 66. Hansard, June 2nd, 1948, column 195; 67. Gardiner and Curtis-Raleigh, op. cit., pp. 18 f.; 68. Ibid., p. 19; 69. Ibid., pp. 20 f.; 70. Ibid., p. 20; 71. Ibid., p. 21; 72. Ibid., p. 14; 73. Radzinowicz, op. cit., p. 251; 74. Sir James Stephen, *History of the Criminal Law*, vol. i, p. 479. Quoted by Gardiner and Curtis-Raleigh, op. cit., p. 13; 75. Quoted from Gardiner and Curtis-Raleigh, op. cit., p. 13.

Chapter II (Pages 208 to 220)

1. Templewood, op. cit., p. 76; 2. R.C.R., Appendix 6, p. 5;

3. Ibid., Appendix 6, p. 5; 4. Hansard, June 2nd, 1948, column 115; 5. Hansard, June 2nd, 1948, column 119; 6. S.C.R., 38; 7. S.C.R., 455; 8. Ch. Phillips, *Vacation Thoughts on Capital Punishment* (fourth edition, London, 1858); 9. Report of the Royal Commission of 1866, Appendix, p. 632; 10. *The Case Against Capital Punishment*, The Howard League (London, 1953), sheet 15; and B. Duesing, *Die Geschichte der Abschaffung der Todesstrafe* (Offenbach/Main, 1952), pp. 232 ff.; 11. S.C.R., 453; 12. R.C.R., 790; 13. R.C.R., 61; 14. R.C.R., 65; 15. R.C.R., 64; 16. R.C.R., 66; 17. R.C.R., Appendix 6, p. 54; 18. S.C.M., 3050; 19. R.C.R., Appendix 6, p. 6.

Chapter III (Pages 221 to 225)

1. Paris, 1872; 2. E. P. Evans, *The Criminal Prosecution and Capital Punishment of Animals* (London, 1906), p. 150; 3. Ibid., p. 334; 4. Dr. J. A. Hobson, 'Psychiatric Evidence in Murder Trials', *The Howard Journal*, vol. ix, no. 2 (1955); 5. R.C.R., 292; 6. R.C.R., 374; 7. R.C.R., 141; 8. R.C.R., 128; 9. R.C.R., 137; 10. R.C.R., 137; 11. R.C.R., 74; 12. R.C.R., 74; 13. Quoted by Templewood, op. cit., p. 34.

Chapter V (Pages 234 to 244)

1. H. Sidgwick, *Methods of Ethics* (London, 1874); 2. William James, *Textbook on Psychology* (Macmillan, New York), p. 237; 3. *Encyclopaedia Britannica* (1955), vol. xix, p. 749.

Chapter VI (Pages 245 to 253)

1. *Daily News*, March 16th, 1846; 2. St. Augustine's Epistles, nos. CLII and CLIII quoted by S.C.R., 292; 3. R.C.R., 374; 4. R.C.R., 606; 5. R.C.R., 606; 6. R.C.R., 605; 7. R.C.R., 611; 8. R.C.R., 790 (46); 9. R.C.M., 3231; 10. R.C.M., 3153.

Chapter VII (Pages 254 to 272)

1. Capital Punishment Commission, 1866, Minutes, 1054–5; 2. Ibid., 1063–74; 3. Ibid., 1060–3; 4. Clifford Sully, *Mistaken*

Identity (London, 1925), p. 15; 5. C. H. Rolph, 'Personal Identity', to be published in 1956; 6. S.C.M., 4386; 7. *The Times*, September 13th, 1955; 8. Hansard, February 10th, 1955, columns 2085–6; 9. Templewood, op. cit., p. 66; 10. Quoted from Paget, Silverman and Hollis, op. cit., p. 113; 11. Ibid., p. 87; 12. Oxford, 1933; 13. Ensor, op. cit., pp. 11 f.; 14. Ibid., p. 22; 15. Archbold, *Criminal Pleading, Evidence and Practice* (Edinburgh, 1949), p. 325; 16. All quotations in this section (pp. 265 to 266) are quoted from Paget, Silverman and Hollis, op. cit., unless a different reference is given; 17. Hansard, February 10th, 1955, column 2090; 18. *The Times*, September 9th, 1955; 19. 'Psychiatric Evidence in Murder Trials', *The Howard Journal*, vol. ix, no. 2 (1955); 20. Paget, Silverman and Hollis, op. cit., pp. 42 f.; 21. *The Criminal Law Review*, September, 1955; 22. *The Times*, September 7th, 1955; 23. *The Times*, September 15th, 1955.

Chapter VIII (Pages 273 to 280)

1. Letter to *The Lancet* by a medical practitioner, August 20th, 1955; 1a. *The Times*, November 19th, December 8th, December 16th, 1926; 2. Hansard, June 23rd, 1926; 3. Hansard, April 14th, 1948; 4. Statement by Miss Margery Fry to the Royal Commission. R.C.M., pages 282 and 283; 5. R.C.R., 732; 6. R.C.R., 714; 7. *Encylopaedia Britannica*, vol. xi (1955), p. 151; 8. R.C.M., 8412–3, 8417–8 and 8428–31; 9. R.C.M., p. 627; 10. R.C.R., 732; 11. R.C.R., 746; 12. Quoted by Calvert, op. cit., p. 32; 13. R.C.R., Appendix 6, p. 4.

Chapter IX (Pages 28 to 287)

1. Quoted from Duff, op. cit., p. 56; 2. Statement by Sir William Joynson-Hicks in the House of Commons, June 23rd, 1927. Quoted from Howard League, op. cit., Sheet 17.

Index

to Reflections on Hanging

Israel and capital punishment, 213
Italy abolishes capital punishment, 213

James, William, 237
Jones, Mr. Justice Glyn, 264
Jordan, N. M., 267
Joseph II, Emperor, 185
Jowitt, Lord, 195, 201
Judiciary, English: oppose reduc-
    of capital offences, 190–6;
    and high treason, 196–7;
    and non-capital punishments,
    198–9; and the rights of the
    accused, 199–201; opposition to
    reform, 201–7; oppose abolition
    of capital punishment, 209–10
Julian, Emperor, 248
Juries, their dilemma at murder
    trials, 261–3

Kelly, Sir Fitzroy, 254–5
Ketch, Jack, executioner, 171

Law Journal, 260, 264
Lloyd George, Major G., 208, 282
Lords, House of, 224, 286
Loughborough, Lord, 197
Luxembourg abolishes capital
    punishment, 213

Macdonnell, Sir John, 278–80
M'Naghten Rules, 223, 243
Malice aforethought, 225
Martin, Lord, 200
Maximum severity, doctrine of,
    201–7
Mental Deficiency Acts, 223
Mexico abolishes capital punish-
    ment, 213
Mill, James and John Stuart, 190
Montesquieu, 185, 190
Morton, Dr., Governor of Hollo-
    way, 275
Murder trials: conviction of inno-
    cent persons, 254–8; fallibility
    of witnesses, 258–9; expert
    testimony, 259–60; dilemma of
    juries, 261–3; the summing up,
    263–5; the Court of Criminal
    Appeal, 265; Home Office
    enquiries on Rowland and
    Evans cases, 266; the Home
    Secretary and reprieves, 266–7;

defence of poor prisoners,
    267–70; probability and cer-
    tainty, 270–2
Trials cited or discussed:
Bentley, Derek, 184, 257, 267
Biggadyke, Mrs., 256
Christie, 279, 281
Craig, Christopher, 184
Crippen, 279
Cumming, 212
Dodd, Dr., 212
Ellis, Mrs. Ruth, 285
Evans, Timothy, 256, 257, 266
Ferguson, 212
Habron, William, 257, 260–1
Haggerty, 179
Haig, 279
Heath, 279
Heywood, 212
Hilsner, 256
Holloway, 179
Hoolhouse, 257
Klundert, 256
Ley, 243
'Martin, Donald', 226–33, 236
Merrifield, Mrs., 260, 264
Misters, Josiah, 178
Peace, Charles, 261
Podmore, 257
Rowland, Walter Graham, 257,
    266, 267
Slater, Oscar, 256
Straffen, 223
Thompson, Mrs., 181, 257, 274,
    275
Thorne, Norman, 257, 260, 267
Tonka, Steven, 256
Tuennisen, 256
Woolmington, Mrs., 267
Woolmington, Reginald, 263–4
York, William, 183
Murderers, kind of, 206 n, 209;
    suicide amongst, 209; case of
    'Donald Martin', 226–33; as
    a class, 278–80; behaviour
    after release, 280
Murray, Rev. Glanville, 275

Nepal abolishes capital punishment,
    213
Netherlands abolishes capital pun-
    ishment, 213
New Zealand and capital punish-
    ment, 215